The Curious Gardener

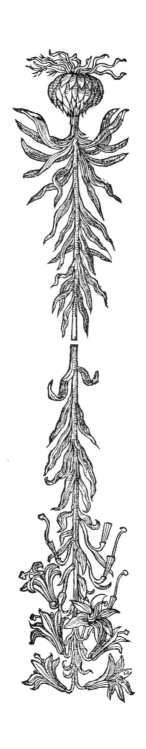

THE
Curious
Gardener

JÜRGEN DAHL

translated by
Claudia Heidieker

with a foreword by
Noël Kingsbury

Timber Press
Portland · Cambridge

Der neugierige Gärtner copyright © 2002 by Manuscriptum Verlagsbuchhandlung Thomas Hoof KG Waltrop und Leipzig.

The present volume incorporates revised versions of three works by Jürgen Dahl: *Der neugierige Gärtner* (1998), *Der Stinkgarten oder die Faszination des Gegenteils* (1997), and *Vom Geschmack der Lilienblüten* (1995).

English translation by Claudia Heidieker copyright © 2004 by Timber Press, Inc. Foreword copyright © 2004 by Noël Kingsbury. All rights reserved.

Published in 2004 by
Timber Press, Inc.
The Haseltine Building
133 S.W. Second Avenue, Suite 450
Portland, Oregon 97204-3527, U.S.A.

Timber Press
2 Station Road
Swavesey
Cambridge CB4 5QJ, U.K.

www.timberpress.com

Printed in China

Library of Congress Cataloging-in-Publication Data

Dahl, Jürgen, 1929–
    [Neugierige Gartner. English]
    The curious gardener / Jürgen Dahl ; translated by Claudia Heidieker ; with a foreword
      by Noël Kingsbury.
        p. cm.
    Includes bibliographical references and index.
    ISBN 0-88192-657-4 (hardback)
    1. Gardening. 2. Gardens. 3. Gardeners. I. Title.
    SB455.D2413 2004
    635—dc22
                                                                            2004001611

A catalog record for this book is also available from the British Library.

For Hella

Contents

All Over the Garden   179

Unexpected Arrivals, Arriving Daily 179, Ninfa Is Everywhere 181,
The Meadow Does Not Exist 184, Angelica Around the Neck 189,
The Mice Have to Go 192, Thoughts at Bedtime 195, Suggestions for
Front Yards 197, In Honor of Vita 199, The Many Uses of Blackberries 200,
Of Wind and Threshing 201, A Failure to Appreciate Rushes 203,
Long Live Pumpkin Seeds 205, The Berry That Is Really an Apple 207,
A Fern Path 208, Two Kinds of Mushrooms 209

Love, Death, and Animals   213

Where Love Shines 213, The Garden as a Place for Courtship Displays 213,
Images of Death . . . 216, . . . And of Continuing to Live 218, Caterpillars
in May 219, Quarrels Around the Pond 220, Sensitive Orloffs 221,
Earthworm Piles of the Third Kind 222

Wintry Things   224

Let Us Booze by the Embers 224, The Shades of Decay 226, Before the
Frosts Arrive 227, Roots and Horseshoes 230, Wintergreens 232,
The Enjoyment of Papermaking 233, Dried Beauties 235, Winter's End 237,
Time of the Gardener 239

Index of Plant Names   251

Foreword

Gardening for most of us is about ornament, about creating color and spectacle to brighten our lives and lift our spirits. But as gardenmaking becomes more and more popular, it moves increasingly further from its roots in survival. Our ancestors gardened out of necessity: to provide food, fodder for their animals, medicine, materials for crafts and construction. Anything grown for ornament or pleasure was purely peripheral.

Gardening in most of the English-speaking world is now dominated by the ornamental, and by the multimillion dollar industry behind the plants and products that fill the garden centers. In much of Europe though, a more traditional style of gardening can still be seen, where fruit, vegetables, and herbs are the priority. There are flowers, but they are grown in a way that reflects their relative lack of importance, usually at the margins or perhaps at the very front of the garden, where they provide a decorative façade for the more serious business going on behind. They are grown for the sheer joy of growing them, with no thought for design. Such gardens are real "cottage gardens," far more utilitarian and more artless than the self-conscious cottage gardens created by the middle classes of cultures with a more "sophisticated" gardening culture. Some of the best of these gardens can be seen in the former communist countries of Eastern Europe, where economic necessity forces much of the rural population to grow as much of their own sustenance as possible, either for themselves or for barter with city-dwelling friends and relatives. But many can still be seen in Germany, which despite its wealth and high per capita spending on the products of the garden center, still retains a vigorous traditional gardening culture.

It is with this world of gardening that Jürgen Dahl connects. His garden is one that is rooted in folk tradition, but also in considerable learning. Plants for him are not isolated beings or artistic materials to be placed next to each other in elaborate designs, but entities that inhabit a number of different and interconnected worlds: myth, folklore, traditional usage, history, local culture, superstition, old wives' tales. Reading Dahl introduces us to the sheer complexity of the culture of plants, but also his own personal world, that of memory and evocation. White honesty (*Lunaria annua* 'Alba') is the plant that evokes Vita Sackville-West, a sea holly relative (*Eryngium giganteum*) Miss Willmott, who scattered the seed in gardens she visited, "opium lettuce" (*Lactuca virosa*) the medieval Hildegard von Bingen and Albertus Magnus, and their advice on its painkilling properties.

Observation is at the core of Dahl's gardening, a quality absent from too many modern gardeners. Observation requires a kind of emptying of the mind, to allow impressions to enter through any of the senses, and space for the imagination to work. Our attention is drawn to the decaying forms of plants in early spring, when "mysterious pictures" are left after the elements and munching invertebrates have eaten away at stems and leaves, and to the "severe," "minimal" wild rushes that have seeded themselves in his garden. Scent in particular attracts his interest; one whole section is indeed called "The Stinking Garden," with the olfactory aspects of a wide range of plants examined, the fact that most of them are unpleasant not being seen as any reason why they should not be explored and recorded.

One aspect of traditional cultures that we have almost entirely lost (at least in the English-speaking world) is the use of wild plants for food, especially in spring, when so many species emerge tender and vitamin-packed from the earth. Dahl discusses many of these plants, but extends his gastronomical curiosity to garden plants too. He reminds us that buckwheat (*Fagopyrum esculentum*) can be eaten like spinach, that ginkgo nuts can be roasted like chestnuts (they make a "spicy snack"), and mahonia berries can be eaten "straight from the bush" or made into a delicious jelly. He even suggests harvesting the buds of sunflowers, to be cooked, as a kind of mini–globe artichoke, and helpfully includes a long list of edible garden plants and weeds.

Constant experimentation and careful observation of the results are crucial to Dahl's gardening. This desire to constantly push the limits of the known, to take risks, to explore and adapt, is part of what distinguishes a merely competent from a great gardener. Whether it is using a tub beneath an overflow pipe to grow watercress, trying indoor plants outside, attempting to grow sweet potatoes, or cooking with forgotten herbs, he is always on the lookout for new experiences and new ways of doing things. One forgotten art he has revived is the making of an herbarium, that is, a collection of flowers and leaves picked from the garden and pressed, a practice that has long since been discontinued by gardeners, but for Dahl is a way of keeping a record and storing memories.

Dahl is one of those gardeners who has endless curiosity and an ability to adore minutiae, an attitude that can enable him to make separations in his mind that perhaps few other gardeners make. An example is his ability to appreciate the beauty of hairy bittercress, a weed notorious around the world, but for Dahl a herald of spring. The origins of plant names is another area where his attention to detail turns up many a small but sparkling nugget of information. And of course the variety of unpleasant smells that make up the "stinking garden."

Much of Dahl's interest lies in his patience, a quality essential to gardeners, but in a world where instant gratification is so easily achieved at the garden center, one that is all too often liable to be overlooked. The rhythms of the seasons, the life spans of plants, the endless cycle of death and rebirth are all recorded and celebrated. His gardening, as with all traditional gardeners, is about process rather than end result. Making his writings available to the anglophone world will hopefully teach the virtues of patient observation to a wider audience.

Above all, it is his ability to make connections that distinguishes Dahl's writing. His mind is one that wanders sideways, musing on whatever he has discovered in the garden that morning; he moves on to consider the science behind his observation, or quote an ancient herbalist, or folk knowledge. Such an ability connects the garden with a wider world, and makes it an immeasurably more interesting place.

NOËL KINGSBURY

Publisher's Note
An Invitation

We hereby invite you to be infected with the curiosity of the gardener, to follow him on less-well-trodden paths, to ponder with him, to experiment, to enjoy, to worry, and to rejoice with him.

With more clarity and depth than most people, Jürgen Dahl viewed gardens as mirror images of the world at large. His insights and interpretations often are like parables, leading his reader into a universe governed by continuous change and infinite variation. This universe obeys its own laws, which we, in turn, are obliged to respect.

The present volume contains the last three gardening books that Jürgen Dahl wrote: *The Curious Gardener* (1998), *The Stinking Garden* (1997), and *How to Eat a Lily* (1995). Some of the text originated in his beloved weekly gardening column; some of it has been shortened and adapted, and botanical names have been added, as have photographs, which previously appeared only in *The Stinking Garden*.

Jürgen Dahl was able to participate in the editorial preparation of this book for only a short time. He died on 6 October 2001. Mrs. Hella Dahl has been very helpful in continuing his work as he would have wished, particularly in selecting pictures and picture captions to be included in this book. For this we are very grateful to her.

The
Curious Gardener
Gardening Virtues and Botanical Surprises

Turkey tails are distinguished by the subdued harmony
of their shading and their delicate sheen.

The Curious Gardener

I am still in my pajamas when I take my first walk in the garden. Curiosity spurs me on to see what might have happened overnight.

Has my white quince finally started to flower?

Have my radishes come up?

Have the bleached dandelion leaves under the cloche grown long enough to make dandelion salad today?

Has the fox been at the chickens again?

Have the boxwood cuttings from the autumn put down roots? (Yes, they really can root overnight, even after months of waiting.)

Has the bud of my white peony—the one that is attempting to flower for the first time this year—gotten a bit fatter?

Have any slugs survived this frosty winter and, if so, have they been at work anywhere?

Can I detect one last whiff of the resinous scent given off by the buds of the balsamic poplars? Each year I eagerly await the arrival of this wonderful fragrance. For the past few days, the garden has been filled with it, but it disappears as soon as the shiny leaves unfold.

And where are the bumblebees? Today I may finally succeed in pursuing one in its flight until it disappears into a hole in the ground and stays there to build its nest. Mind you, I have never managed to trace the location of a bumblebee's nest in this way, so the question of where these creatures actually live may yet go unanswered.

Bumblebee nests notwithstanding, the gardener will find many more answers than questions when he says "good morning" to the garden if he is curious and observant enough to perceive the many small changes that occur every hour. This curiosity is a virtue, presenting a wealth of discoveries that together form an image of the garden. It is a patchy image that has little in common with the lush, pretty pictures found in many gardening books. The curious gardener focuses not on the overall prettiness of the garden but on the boundless abundance of detail. If there are enough details, prettiness will take care of itself.

My curiosity may not be quite so virtuous when I visit other gardens as a guest. Intermingled with the joys of discovery is a spirit of competition. I may even experience jealousy and envy, though of course only in their most civilized form; I hardly ever commit actual crimes against a host's property. Even so, when my host owns the exact species of plantain missing from my own collection or when the yellow bellflowers of Mongolian clematis—a real beauty— cascade down his fence in a shimmering wave throughout the season, it can be difficult to bear. I myself have never succeeded in keeping the tender Mongolian alive for more than two years and only as a most feeble individual at that. How does he do it? And how is it possible that Alpine snowbell, appearing so modest and yet so demanding and sensitive, obviously thrives here in well-established drifts?

Never mind. Competition soon gives way to inspiration and ambition. I start filling my notebook with names and good intentions, sometimes followed by exclamation points. And sometimes I fill the little box that my host so thoughtfully provides to carry home cuttings and starts. (In botanical gardens, the situation is quite different. Plenty of exemplars fuel one's curiosity, but great value is understandably placed on preventing enthusiasts from walking off with anything, even by mistake.)

A gardener's curiosity is never at rest, not even indoors. I hunt through books and magazines just as I do in the garden. Hidden between the known and the ordinary, I find news about other gardeners' experiences and practices and information about unfamiliar plants. Every book and newspaper article has something of value to impart.

For example, in the gardening column of a Dutch daily (in Holland and England, even daily newspapers boast a gardening column), I discovered the source for the widely held and yet erroneous assumption that caper spurge (*Euphorbia lathyris*) deters wood mice. Here is how it happened.

A horticultural writer noted that caper spurge is sometimes called mole plant in English. He concluded that the plant must be effective against moles, and to top it off, he recommended it against wood mice as well. Thus he played a role not only in the dramatic sales increase of *Euphorbia lathyris* but also in amusing generations of wood mice. One can sometimes hear their tiny peals of laughter when yet another gardener plants a caper spurge somewhere. This well-meaning expert had overlooked the fact that the word *mole* may also refer to a skin growth and that mole plant had long been valued as a remedy for warts and skin discolorations. This explanation for the plant's common name may or may not be true; word of its effectiveness against wood mice, however, is based on a slight error in translation, and wood mice, for one, did not fall for it.

By the way, treating warts with the milky juice of caper spurge can result in painful blisters and sustained inflammation—another example of how risky it can be to follow the highly touted herbal wisdom of our ancestors. Never let your curiosity cause you to put your health at risk. What will become of the garden if you do?

Spring

Geese in Pain and Pruning Wisteria

Yesterday a fox came to get another goose, and now only one remains. Today this last one is crying out constantly and heartbreakingly for its companion. The only thing that makes its grieving bearable is the hope that its tiny head, unable to grasp very much, cannot feel the amount of pain and agony we think we can detect in its cries.

I am well aware that people may now accuse me of callousness and tell me countless stories of grieving geese. In response, I would like to point out that one must think of the fox as well! Speaking in the abstract, is a starving fox preferable to a dead goose? Here human emotion is governed by irrational preferences and sympathetic assumptions. The cries of a distraught goose do indeed sound like cries of agony, but we would really need to discuss this with the goose before making such a judgment.

When the local press asked the owner of some Galloway cows imported from England about the imminent slaughter of his animals, he said, "These animals are part of our family. We eat them all ourselves."

Stewing and frying family members may sound horrifying, but it is an ancient rural way of thinking. Most arguments against it express conflicting feelings, fickle sentimentalities, and many well-chosen words—especially from people who would never go without ground beef—that in the end turn out to be high-handed maxims, opportunistic and spurious at that.

When it comes to plants, things are easier because emotional ties to foliage are not quite so binding. However, this does not stop people from reacting with indignation when I, upon being asked for advice regarding a sick plant, suggest replacing it with a new, healthy one. "How cruel!" people say, claiming to be much too attached to the plant.

In light of my attitude, people at some point want to know if I talk to my plants. Of course I talk to them, but I am always aware that I am holding a monologue. Any scientifically proven benefits of this discourse (the experiment itself being highly unscientific) are probably due solely to the fact that I naturally give more attention to the plants that I address.

Sometimes I ask people what they have to say to cabbage, which is beheaded, ripped to shreds, and seared with salt and pepper before being eaten. I once got

Hemi-parasitic cow wheat gets its particular charm from the differing shades of its leaves and flowers.

the following response: it is the will of a cabbage to be eaten. How easy it is to make the way of the world conform to one's own wishes!

Speaking of chopping, the wisteria on my wall needs a radical pruning. Now, in February, is our last chance to cut back all (and I really mean *all*) of the side shoots. Many of them are a meter long or more, and if they are not cut back to short stumps with only four eyes, about the length of a finger, all the flowers will simply drown in a cascade of leaves. Midsummer is really the proper season for this severe treatment. At that time, the wisteria still has time to respond to the curbing of its expansionist ambitions by producing hundreds of flower buds for the following spring. By the way, those who profess to talk to their plants should be careful not to call the wisteria by an incorrect name. It is *Wisteria frutescens* not *Glycine frutescens*, as the first American species was once named. Calling it by the latter name might upset it and prevent it from flowering.

The long, pencil-thin shoots of the wisteria are eminently suitable for weaving. One can make them into baskets and bowls (if only to discover how difficult this is to achieve) or into solid, endlessly intertwined balls that can then be left to get covered in moss and rot away among the herbaceous perennials. This process of reclamation can take years and shows us just how the garden absorbs everything we give it, slowly but inexorably nibbling, rampaging, encompassing the offering until it is no longer recognizable or is altogether obliterated. Not even iron withstands this process: flaring up when it rusts, iron displays magnificent shades of red and brown and then disintegrates into grainy shreds. In the ruins of a garden, time itself is made visible and invisible again, as Adalbert Stifter describes in *Fool's Castle*: "Garden beds deeply sunk, little lead labels amidst the grass."

Evidence of this process can be seen in the thick branches of willow and cherry, piled up in the yard to be chopped up for firewood during the summer. They are displaying the first signs of decay as gray and green lichens take possession of them, barely pinpoint-sized colonies that will expand into circles. Even more compelling are the masses of turkey tail mushrooms, sprouting from the wood like a hundred blossoms. They are leathery to the touch and seem to imitate their host, the tree, by developing growth rings that indicate weeks rather than years.

The fungi will have died long before this wood is chopped up, and they will have gone dry and tough in the meantime. In an old book on fungi, one can read that with their beautiful stripes and their reflective surface, turkey tails "used to be worn by ladies as adornments on their black velvet hats." We may not attach these turkey tails to our black velvet hats, but they will still sparkle festively one last time. In our open fire, they will flare up like dry tinder, and it will look as though the wood had been studded with a thousand little lanterns.

The Navel of Venus

"This is paradise!" our Dutch friends said. They were seeking refuge from the flood and arrived here at Lindenhof with their horse-drawn cart, grandmother, and baggage. Within a few hours, paradise was threatened by the rising waters. Sandbags were piled high outside the front door, and on the ground floor, we tried to determine which of the books from the lower shelves we needed to rescue and which we were prepared to let go.

Then came time for another, perhaps last walk through the garden. It was somewhat spooky. The sun was shining. The snowdrops were flowering. The winter aconites had started to appear. The first leaves of caraway, brimming with health, offered themselves up for an early spring soup. And yet I knew that in just a few hours, everything might be buried under a murky, gurgling mass of water.

But the dikes held, and the flood passed us by. Our Dutch friends are homeward bound, along with their horse-drawn cart, grandmother, and all their baggage; the sandbags can be cleared away for now; and the garden looks as though nothing happened at all. Well, this time nothing did happen.

If the waters had come, not only would they have choked the garden, they would also have liberated a prisoner, navelwort (*Hydrocotyle aquatica*), which has so far been contained in the ditch. Throughout the summer, navelwort has so completely covered the ditch that not one bit of water remains to be seen. The leaves poke up like miniature umbrellas, one next to the other, and beneath them, a thick carpet of stringy runners and felted roots cover everything. If the flood had washed these tangles out of the ditch, they would quickly have developed into a plague; navelwort is amphibious, so it can also live on dry land.

In navelwort's tropical home countries, elephants are said to enjoy it as a salad. However, we do not have any elephants, and our geese do not seem to like it. Even the frost has not managed to do it any harm. It is no consolation that a bitter substance it contains has a diuretic effect; pharmacies used to sell its dried leaves as *Herba cotyledonis aquaticae*, a remedy for rheumatic disorders. Its side effects are very dangerous, however, and so one cannot even think of cultivating it as a medicinal herb.

The only way that we have managed to keep it contained is as a potted plant in the bathroom, for it will thrive in any pot of water and continuously produce long, stringy shoots with almost perfectly rounded leaves the size of a five-mark piece (U.S. half dollar). The leaves have a serrated edge and are slightly depressed in the middle where they join the leaf stalk, hence its name, navelwort. In French it is called the very charming *nombril de Venus*, which I think is somehow fitting for a bathroom.

For the gardener, there are two sides to this rampaging, vegetative abundance. Some plants, such as ground ivy (*Glechoma hederacea*) and quack grass (or couch grass, *Agropyron repens*), drive you up the wall with their merciless vitality and their almost cunning speed. Others you might like to see in even more abundance, such as *Fragaria* 'Florika', a breed of strawberry protected by patent legislation. We planted 'Florika' in late summer. Its claim to fame is that it produces runners tirelessly, and in a very short time, it can cover a large area so densely that no other plant has a chance of popping up. The resulting strawberry meadow is then supposed to grow by half a square meter every year. One does not need to cultivate this ground or worry about strawberry mold—'Florika' is immune to it. And though its fruit does not quite grow right into one's mouth, the berries are held on long stalks above the foliage rather than hiding deep beneath it, as is the case with other varieties.

Again, this is a scene from paradise: fertility without work.

In the chicken pen, however, the opposite of paradise can be observed: our rooster has a blood red mark on the back of his neck. A buzzard must have tried to make a meal of him and failed—this time.

Cloches of Glass and Clay

Early sowings—especially those of plants that need frost to germinate and should be sown by now at the latest—must be protected from being washed out by the rain, and many outdoor seedlings need protection from wind and weather. A certain tool comes in handy here, one that was formerly used to protect tender tree shoots in French nurseries and is often sold as decoration in flower shops: the glass cloche.

Glass cloches are tiny, portable greenhouses, and once you have used one, you will not want to be without it again. Of course, the soil under the cloche must be checked at regular intervals for moisture, and just as in a real greenhouse, some shade must be provided to prevent burns. Small twigs or boards stuck into the soil on the sunny side of the cloche are most suitable for this purpose. If a glass cloche proves too expensive, you can simply use a glass or transparent plastic salad bowl instead.

Cloches not only provide protection, they also serve to distinguish sowings and seedling plants that might otherwise be overlooked or inadvertently ripped out. In winter, a cloche can protect plants that are sensitive to wet climates and

Seakale forced under a clay cloche is a tender white vegetable.

that rot easily, such as some stonecrops, or that should really be grown in a cold greenhouse, such as the beautiful white-haired plantain *Plantago nivalis* from the Sierra Nevada.

By and by, the time for a glass cloche will give way to the time for putting the clay cloche to good use. Seakale (*Crambe maritima*) and dandelion (*Taraxacum officinale*) can be covered with a clay cloche to cut out the light completely, producing yellowish leaves that are far less bitter than the usual green ones. In England, this type of forcing or bleaching is very popular, and large, beautiful clay pots are designed specifically for this purpose. These "forcers" are really quite expensive, however, and a homemade clay cloche will do just as well; if you just want the vegetables and do not care about beauty, you can simply use a black plastic bucket.

In the autumn my wife brought home two heads of ornamental cabbage from the market, just as she does every year. Far into the winter, these have been standing on either side of the front door. They need cold temperatures for the leaves to develop their gaudy shades of yellow, green, red, and purple. I feel that their cheerfulness is a part of the winter season. And far from being artificial, they exemplify the inexhaustible potential of *Brassica oleracea*, ornamental cabbage, whose wild form can still be found on the Atlantic coast. Every useful variety of cabbage grown in today's garden is derived from this one ancient cabbage—from kohlrabi to green cabbage, from cauliflower to white cabbage—a genus in transformation that offers an abundance of culinary varieties that are both known and yet to be discovered.

Ornamental cabbage is edible, but store-bought varieties are bound to be steeped in noxious chemicals. Raise them from seed yourself if you want to use them to make a rainbow-colored dinner in November with fried eggs and potatoes.

Some cabbages need the frost to fully develop their taste. The decorative ones by our door, however, usually give up the ghost at some point. Now, in spring, when the crinkled, finely slit leaves have long since fallen off, only the trunks remain, with trapeze-shaped leaf scars and minute buds. The buds seem to want to develop into miniature cabbages, but the plants' power is spent.

Especially in these first weeks of spring, the garden is full of forms and figures, relics of old vigor, and the stripped structures of skeletons. Everything soft has been scoured away, leaving only the framework of what was once rigid. Often, mysterious shapes develop, and even the experienced gardener has trouble telling just whose remains are momentarily suspended here, graphic treasures about to be done away with by awakening larvae, bugs, and wood lice. Many of these images remain unrecognized because the gardener is too busy clearing things away to notice the details.

If this trunk of an ornamental cabbage were not identified, it could be a magnificent puzzle.

To the gardener, the first signs of new life are more important than the last signs of death. For example, take the seedlings that are raising their heads everywhere now. Their first two seed leaves are mostly anonymous and oval, while their first two true leaves, growing between the seed leaves, allow the gardener to identify unwanted, everyday weeds and plants such as wolf's bane (*Aconitum vulparia*) or pasqueflower (*Pulsatilla*) that are expanding their territory by self-seeding. The gardener puts down the hoe, puts on his spectacles, squats down, makes a studied determination, and then plucks and plucks with careful fingers.

A new guest in the garden that needs special care is cow wheat (*Melampyrum*). Its seedlings, which appear early, need to be protected from the competition of sturdy herbs and grasses. Yet it is dependent on such neighbors and could not live without them because it drives its roots into the roots of other plants and taps them for water and minerals. Cow wheat is therefore a parasite, or to be botanically accurate, a hemi-parasite, since the nutrients it steals cover only half of its needs; it produces the rest in its leaves, just as any other plant would do.

The different types of cow wheat are very particular about who their host plants are, so the gardener who wishes to grow these curious plants must be extremely circumspect from the moment of sowing and cannot let up in their care until they are firmly established and have started to spread into the garden independently.

I have the gardening couple next door to thank for my cow wheat (which, incidentally, is not related to wheat at all but is a spindly herb belonging to the snapdragon family). These neighbors have given new life to the German saying that translates literally as "letting something grow across" (meaning "passing something to somebody"). Their garden abounds in wild plants. Other parasitic plants besides cow wheat that they have allowed to "grow across" include eyebright (*Euphrasia*), yellow rattle (*Rhinanthus*), and coral root bittercress (*Cardamine bulbifera*). All these plants have become rare in the wild because they have not been able to withstand the onslaught of our field, forest, and meadow economy.

Other parasitic plants in my garden are dodder (*Cuscuta epithymum*), a fragile liana that is parasitic on thyme (*Thymus vulgaris*), which I obtained from a nursery in southern Germany, and mistletoe (*Viscum album*), which has for years been at home on the apple trees and willows of Lindenhof; soon we will be able to cut our own bunches of mistletoe for Christmas.

What is it that makes us dedicate ourselves to these rather abnormal and difficult plants? Maybe an irrational kind of ambition is at play here, the necessity of proving to oneself and others that one really does have a green thumb. Usually I am more inclined to follow the principles of the great gardener Vita Sackville-West. According to her, plants that take too much trouble getting established in our gardens should not be needlessly coaxed into staying because this is no joy either to them or to us. So why do we keep getting involved with all these parasites?

There is something spooky and a bit immoral about them, living off their hosts' sap like vampires. Maybe this is the point? Maybe the gardener is just venting a deep-seated desire to be parasitic? Or is it the other way around? Is he trying to make his own parasitic weakness socially acceptable simply by changing the object? Is he intrigued by immorality?

Perhaps it would be best to stop talking about this.

A Brazilian Lady in the Frost

Our passionflower has so far survived three winters outside, and no harm has come to it. Even though its leaves and side shoots may freeze off, normally it quickly turns green again in spring. The shining coat in its sheltered corner gets denser every year, and in summer it is ever more richly speckled with blossoms and buds.

True, this is a question of climate, and it would not succeed everywhere. But the least we can do is to create a favorable microclimate and, in a sheltered corner (it does not need direct sunlight), attempt to let this tropical beauty pass its winters in the open.

The only winter protection that my passionflower enjoys is having its feet wrapped in straw, and sometimes I water it a little when the weather is dry and frost-free. One can easily recognize that this is a marvelous and powerful plant, but one can only imagine how it manages to cover entire trees in its Brazilian homeland. In our area, it is mostly forced to vegetate in a much-too-small pot or twist along a wire frame, like a tiger circling its cage.

It is said that through artificial pollination using a brush, one can obtain its reddish-yellow, edible (but not very tasty) fruits. I have not yet managed to do this. I sometimes compensate by eating a few flowers, fried briefly in oil and then sprinkled with sugar. People who like bittersweet dishes should try them.

In addition to our *Passiflora caerulea*, which I have been referring to, this genus has several other species. The most important one is *Passiflora edulis*, whose fruits are sold as maracuja; under their crinkled skin, their greenish pulp is full of small seeds. It looks similar to gooseberry pulp and tastes very exotic and aromatic.

One can certainly raise plants from those seeds, but they are definitely not frost hardy and require a large amount of space, warmth, and light if they are to develop. If you can offer them these conditions, you will even be able to harvest the fruit after a few years.

Another "indoor plant" that has survived even the hardest winters quite well outside here is *Tolmiea menziesii*. It continuously grows little plantlets on its leaves and therefore boasts such colorful vernacular names as mother and child, piggyback plant, and youth on age. However, the plant displays its high flower stalks only on the West Coast of the United States, where it is at home. Even so, in areas of moist shade, it forms beautiful, dense stands that spread by runners and also by the "mother" sinking to the ground and rotting while the "child" puts down its roots and starts to grow.

More or Less Hardy Ones

Every year—this year just a few weeks later than usual—the gardener repeats the same springtime ritual. Arms and mouth hanging, he stands gaping at plants that have not survived the winter and then raises his hand to make an oath. Once and for all he vows to be done with any plants that simply cannot cope with our winters: those that have to be wrapped up in tents and blankets of straw or pine branches or worse, those that must live in boxes and tubs, and those that must be sheltered in the vegetable cellar where some of them just rot away quietly if one is not careful. If these strenuous moves have inadvertently been overlooked when the first frost arrives, the pineapple-scented sage and the lemon shrub will be gone, and the bulbs of the voodoo lily will simply have turned to mush.

Even gorse (*Ulex europaeus*) was not spared this year. This brave shrub needs a mild, moist climate, and its death was most likely due to a kind of freeze-drying. The worst thing about this winter was not so much the subzero temperatures as the drought that spelled disaster for my evergreens.

Gone are our fuchsias, of which there are always more and newer hardy varieties on the market, as is our marvelous *Gunnera*, which grows the most bizarre flower stalks under huge leaf umbrellas. We tried to protect it with suitable hoods of baskets, straw, and twigs, following the advice of our gardening books, but to no avail. It has said good-bye just like the passionflower (which had survived three winters previously), the borage (*Borago officinalis*), and the balsam of Tolu (*Myroxylon balsamum*).

Hoping against hope, one really ought to wait until May before digging up the casualties of winter and dumping them on the compost heap. Some may only be playing dead and will suddenly spring back to life when the last frosts are over. Like an unexpected arrival, they help compensate for the many departures.

The most painful thing is that last spark from the plants that seem to have survived the cold and then collapse. The tiny amount of fresh greenery they produce is not a new awakening, but a gesture of good-bye.

Again and again, in man and beast, in plants and flames, we can observe the same thing—just when they die, there is a final moment when all their strength seems to culminate in one last effort, and then they perish. Is this simply a natural phenomenon—and if so, which one? Is it a last farewell or a rebellion? Even if it is none of these things, our feelings of melancholy and loss remain.

In the meantime, we are busy starting over, procuring just those not-quite-so-hardy plants that we only recently vowed to forsake. Rather than inconsistency, this represents a new resolve to look upon a plant as a summer visitor that is going to leave us again when its time is up, as a companion of a few months that we need not use all our gardening art and technique to force to stay. There is a new variety of allegedly hardy fuchsia, the exotic French lavender (*Lavandula stoechas*), flowering maple or Chinese bellflower (*Abutilon*), and curry plant (*Helichrysum italicum*). This last one is widely held to be frost hardy, but it has never managed to survive a winter in my garden.

Much more reliable, even though its name might lead one to surmise otherwise, is warty cabbage (*Bunias orientalis*). It is native to eastern Europe and can also be found in Siberia, so it is not apt to be scared by any of the winters we have here. Warty cabbage is a robust perennial of medium height. It bears an abundance of yellow flowers on richly branched stalks, yet it has never been recognized as a valuable perennial for the garden. As a restless weed, it can be found meandering on derelict land and in river valleys.

I read that in Turkey and in Russia, warty cabbage has always been valued as a vegetable, so in early spring, I put a bucket over my plant just as it was beginning to grow. Growing the first leaves in the dark makes them milder and more tender, just as with chicory and seakale.

When we lifted the bucket and harvested the leaves, we found that they made a delicate and exotic-tasting vegetable that needed no extra spices when briefly boiled. Their aroma is slightly reminiscent of cabbage (to which, as the name suggests, this plant is loosely related) with a whiff of mustard that one might easily reinforce by means of a creamy mustard sauce. Anyway, it is a plant that hardly needs any care apart from harvesting. We are now going to try the unbleached summer leaves to see if they, too, can be eaten.

Bunias flowers make delightful, large bouquets to brighten the indoors. We will be able to cut the first blooms for the house in only four weeks, as the gardening year is really picking up speed now. It is catching up on all its delays and has nearly made us forget how hard the winter was and how many plants fell victim to it.

Flower Foam

Very early in the year, the gardener welcomes a small species of bittercress that heralds the coming of the larger form. Both are beautiful. Anywhere that the soil is still bare at the beginning of the season, hairy bittercress (*Cardamine hirsuta*) seizes the moment while its competition is still dormant.

This little herb makes good use of its time. In only a few days, pretty rosettes start to sprout, and shortly afterward, tiny flowers appear. Then almost overnight the seed pods pop up and scatter a huge number of ripe seeds over several square meters. Most of the time, this activity is over within a matter of weeks, and the seeds rest in the ground until the next year.

In the meantime, the evergreen rosettes of lady's smock or meadow bittercress (*Cardamine pratensis*) begin to swell. Slowly their flower stalks emerge, and in May, their loose, white or bluish inflorescences seem to hover above the fresh greenery like the hood of a cloak. Botanists disagree about whether its traditional name of foam weed originates from this display of flowers or from the foam that is often found on the flower stalks, protectively enclosing the larvae of the foam cicada.

Wherever the ground is moist enough, lady's smock will also easily spread by means of seeds. More proof of its vitality is that offsets grow in the moist shade of its leaves and put down roots, thus adding to the spread of these plants in the garden.

Toward autumn, while the first seedlings of lady's smock are growing, a third species of this fertile genus appears. Forest bittercress (*Cardamine flexuosa*) rushes through its life cycle. Its flowers are so inconspicuous that most of the time, it goes undetected until its seedpods appear, forming dense stands resembling a lawn.

Like hairy bittercress, forest bittercress makes use of a short timeframe when it is not in competition with other plants, and because its ecological niche often extends to nurseries and garden centers, gardeners can obtain it for free through the seedlings that stow away in the pots of other purchases. Consider the accidental acquisition of this plant to be a bonus, if only because its tender leaves are a spicy addition to any salad.

Morning Glory Potatoes

East Asian food shops found in big cities harbor many surprises, especially for the gardener, and one in particular is the sweet potato. These pink-skinned tubers have nothing whatsoever to do with our common potato and are, in fact, a species of morning glory native to South America. Columbus found four distinct cultural varieties of it in his travels. The botanical name is *Ipomoea batatas*, from which the ancient Indian name *batata* has survived.

When the *batata* arrived in England, it came to be called potato, and only much later was this name transferred to the common potato. All attempts at cultivating the *batata* in Europe ended in failure. The plant requires large amounts of light and warmth and will grow only in tropical and subtropical countries, where it is now widely cultivated; China leads the world in today's production.

Place one of these tubers on moist sand in a greenhouse or by a window to coax it into producing sturdy shoots with heart-shaped leaves. The shoots can be trained along several meters of cane and wire, but will never produce a single flower. However, when the shoots are guided to new pots containing nutrient-rich, limy soil, with a bit of luck they may produce a few new tubers before the shoots die off in the autumn.

The tubers contain starch and sugar and just as much vitamin C as an apple or a handful of cherries. Wherever they are cultivated, they are an important staple and are also used to make flour and brew alcoholic beverages.

Everyone really ought to try sweet potatoes in their own cooking. When boiled they have a sweet and rather bland taste, but when sliced and panfried,

In our latitudes, sweet potatoes unfortunately do not fruit in the garden but can be grown in pots as ornamental climbing plants.

they give off a distinctive and appealing aroma. As early as 1633, the English doctor and botanist John Gerard recommended this cooking method, adding that one could then serve the slices with oil and vinegar. Such a meal was alleged to strengthen one's body as well as one's libido.

Allium, *All Sorts*

The genus *Allium* is friendly to us humans. All of its species, from *Allium acuminatum* to *Allium zebdanense*, are edible, without a poisonous plant in the bunch. I say all of its species in a general sense; there are about 500 of them, and nur-

Hardneck or topsetting garlic looks almost like a lively dancer.

series and plant catalogs usually offer only the so-called most important ones for the kitchen and herbaceous garden. It can take a long time to hunt down the others. The *PPP-Index* published by Ulmer, among other sources, lists suppliers for more than 100 species with more than two dozen varieties and cultivars for each, and this does not even include the common cooking onion.

I am not going to discuss the proper cooking onion (*Allium cepa*). Its manifold varieties, from Stuttgart Giants to Brunswick Reds, are a law unto themselves, and everyone must identify their own favorites. (However, do not forget, of course, the mild shallot *Allium cepa* var. *ascalonicum*!)

In the kitchen area of our bulb garden, we naturally have lots of chives (*Allium schoenoprasum*). We add their flowers to salads, or we fry them in butter and eat them as a starter. Harvesting these flowers stops the plant from seeding all over the place. The exception is 'Profusion'. Its flowers remain sterile and so do not produce seeds. An added advantage is that its flowers are noticeably more tender and thus perhaps even more suitable for use in salads.

The tree onion (or Egyptian onion), *Allium ×proliferum*, produces an abundance of sturdy and long-lasting bulbs instead of flowers. We value them not only in the kitchen but also as a spectacle. No other plant grows such large bulbs on aboveground stalks.

Parents of this tree onion are the common onion and the Welsh onion (*Allium fistulosum*). In my opinion, the Welsh onion is second only to garlic in importance and truly lives up to its vernacular name, eternal onion. Year in and year out, it grows in dense stands that are impervious to weather if the winter temperatures are not too low, providing us with a year-round supply of chives for cutting. Throughout the year we can also harvest the entire plant instead of just the tubular leaves and use it as we use leeks.

The leek (which, as we know, is biennial) is prized for its dense, thick, star-shaped flowers. When it wilts and produces seeds, something very strange indeed happens at the base of the plant: a shiny white bulb develops. This growth is so distinct and completely different from the parent plant that botanists have given it its own identity, calling it not simply *Allium porrum*, but *Allium porrum* var. *sectivum*.

Left to its own devices, this bulb will produce leaves in the following year, but it will not flower, having irrevocably lost the ability to reproduce by seed.

Instead, it will surround itself with a dense cluster of new, delicate bulbs. These onions will continue to propagate in this way indefinitely. One can let them run wild in the garden, since they avoid the perils of seed production and all the more zealously dedicate themselves to ceaseless vegetative multiplication. A pensive little onion might easily get depressed and start thinking about the meaning of life. When this happens, tell it that it is the finest and mildest type of onion in existence and that you cannot live without it.

The pinnacle of the *Allium* garden is, of course, the garlic. Its current botanical name is *Allium sativum* and its slightly milder variation, *Allium sativum* var. *ophioscordum*. Year in and year out, we look forward not only to fancy braided garlic, but also to the annual bulbs that we get by harvesting the tiny bulbs from the flower heads and pressing them into the soil in autumn. By the following July, a new bulb will have grown from each one. Why don't gardening books tell one these things?

I grow two species of *Allium* that can be used as chives: *Allium tuberosum*, or Chinese chives, the common chives from East Asia; and *Allium ramosum*, formerly *Allium odorum*, or fragrant-flowered garlic.

The last two alliums that I grow in the kitchen part of the bulb garden are native to our area. These are ramsons (*Allium ursinum*), whose leaves are suitable for a springtime salad, and wild garlic (*Allium vineale*), which produces round heads with countless tiny bulbs. Both are edible as long as they have not developed a thick outer skin.

Other native species are frequently sold in perennial nurseries. Among the most common is *Allium sphaerocephalum*, the round-headed leek with magenta-colored flowers. Sometimes one can also find *Allium carinatum* subsp. *pulchellum*, which is all but extinct in the wild, and *Allium victorialis*, a rare alpine plant.

Then things get tricky. A dozen or so native alliums are well-nigh impossible to get hold of, such as the nearly extinct *Allium multibulbosum*. Every so often I have found seeds of *Allium angulosum* or of *Allium montanum*. However, my collection remains incomplete.

Part of the bulb garden is devoted to the decorative species of *Allium*, and herein lies our reward. Most—such as yellow onion (*Allium moly*), which in former times was truly thought to aid in the making of gold—are native to the Middle East, China, or North America and are readily available in the trade.

My favorite is *Allium christophii*, whose large flower balls have a metallic sheen to them and are attractive even when dried. Some alliums are widespread, but others seem to be quite rare, such as *Allium cyaneum* with its stringy leaves, or *Allium narcissiflorum*, which still lacks an accepted common name but lives up to its botanical name by dint of its daffodil-shaped flowers. This narcissus-flowered *Allium* is native to the southwestern Alps. Like most other species of *Allium*, it is a wild plant that is largely untouched by cultivation. Even the huge flower balls of *Allium giganteum* native to the Himalayas are the result of natural phenomena rather than breeding success.

Nothing should prevent you from growing any number of the abundance of *Allium* in your own garden. Plant them in suitable places with open soil and sunlight or semishade, or simply let them run wild. Many species propagate themselves through bulbs without any intervention, and of course, you can try raising them from seed as long as you keep in mind that most species need cold conditions to germinate.

If we ultimately end up with rather too many alliums in the garden, we can always put them to practical use: as I have already said, all species of *Allium* are edible.

The Use of Shallow Tubs

Water in the garden does not have to mean a pond, puddle, or ditch. It can also be a shallow tub. Once you have had a large, shallow tub in the garden, you will never again want to do without it. Moreover, you will want to add a second or even a third. Birds get the fun, and gardeners get the use.

For example, Mary's grass—aptly called vanilla grass because of its scent—spreads so vigorously that there is scarcely a place in the garden where anyone would want to put up with it. Thank goodness it likes swamps. When it is planted in a pot and immersed in a shallow tub, it is continuously moistened from underneath and is quite happy without making a nuisance of itself.

In fact, I keep different bog plants in pots set in a tub or in my pond. It is a good way to keep these plants contained, and it is also a good way to raise them from seed, which would otherwise be difficult.

Shallow tubs can actually be useful for raising other plants from seed if you place the pots on bricks above the water. This arrangement presents a foolproof defense against slugs, who never again will gobble up a whole batch of seeds overnight.

A base layer of limy soil in a deeper pot placed under the overflow pipe of a rainwater tank gives watercress (*Nasturtium officinale*) exactly the conditions it needs—running, oxygen-rich water—without clogging up the pond and rewards us with good growth and a long life.

Sometimes a butterfly or fly or other winged insect mistakes the shining reflection of the sky for the real thing and meets its end on the surface of the water, wings outspread. Rather than doing without a shallow tub to avoid this hazard, seize the opportunity to get a closer look at the insects captured there. After all, they usually fly off just when you want to take a closer look at them.

Shallow tubs have myriad uses for both plants and animals.

Summer

So-called Groundcovers

What nurseries advertise as groundcover may look tempting at first sight. Usually they are low-growing, sometimes cushion-shaped plants. Many of them are evergreen. Some can almost tolerate being walked on.

Just the word *groundcover* conjures up the image of a green carpet. Like a lawn, it is restful to the eye; unlike a lawn, it does not require continuous care. Piri-piri bur, low-growing species of stonecrop, thyme, creeping bugle, and many others are all touted as being easy groundcovers. Only later does one discover the downside, literally. Even dense groundcover makes a fabulous seedbed for all kinds of wind-borne seeds. Weeding these groundcovers never ceases.

Finding a more maintenance-free groundcover, therefore, means searching for plants that have leaves so dense and roots so tough that they let nothing else appear in their midst.

Embarking on this search may mean watching herbaceous perennials and wild plants very closely to find out how well they cope with chance competition (such as grasses, whose seeds are just about everywhere) or with their own neighbors. Those that cope well are always plants that also propagate freely because they are so strong, and it is easy and inexpensive to use them for groundcover in areas that you want green once and for all.

For example, one need only see the roots of orpine (*Sedum telephium*) to understand why it does not tolerate competition. In early spring, the leaves of its winter buds unfold and then keep the ground shaded for an entire summer. No other plant can crop up under them. Slowly but powerfully, orpine then spreads out in all directions, its beautiful flower spikes joining up to form a large-scale pattern. Propagation could not be simpler: from May to September, one can simply cut finger-long pieces of stem and poke them into the soil. Each one will develop into a new plant. At some point toward the end of the winter, the only work required is to clean up the meadow by trimming off the rigid stems of the wilted but still decorative flowers.

Comfrey can make life even easier. If the mighty perennials that the larger species turn into are simply too big on a grand scale, use the low-growing relative from the Caucasus (*Symphytum grandiflorum*). It grows freely in the shade and produces cream-colored flowers in early summer. There is also a blue-flowering variety. In winter, it simply wilts, and like its larger relative, it leaves a dense, black carpet of rotting foliage. The new shoots have no trouble making their way up through it in the spring.

An added advantage of comfrey is that, unlike orpine, bulbs can thrive for several years in the carpet it forms. Snowbells and daffodils flower while comfrey is still dormant, and they retract as soon as it awakes.

Bistort (*Persicaria officinalis*) is another plant that saves us from spring cleaning. Its young leaves can be eaten as a salad, and its flower spikes, shaped like ears of corn, delight us for many weeks. It loves moist soil and semishade, but it is prone to wander and is therefore mainly suitable for places that can reliably be fenced in by walls or pathways.

Species of lady's mantle (*Alchemilla mollis* or *Alchemilla vulgaris*, for example) do equally well in sun or shade. They feature small, greenish-yellow flowers in dense umbels and rich foliage that completely covers the ground. Maintenance is low except for raking off old leaves in the spring.

In semishade, sweet cicely quickly grows into a dense, tall shrub that self-seeds to become a veritable hedge. From a distance, it looks similar to a clump of ferns, but in spring it is covered in beautiful white umbels. Its dry remains are often blown away by the wind, and if not, one has to help them a little. The same is true for black-eyed Susan or orange coneflower (*Rudbeckia fulgida* var. *sullivantii* 'Goldsturm'). Although it is really a perennial for woodland edges, it is equally well suited for large-scale plantings. When its flower bases turn black in winter, they create a beautiful pattern of dots hovering above a carpet of gray foliage.

Finally, evergreen fringe cup (*Tellima grandiflora*) does well in deepest shade. Planted in large stands, it gives off an intense fragrance of lily-of-the-valley that is widely noticeable when it flowers.

All of these are examples of plant species that can be used as groundcover and require very little work. Such monocultures are not at all unnatural, either, since these plants tend to form large stands in the wild. Of course, mixed plantings are also possible, but one must pay attention to the different needs of the plants one combines.

The biggest incentive for continuing the quest for the perfect groundcover is the prospect of making new discoveries. In the process, one finds new ways of looking at the growth forms and qualities of many garden plants.

Butterbur and Opium Lettuce

Butterbur (*Petasites hybridus*) seemed like a good idea. Our moist area to the north, where the drainpipes distribute our domestic sewage below ground, needed to be planted with something "easy to look after." Shrubs and trees were out of the question because their roots could get into the pipes and eventually block them. So we chose butterbur.

In the deep shade of its six-foot-high forest of leaves, nothing else grows, so there is no need for weeding. Early in the spring, cylindrical flower heads mushroom from the soil on short, tubular stems, densely packed with small, Michaelmas daisy–like flowers—real jewels on bare winter soil. Only afterward do they develop their giant leaves, which from a distance are reminiscent of rhubarb and are the biggest of any native European plant.

Hildegard von Bingen called this plant great coltsfoot and recommended it, among other things, against malignant abscesses. Later, when the plague hit Europe, it came to be called plague root and was touted hopefully but unsuccessfully as a remedy. In the Walachei region of Romania, where things have always been quite rough, its bitter-tasting leaves were eaten as a vegetable. One leaf was enough for four people.

The intricate pink flowers and outrageously large leaves seen above ground are sustained by an underground stem that is both strong and relentless. Initially the tufts of butterbur were modest and picturesque in our garden, but in the space of only a few years, they turned into a real jungle. The runners just kept going, growing underneath a stone pathway and continuing straight into the herb garden. There they spread out their leaves and overcame anything that dared cross their path. The name of plague weed suddenly acquired a whole new meaning, and the image of such a plant taking over the entire garden,

Children are not the only ones who can play hide-and-seek in the giant stands of butterbur. Photo by Hella Dahl

meter by meter, became more and more alarming, a bad dream from which I would awake at dawn.

Saying good-bye to the butterbur is also causing its share of sleepless nights, for clearing 200 square meters of butterbur root is not child's play. Apart from that, we are going to miss the peculiar smell of its leaf sap, a combination of coriander and fresh water (or of "bugs," as botany books put it), like an evening by the lakeside.

Perhaps we could plant opium lettuce (*Lactuca virosa*) in place of the butterbur and, in doing so, continue a practice that began in ancient times but petered out about 100 years ago. Opium lettuce is a close relative of our green lettuce, which was prized by the ancient Romans for its soporific effect. This is why they used to serve lettuce for dessert rather than as an appetizer. If a stronger narcotic was needed, they used opium lettuce, not as a salad but as lactucarium, the brown, resinous grains obtained from drying the milky sap of the plant. Lactucarium was valued as a medicine of many uses and particularly as the best sleeping pill and painkiller next to the poppy. Just a quarter-gram of lactucarium was enough to bring sleep and a respite from pain.

The Romans were not the only people to value lactucarium. Hildegard von Bingen advised careful use, Albertus Magnus praised its painkilling effect, and North American Indians ground it into a paste and made tea from it.

As time went by, opium lettuce was all but forgotten until the Viennese doctor H. J. Collin rediscovered it in 1771 and sang its praises once more. The advantages of lactucarium over opium are that lactucarium has no side effects and is not addictive.

In several countries in Europe, opium lettuce cultures sprang up where people cut the plants by a few centimeters several times a day to collect the sap that exuded. In Zell on the Moselle, a pharmacist named Alois Goeris started growing opium lettuce commercially in 1847, but he was a little too late to make a go of it. One year earlier, an American dentist used ether as an anaesthetic for the first time, and its success soon spelled the end for lactucarium, though it continued to be found in American medical handbooks until the end of the nineteenth century. So opium lettuce enjoyed a long medicinal history— starting with the Emperor Augustus, who dedicated an altar to lactucarium because he was so grateful for it—until it was removed from medical texts altogether. It is not surprising that a sleepless gardener was tempted to try it. The seeds of *Lactuca virosa* were easy to get hold of, the plants thrived, and harvesting the milky sap was no problem, but the beverage, prepared by the book, remained without effect, even though I increased the dosage a little every day.

I can unequivocally say that opium lettuce, at least in moderate doses, is

Opium lettuce is clearly a relative of our common lettuce. Its sap has a narcotic effect.

not at all poisonous. By the way, if mixed with alcohol and a little sugar, it has a most distinctive taste reminiscent of plums. That is reason enough to extend the lettuce field this year and to continue the experiment, concocting the delicious beverage or using the leaves to brew a tea that the Meskwaki Indians prepared and declared useful. Augustus, Hildegard, Albertus, Dr. Collin, the Meskwaki—surely they cannot all have been wrong!

If I should succeed in getting some slumber with the help of this lettuce, I really am going to plant a field of it in the area that is now costing me so much sleep, as it is still covered in butterbur. And then we are going to check the laws to see whether we might be able to open a very small factory for sleeping tea. It is probably forbidden.

And, of course, if any of you want to try this lettuce, do so at your own risk!

The Joys of Collecting Sempervivums

No plant genus grows nearly so easily as *Sempervivum*, or houseleek, does. Stack three flowerpots of different sizes into a pyramid, fill them with some soil, and plant each one with a few rosettes. In one or two years, without any work, a cascade of kids and grandkids will delight you, the oldest ones producing magnificent flower heads in the summer.

Sempervivums need nothing but sunlight and will even put up with semishade if they have to. They need little water and appreciate never being fertilized.

And of course, they do not really need a pot pyramid. Any stony, lime-free, well-drained ground will do. If they get wet feet, they soon die and are therefore unhappy in normal garden beds. They love stony hillocks, dry-stone walls, roof tiles, stone troughs (with a hole at the bottom!), and balcony flowerpots.

Thanks to their mastery over hunger and thirst, they are not insulted when we take off on our summer holidays and leave them to their own devices for weeks on end. Their fresh colors will welcome us back, and their firm, succulent leaves, in which they can store water for weeks or even months, will put on a show.

These plants learned such unpretentious survival skills in their home country, where they nest in rocky gorges high in the mountains. They form dense cushions over the years and then live off their own humus, similar to those cushions of houseleek that people used to grow for decades on their rooftops in the hope that they would protect the house from lightning.

When a rosette is mature and flowers, it consumes itself in the process: it sends all its vitality into the flower head and then dies. In the meantime, however, it forms new rosettes all around itself. In the genus *Sempervivum*, these are more or less long offshoots that one may cut off, trim to size, and plant out; in the space of only a few days, they will grow some roots. In the genus *Jovibarba*, a close relative, the "daughters" detach themselves when they are big enough and immediately take root where they fall.

Only *Jovibarba heuffelii* proves an exception to this rule. This species propagates itself by division of its rosettes, giving its cushions a very strange look and making it recognizable even from long distances. Apart from this, species names are the only area in which houseleeks give us a hard time. Even specialists do not agree on the allocation of species and subspecies. The number of hybrids and local variants is immense and just continues to multiply, and successful breeding has increased the number of cultivars by so much that one needs a lot of patience and a good eye to find one's way through the thousands of known variants. The names that cultivars or species are sold under are often just plain wrong, and for this reason, some nurseries will offer only unnamed assortments. If one does not fear the upturned noses of proper *Sempervivum* collectors, one may happily put together all the varieties that one likes, even without their proper names.

Yet one should take delight in the small differences: the white felt of the spider web houseleek, the large leaves and flower heads of the *Sempervivum tectorum* group, the changing color of the leaves (from gray-green to dark red) through the seasons. They flower all through the year, offering a whole range of colors—white, pink, red, and yellow in many different shades—in nice subdued tones rather than a spectacular riot of color.

If one is wondering just how the spider web houseleeks manage to cover themselves in such an even felt of white hair, pick up a strong magnifying glass. It will reveal that every leaf grows hairs to its neighboring leaves. The hairs meet in the gap and are so closely intertwined that one they appear to be a continuous mat of felt. This examination does not, however, solve the riddle; it merely describes it in other words.

Hay Scent at Bedtime

Not all hay is scented, and not everything that smells of hay is indeed dry grass. The strongest smell of hay, in fact, comes from a Brazilian plant in the pea family, tonka bean (*Dipteryx odorata*). Its black, elongated fruits are sold in pharma-

Bouquets of Bokhara clover can make a whole house smell intensely of hay.

cies as *fabae tonco* and are mainly used for adding aroma to tobacco, liqueurs, and biscuits. Their scent of hay is so intense that it approaches that of vanilla.

Tonka beans owe their scent to cumarin, the same substance that adds the characteristic aroma to hay and woodruff (*Galium odoratum*). Unfortunately, cumarin has turned out to cause headaches in sensitive people. Over long periods of time it can also cause heart and liver damage, which is why traditional woodruff punch has fallen into disrepute.

However, that should not stop us from enjoying the hay scent many grasses exude after being dried, and two species in particular: sweet vernal grass (*Anthoxanthum odoratum*) and holy grass (*Hierochloe odorata*).

Both of these are perennial grasses that occur naturally in meadows and can also be accommodated in a garden. But be careful with holy grass! It is very vigorous, and its strong rhizomes can run for meters. It is difficult to catch once it has escaped and is best confined to a large pot. Holy grass smells sweet even when it is fresh. Its vernacular name used to be Mary's bedstraw. In Poland, some types of vodka contain a straw of holy grass for a touch of softness in what otherwise is pigswill.

The most beautiful cumarin plant for the garden is Bokhara clover (*Melilotus*), a biennial species that grows as upright, richly branched bushes. We harvest it in large bouquets and let them dry inside the house. For several weeks, the house is then filled with their wonderful hay scent. If one is not prone to headaches, one may place a small bag of Bokhara clover leaves under one's pillow. Pressure and warmth will then for months sustain the illusion that one really is lying in a meadow on a beautiful summer's evening. This can help one fall asleep and it is certainly safe, though one should dispense with the old-fashioned applications of Bokhara clover (for coughs and circulatory disease) in view of the dangers that cumarin poses.

Would Not Hurt a Fly?

My birdwatching visitor, nodding appreciatively, asserted that he had just heard a chiffchaff. If birds were unable to fly, I might be quite interested in studying them myself. But like this? One learns that the greenfinch has a yellow dot on the side of its tail and that its call sounds like *djui* (whereas that of the chiffchaff sounds like *huid*), and just when one tries to focus on the tail, the greenfinch flies off and might have been something else altogether. Its song just slips away into the bushes and does not remain in one's memory, at least not in mine.

Disappointed by the futility of my early ornithological endeavors, I turned to stones that neither flew off nor sang, and only via this detour did I then turn to plants. One can identify plants in peace and quiet and then archive them in an herbarium.

The famous German poet Joachim Ringelnatz once suggested something similar for animals, the "terrbarium": "Above all, one must press the animals alive." Ringelnatz was much too gentle to have been serious, but this is hardly a laughing matter in view of all the things that are done to animals today. As meat consumption has increased, so has our sensitivity, so that even the gardener becomes embarrassed when asked what he does to his snails and slugs. Does he relocate them (permitted), does he scald them with boiling water (tolerated grudgingly), or does he chop them up with his hedge clippers in passing (taboo among animal lovers)?

Of course, we take such drastic measures only against slugs, who attack our seedlings or who manage to munch up the tender shoot of a toad lily in such a way that it will never come back. Snails, however, with their joyful shell colorings, deserve protection and not just because they are pretty. They never gnaw fresh greenery, but only algae and rotting leaves, and they also feature on a sensitive gardener's coat of arms. With eyes on stalks and tender feelers, they explore the realm of the garden. They destroy nothing, they make no noise, and above all, they are slow and patient. At dusk, when the pathways are moist, they come out of their hiding places. Then we have to take care that they do not meet an untimely death beneath our boots.

In former times, one was less worried.

The gardener, if his garden has an agricultural element as well, has to decide. Should he create an artificial paradise where death does not exist and where moles are rescued from attacking cats? Then he would have to do without chickens, too (nor could he simply go out and buy eggs, since delegating the killing would be almost hypocritical). Or should he regard himself as part of the terrestrial ecology by dealing with chickens as chickens deal with earthworms or martens deal with chickens?

He has to decide, and if he does not live up to the Franciscan ideal, then he must live with the constant reminder that all the reasons human brains can furnish to justify any killing are not enough to make it absolutely necessary.

May I, sitting by the pond, kill the mosquito that is biting me? There are good reasons for doing so, in spite of those gentle people who would not even hurt a fly. On the other hand, once a gentle person gets into a car, hundreds of mosquitoes get squashed on the windscreen.

Despite my scruples, I have started a small collection of insects, which gives me at least the most important groups and species for identification and comparison. Some of them I find dead in the rainwater tank or lying on the pathway, some I kill with a drop of ether. Naming them is a difficult undertaking. In many cases I can identify them only roughly. When I see 10 or 20 creatures spread out, I realize that I can never hope to know more than a fraction of the diversity in the garden. Politeness would dictate that I should address every creature in the garden by its proper name, and yet I feel proud when I can point to the little moth circling the lamp and say that it may be a type of pyralid moth. I wisely do not add that there are at least 300 different species of these moths in Germany alone.

It is only when one begins to distinguish the large groups and then the genera and species that one gains any insight into the way of life of the different bugs, bumblebees, wasps, and all the other flying and crawling and chewing insects. This takes a number of books in which the fruits of several hundred years of research have been collected.

How much time and energy must have been invested in finding out that male mosquitoes, hovering swarms of which can often be seen at dusk, give their females a wrapped up insect as a wedding present before getting down to business (during which act the female remains totally unruffled and proceeds to eat her present). One can discern months and even years of dogged observation behind every cut and dried sentence. To this day, insects spend most of their lives in secret. Only short episodes from different stages in their lives are revealed to us. Female glowworms lie in the grass and blink at the searching males; the Bokhara clover leaves are once again nibbled around the edges and we still do not know who the culprit is; punctually as ever, the beautiful brown-white-yellow larvae of water betony have reappeared, yet we still have not seen the real thing.

The more one knows, the more the image of animals as guests in the garden starts to turn on its head: they are not the guests, we are. We are guests at the edge of an insect universe about which, judging from its size, we still know next to nothing.

When we discover the larva of the elephant hawk moth, it displays its threatening posture and seems like a Cerberus to us, guarding an immeasurable kingdom and clearly preferring that we not exist at all.

Speaking of glowworms, the other day I wanted to lift a glowing female from the ground for the collection. It turned out not to be a glowworm but the stub of a cigarette. That hurt! It was as though St. Francis had pinched me just as I was about to kidnap a glowworm.

Does a Stinging Nettle Defend Itself?

Our goose meadow has been grazed bare, nibbled down nearly to soil level with only a few bushes of stinging nettle and sorrel rising up like islands on the plain. Our hawthorn hedge has also escaped unscathed.

It is remarkable how these plants manage to defend themselves against voracious animals. Hawthorn does it with long, hard spines, stinging nettle with its stinging hairs, sorrel with oxalic acid. But do these plants really defend themselves? Can one say, even figuratively, that they protect themselves?

The answer is yes. Biologists are totally sure of this. Without any hesitation they talk of "protection" and "defense strategies" and can bring into play many other obvious examples, apart from hawthorn, nettles, and sorrel. Prickles on roses? Protection. Thorns on thistles? Protection. Poison in belladonna? Protection.

Once on this road, biologists go one step further. Some very remarkable things were recently reported at a congress on evolutionary biology in London. For example, they interpreted the soft hairs of the dead nettle to be a form of mimicry, meant to be a deceptively real and deterring imitation of the burning hairs of stinging nettle. The narrow, grayish-brown leaves of some New Zealand vines are also interpreted as being a cunning deception. Moas, a species of birds that are unable to fly, are supposed to mistake these leaves for thin branches, as if, in the course of thousands of years, they have not been able to figure out the deception.

Furthermore, evolutionary biologists assert that dented or serrated leaves are meant to trick visiting insects into thinking that others have already been feeding on the leaves and nothing worth bothering with is left. The same is true of the swiss cheese plant (*Monstera*), a tropical plant that used to be commonly found in butcher shops but that nowadays is more likely to live in open-plan offices. Its leaves are full of bizarre holes and slits, a distinguishing feature meant to signal traces of feeding to foraging insects.

Finally, in a recently published book on plant ecology, one can read, "A further defensive strategy against being eaten is the fact that the nutritional value of many plant species is indeed very poor."

On this point, at least, one's admiration for the acumen of those scientists may turn to skepticism in light of their hasty conclusions. So we ask again: Do plants defend themselves? Can the poor nutritional value of a plant, which may indeed be favorable to its existence, really be called a strategy?

Upon further study, one can see that the explanations for these conclusions, even if they are merely used in a figurative sense, are in stark contrast to the fundamental assumptions of evolutionary biology, the very science on which the discoveries are based.

After all, evolutionary biology teaches that all characteristics of living organisms have, in the course of history, come about totally at random through chance mutations that were not at all aimed at some purpose. Depending on their value for the survival of the species, these features were then confirmed or discarded by selection. Prickles, thorns, poison, and stinging hairs have all developed by chance and, as their existence shows us, they have turned out to be useful for survival.

Such unplanned and aimless development, however, is exactly the opposite of a strategy. Strategy defines an aim and maps out a way to achieve it, whereas evolution progresses blindly and mechanically in minute steps through the process of trial and error. Because one thing leads to another, it may sometimes look as if the steps lead in a particular direction. However, the laws of scientific investigation do not permit us to present "as if" as hard fact.

If characteristics such as those described above have developed through chance mutations, then we may be permitted to state the following. During the course of their evolutionary history, some plants have by chance acquired characteristics that make them inedible to some animals. This in turn may have helped them survive, even though dandelions, which are really tasty, have not yet been driven to extinction by their enemies.

Rather than splitting hairs, I am making an important distinction that can open the mind to a way of looking beyond the details to view an entire problem, and by entire I mean the totality of all organisms as well as the entire organism of a plant species.

Viewed in connection with all other plants, the comment that some animals avoid some plants seems self-evident, a statistical platitude. Among roughly 250,000 distinct plant species and far more species of animals with different demands, it is almost unthinkable that some plant species are not protected by some random quality from being damaged by some animal species.

Stinging nettles, for example, are in fact avoided by many animals. Our geese do not eat them. To make up for this, however, there are dozens of beetles, bugs, mining flies, gall wasps, cicadas, and above all butterfly larvae that are not at all deterred by nettle hairs and can sometimes be devastating to the plants. So one can really speak of protection in only a few specialized cases, namely those in which one assumes that the animals would indeed feed on the nettles were it not for the stinging hairs. This is not a very convincing basis on which to assert a defensive strategy.

One can look at the entire organism of a plant and draw similar conclusions. All of the details and qualities that might be useful in protecting a plant against some animals actually have a role to play in shaping a plant's life story. For example, the hairs of many plants may be interpreted as providing protection but also have a cooling effect by reducing transpiration, the prickles of blackberries are useful as a climbing aid, the transformation of thistle leaves into thorns enables some thistles to survive in extremely dry environments, and so on.

Things get even more uncertain when it comes to plant poisons. Plant poisons are part of a metabolism operating with thousands of different substances. In the large chemical laboratories that work with different formulas to make up a plant, it is impossible to tell whether these toxins have been produced for their own sake (as weapons, so to speak), are supplementary products of other production processes (such as the production of proteins or energy), or are by-products of a plant's physiology (such as waste products).

It therefore seems bold to assert that the poison of a plant, which is bad for some animals, was developed as a defense mechanism against those very animals, since one often discovers animals that find this same poison very tasty indeed. Thrushes are mad about the berries of deadly nightshade, for example, so in this instance the taste actually helps to distribute the seeds.

All this literature about defense strategies of plants finally boils down to one simple, not very surprising sentence: some plants have some qualities that make some animals avoid them.

Such thoughts are not arguments against evolutionary theory. On the contrary, they are a plea for keeping its system free of metaphorical expressions that only get in the way of what evolutionary theory can and cannot describe. Where only chance exists, one cannot and must not talk of any kind of purpose, not even in the sense of "as if."

Risky Umbels

The flower plates of the parsley family beam at us benevolently both inside and outside the garden. Most of the time, these flower heads are white; more rarely, they are greenish or yellowish. Most of the time, they are spicy; sometimes they are also poisonous. Many important spices and medicinal plants belong to this family, and they all have vastly different scents: caraway (*Carum carvi*) and aniseed (*Pimpinella anisum*); fennel (*Foeniculum vulgare*) and dill (*Anethum graveolens*); parsley (*Petroselinum sativum*), chervil (*Anthriscus cereifolium*), sweet cicely (*Myrrhis odorata*), lovage (*Levisticum officinale*), and angelica (*Angelica archangelica*); not to mention one of the few perennials in the parsley family, the mostly unknown (alas) baldmoney (*Meum athamanticum*), which even in the earliest part of the year supplies us with feathery leaves that taste similar to dill. Last but not least, there are also three vegetables in this family: celery, carrot, and parsnip.

Many of the umbels and finely slit or feathered leaves found in the parsley family are very similar, which unfortunately makes them very dangerous.

Along with the species listed above that are used as spices, medicines, or food, there are a host of poisonous species. People who have confused them have often paid with their lives. One of the more famous—or infamous—is hemlock (*Conium maculatum*), which the Greek philosopher Socrates used to take his life. Even more poisonous is MacKenzie's water hemlock (*Cicuta virosa*).

Both can be found in the wild and only rarely wander into gardens, though the decorative McKenzie's water hemlock may intentionally be planted in a pond.

Fool's parsley (*Aethusa cynapium*) is a more common and therefore more dangerous plant. It often appears in gardens and then freely seeds itself. It is very similar to two kitchen herbs, namely parsley and chervil, and therefore demands caution. Luckily there is a fail-safe characteristic: chervil and parsley both have a typical and pleasant smell, whereas fool's parsley smells rather disgusting.

If you go out walking to collect wild plants for cooking and healing, take a lesson from the fool's parsley and eat only those plants you can identify with certainty. This does not go only for the parsley family. Years ago, a man died after eating a portion of autumn crocus salad because he had mistaken the poisonous leaves—which do actually smell of garlic—for those of wild garlic.

Who Is the Queen of Flowers?

Only reluctantly will I admit that I just cannot worship the rose as the queen of flowers. First of all, I do not like this expression because it is degrading to a thousand other plants. Second of all, if pressed, I could suggest a few other candidates of equal value that would merit being called regal. Iris is a good example.

In my garden, there are very few roses. One of my favorites is *Rosa roxburghii*, with its prickly fruits and its bark peeling away as if in mourning. It grows into a large, solid bush and does not need worry and care. In addition, there is *Rosa foetida*, the stinking rose or Austrian yellow rose, whose stench never fails to take garden guests by surprise.

If somebody wants to make fun of the fact that they can hardly find any roses in my garden, I tell them the story of Christopher Lloyd, who has been running a famous nursery in East Sussex for years and who has written a dozen well-respected gardening books. The grounds of the vast family estate were designed long ago by Christopher Lloyd's father together with Sir Edwin Lutyens, the famous garden architect, and a large rose garden naturally formed a central part of it. So what did Christopher Lloyd do at the ripe old age of seventy-two? He cleared out the rose garden and got rid of the queens once and for all. "I was fed up with all the trouble that roses bring," he grumbled. "They are constantly getting any old disease, and one cannot replace a weak bush without first replacing the soil. They are not even beautiful, and when they flower, one sees nothing but a sprinkling of blobs. Climbing roses are just about all right, but shrubs are simply horrible."

I do not want to propose a new dogma, nor do I want to start an argument. I merely want to suggest that we now and then question traditions handed down to us. Is every gardening tradition that we hold dear really suitable for us? According to Christopher Lloyd, "It is much easier to imitate something than to think something up oneself."

When it comes to irises, that they are not scented could be considered a deficiency in comparison to roses. Even stinking iris does not stink. But the true iris experts (among whom I may not count myself)—those who work their way through iris catalogs every year—know that there are many sometimes surprisingly scented species and varieties of iris. In my garden, there are four: *Iris graminea*, or grass-leaved iris, smells of plums. Corn leaf iris (*Iris bucharica*) and dalmatian iris (*Iris pallida*) have a gentle, flowery scent, and a brown-yellow-pink variety of bearded iris, the name of which I do not know, smells distinctly of chocolate. For me, this is enough.

True and False Asparagus

There has to be an end to green asparagus. Harvests are plentiful; the nodding heads of their shoots, which look like pipes, are pretty; it is easy to care for; and we will miss the golden autumn color of the six-foot-tall bushes. But green asparagus needs a lot of space, and the taste of its shoots is hardly reminiscent of white asparagus. Instead, it tastes of broccoli, and I do not like broccoli.

Some people praise green asparagus as the asparagus of the hobby gardener. There may be some truth in that. Its shoots can be harvested above ground, it does not need mounds of soil, and a few handfuls of compost suffice as fertilizer. The shoots taste best when harvested very young, before they have developed even the tiniest bit of hard skin. Boil the shoots, drown them while still warm in a spicy vinaigrette dressing, and allow them to marinate for at least three hours.

However, after an entire month of having a bowl full of green asparagus in vinaigrette on the table that has to be emptied day after day to keep it from fermenting, this modest delicacy loses what little attraction it once possessed, and to consume it becomes an obligation.

We are going to keep a single asparagus bush, mainly because of its autumn color but also because of the asparagus chicken, which is not a chicken at all but a beetle with beautiful red and yellow markings. It is called a chicken because it produces a chirping sound with its legs and wings. As chickens do not chirp, this may not be a logical name, but it is a fact.

At the same time we are harvesting our asparagus, people in England are harvesting Bath asparagus, which occurs naturally in large stands in the forests surrounding the spa town of Bath in the county of Somerset.

Bath asparagus is not a type of asparagus, just as the asparagus chicken is not a chicken, and its ornamental species are called Star of Bethlehem (*Ornithogalum*). Several species are available as bulbs. They are planted in September, and in spring they produce wonderful bouquets of shining, white, star-shaped

As long as the buds remain closed, the flower shoots of Star of Bethlehem can be prepared and eaten like asparagus.

flowers. Before the flowers open, the flowering shoots are collected and then bundled and boiled like asparagus. In England and in Holland, one can buy these in the market, but in this country, we have to grow the Star of Bethlehem in our own garden if we want to try it. It turns out that it has only one thing in common with asparagus: it is boiled in bundles. Apart from that, it tastes a little bitter and a little green and little else, but the English seem to be content with it.

The story of the Star of Bethlehem as food dates back to Roman times, and it is connected to a venerable translation error. Generations of Bible readers have chewed over (or maybe not) a strange passage in 2 Kings 6:25: "In Samaria there was great famine, and so strict was the siege that the head of a donkey sold for eighty shekels of silver, and one quarter-kab of dove's dung for five shekels of silver."

What use can dove's dung have had in a besieged city, and why would people pay so much for it? The answer is that dove's dung was the vernacular name for Star of Bethlehem, the wild onion that grows in large amounts in Samaria and in many other places in Syria and Palestine. Perhaps the meadows looked like squares sprinkled with dove's dung.

In countries east of the Mediterranean, the bulbs of the Star of Bethlehem were and still are eaten raw, boiled, or panfried. Why this beautiful, edible plant has not managed to win itself a place in our cuisine becomes clear when one tries it. Both its shoots and its bulbs taste distinctly bitter, probably too bitter for our liking. Yet in Syria and Egypt, its bulbs were dried and carried as food on long journeys.

The raw bulbs contain lots of mucous substances. Given its bitterness as well, Star of Bethlehem should by rights make good medicine. After all, mucus loosens coughs, and bitter substances activate stomach juices and give people an appetite. This combination may also calm a nervous stomach. So this remedy may be worth trying.

Star of Bethlehem is not suitable as an alternative to asparagus, however. For real white asparagus, with potatoes and melted butter and ham, we continue to rely on asparagus farmers and asparagus cutters. Even seakale cannot replace asparagus, though English people are really mad about bleaching its shoots under their outrageously expensive forcers and, in May, preparing it like asparagus. We tried seakale (*Crambe maritima*) grown under an original English forcer. Its pale shoots looked nicely spooky, but it tasted perfectly bland, somewhat reminiscent of cabbage and, at best, suitable as a neutral substrate for distinctive spices. However, we are continuing to cultivate it if only to prevent our forcer from standing idle.

An afterthought: while I was sitting here writing this, my wife was busy preparing a cream of asparagus soup from the last harvest of green asparagus. Delicious! It might be allowed to stay after all.

A Failure to Appreciate Absinthe

Because it is considered a kitchen herb, absinthe (*Artemisia absinthium*) is sometimes planted in kitchen gardens just to be polite. One rarely finds a gardener actually using it in cooking. However, a small leaf (no more!) can add a very distinctive note to many meat and egg dishes. One need try it only once to be convinced.

It is true that if absinthe were useful only as a spice, it would not be worth the trouble it takes to look after the large bush and keep it young through division or through cuttings. But absinthe has more to offer.

The leaves of absinthe are its most beautiful feature. They are roundly incised and can range from gray-green to shimmering white. It is a color that does the garden good, both as a tone that differs from the other, warmer shades of green and as a backdrop that provides a strong contrast for flower colors and contours. Blue bellflowers (*Campanula*) and yellow Himalayan poppies (*Meconopsis regia*) name but two possible neighbors.

I have found no evidence to confirm the widespread opinion that absinthe hinders the growth of anything planted next to it. Everything I have paired with absinthe has done well and has flowered freely, so take advantage of its virtues without any concern. The beautiful gray-green bushes tolerate dry soil and full sun and create an imposing spectacle from spring all the way through to autumn, though the small yellow flowers, which appear in August, are rather insignificant.

One does, however, need to be careful when using absinthe as a medicinal herb, even though herbals have always praised it as a good remedy for stomach upsets. It can irritate the kidneys and the mucous membranes inside the stomach, and there are less risky bitter medicines to get one's juices going. The infamous absinthe schnapps is rightly prohibited by law, though absinthe wines are free of any noxious substances.

People used to put bundles of absinthe among the washing to keep moths at bay, and dry bouquets of absinthe hung up in a room were said to repel all other insects. It is indeed possible that the odor of absinthe has this effect, and the bush of absinthe in the garden will put this theory to the test.

A Display for Patient People

If one has ever taken the time to watch a flower unfold, one will never forget the experience and will seek it out time and again, either during the day, which is when irises open, or in the hour before dusk settles in, which is when the evening primrose makes its appearance.

A bud symbolizes a secret and a promise. Tightly folded, it contains a complete flower. When the hour of flowering arrives, the petals burst out of their cover with gentle, silent force and unfold into a flower. Its size defies the notion that all its parts fit into the bud. This process of unfolding, which happens a thousand times over in the garden but nearly always remains unseen, presents a marvelous display. The plant is actually doing something, and the more an observer gets absorbed in the process, the more a flower appears to be a live and moving individual, compelling and breathtaking.

It naturally takes a lot of persistence and calm to observe this phenomenon. Just as in a game of chess, moves happen quickly but the breaks in between seem to drag on and on. With irises, for example, the first thing to do is to identify a bud that is about to open, understanding that "about to" can take hours. You can go get a chair and make yourself comfortable at your lookout post or—even more comfortable—cut a flowering shoot and place it in a vase inside the house. The only drawback to the indoor method is the lack of wind, which sometimes aids the opening of a flower.

One after another the falls spread out and then turn downward. In the meantime, the "dome" of the bud widens as the standards round themselves to the outside. Casually but persistently, the flower goes through its paces, which in a purely mechanical sense can be compared to pumping something up. The

The unfolding of an iris flower is only for those who are patient enough to appreciate the event.

pressure of the sap, or the turgor, makes the tissues swell in precise areas and in precise ways.

The iris flower wilts by the following day. Its petals turn limp, and the fluid that gave them their shape drips to the ground. A few centimeters lower on the stem, the next bud starts to thicken. It will flower tomorrow.

Notes on Pruning Things into Shape

Just leave your privet in peace this year! Do not constantly clip away at it to make it keep its shape. Let it flower for once if only to encourage the privet hawk moth, *Sphinx ligustri*, to use its long trunk to suck nectar out of the scented flowers and deposit its eggs. In August and September you will be able to marvel at the gigantic green caterpillars with their purple and white stripes.

Privet (*Ligustrum*)—one native species and several East Asian ones are available in nurseries—has some indisputable virtues. Even in the deepest shade, it quickly becomes green and dense. In mild winters, it retains some of its leaves, though the danger of seeing it freeze to death increases as you move into higher elevations.

Privet is easy to propagate from cuttings, which makes it inexpensive. It is an ideal shrub for fast-growing, sometimes evergreen hedges if you are unable to afford boxwood or yew.

The guardians of the town of Kamp-Lintfort may have been thinking along these lines a few years ago when they decided to restore the baroque garden of their Cistercian monastery on the lower banks of the Rhine. They mainly chose privet for the more than 100 cone-shaped trees they needed. It had already been expensive enough to buy up the land for the garden, which had been subdivided long ago, and to reconstruct its old terraces.

The privet trees in the garden at Kamp look decidedly mangled every spring, but that is somehow fitting for this desolate reconstruction, which the dismal mining town of Kamp-Lintfort is now using to attract tourists.

I am never quite at ease with all these ubiquitous efforts to restore baroque gardens. What exactly are we thinking as we recreate the most arrogant and violent symbols of a feudal and hierarchical understanding of world and nature, those drawing-board gardens in which every tulip stands at attention and screams *L'État c'est toi!* while the boxwoods sadly wonder whether there is life outside the barbershop?

Franciscus Daniel, who became abbot of the Kamp monastery in 1733, loved luxury and abhorred the sour wine then cultivated on the monastery's southern slope. Going far beyond the principles of his monastic order and the capabilities of his patron saint, he cleared the vines and began to turn the vineyard into a feudal garden. To the irritation of his fellow monks, he sold monastery property and forests to fund the project. The garden was never actually completed, however, and in due time, secularization finished it off.

Now, 250 years later, people are fervently and earnestly working to reconstruct this vain cleric's folly. They are spending 5 million marks on it and another 5 million for the so-called infrastructure in order to sustain the legend that Frederic the Great passed these gardens when returning to Berlin and was inspired right there in the carriage to draw up his plans for Sanssouci.

In the intervening years, a federal road nibbled off a corner of this "Sanssouci of the Lower Rhine," as the town likes to advertise it. To camouflage this flaw, the architect added a blue gate. Indeed, throughout the garden, metal railings in blue and silver and two ungainly greenhouses attract one's attention. Unfortunately these touches in no way detract from the wide-bottomed four-family house that the local authorities in Lintfort authorized before their baroque inspiration hit them.

So much for the ensemble, which is completed by playing fields and a sports facility to the west.

Stingy flower beds in the ornamental garden, narrow staircases, and the lack of a focal point—not counting the asymmetrically placed, modern wooden sculptures—make for a sad, dreary scene. In fact, baroque gardens were designed primarily to provide a backdrop for parties and celebrations featuring music and dance in an atmosphere of fountains and fireworks. When the guests had gone, the fountains were turned off. The empty scene is attractive only to those who can appreciate its geometry. And to maintain it, servants must continuously prune the plants into shapes that they would never naturally assume, just as the pious brothers of Abbot Daniel pruned people around the world into shape and coerced them through corporal punishment into accepting the Christian doctrine while he strutted around his garden. Paradises were burned in honor of the merciful God.

When contemplating reconstructed baroque gardens, we might sadly and angrily compare the creation and destruction of cultures to the pruning action required for both. However, the mind can filter these thoughts, drawing a clear distinction between the cultural traditions we approve of and want our public officials to sanction and the pitiable mistakes that we as a culture would just as soon forget.

By the way, no one should suppose that people in those days were ignorant of the facts. Even then, there were critical and accusing voices that condemned unchristian and inhuman behavior and practice. These voices were heard but were quickly silenced.

I would give all the baroque gardens of Europe to make Surinam or Haiti or Bali rise again, protected from money-grabbing occidental traders as well as from self-righteous missionaries who had the happiest of people whipped to death simply because they refused to cover their private parts. These people were not indecent. Abbot Daniel in his habit was the indecent one. I do not want to see his garden any more.

The Blue Flower from Romantic Novels

What was attracting him with all its might, however, was a tall, light blue flower standing closest to the spring, touching him with its broad, shiny leaves. All around it, there were countless flowers in all colors, and the sweetest scents filled the air. Yet he saw nothing but the blue flower, and he regarded it with tenderness beyond words. He decided to approach it at last when suddenly it started to move and change. Its leaves became shinier, and nestled against the growing stem, the flower bent toward him. Its petals revealed a blue, open collar with a delicate face hovering inside.

Thus the protagonist dreams of a blue flower and then goes on to spend his lifetime seeking it. This famous novel, *Heinrich von Ofterdingen* by the German romantic poet Novalis, was never completed, but from documents regarding the author's plan for the story's ending, we know that Heinrich finally finds the flower, his lost love named Mathilde.

It is probably futile to ask which plant Novalis thought of as the blue flower, though thereafter it became the symbol of all romantic seeking. As far as I know, neither botanists nor linguists ever pursued the question, and I myself had always assumed the blue flower to be an allegory that was not connected to any particular species of plant.

At least that is what I thought until one day when I was reading a book on edible plants and animals somewhat haphazardly written by Waverley Root, an American journalist. In it I came across the assertion that this blue flower can be identified as borage. Borage, of all things! Borage leaves are rough, not shiny, and even though its flowers are of a heavenly blue, they are quite small and nearly always bent bashfully downward, so that Heinrich would hardly have had the chance to see "an open collar with a delicate face hovering inside."

After this misconception, it is tempting to make further assumptions and speculations as to the identity of the blue flower. What about the forget-me-not? It may not have an open collar, but there is something decidedly romantic about it. But then in the novel we find that Sylvester, Heinrich's doctor, gives him "a forget-me-not just starting to flower." There is no inkling that Heinrich recognizes the forget-me-not as being the blue flower he seeks. He does cry out, but for other reasons.

Still, forget-me-nots bring us a little closer to the heart of the matter. They have always played various roles in the magic of love and, moreover, belong to a group of key flowers praised in folktales and superstitiously respected for their ability to open mountains and gain access to hidden treasures.

More than any other plant, the forget-me-not strikes a romantic chord by linking love and treasure hunts. Its power and lore remind us that the image of the blue flower was not wholly invented by Novalis. It had its origin in familiar, traditional images of magical blue flowers.

Honesty was another key attribute ascribed to blue flowers. In addition, a less valuable characteristic was the belief that blue flowers attract lightning, which is why some of them—including bellflowers, gentian, and chicory—were called lightning or thunderstorm flowers. Anyone picking these flowers and taking them home risked having lightning strike the house shortly thereafter, an occurrence whose impact is not far removed from the magic of love, after all.

In the garden, these somewhat rare blue flowers possess a charm of their own. They shine without dominating; they take a back seat to a color such as red, which jumps to the forefront; and, very romantically, they make us think of the secret depths of the sky, the sea, and even clear precious stones.

Is there such a thing as a most beautiful blue in the garden? Perhaps there is. The cultivars of *Delphinium* raised by Karl Foerster, such as *Delphinium* 'Finsteraarhorn' and *Delphinium* 'Midsummernight's Dream', are both a deep gentian blue. To bring into play a little romantic irony, the wet dark blue of French truffles stays hidden beneath the soil and can be seen only if cut with a knife—trivial damage to witness such a sublime thing.

Please Sow Me Right Away!

Plants sow themselves in the wild. That is, their seeds drop to the ground when they are mature, and they germinate when their period of rest is over. The rate at which this occurs differs from one plant to the next.

Some plants do not need to rest at all and germinate as soon as they are mature. This is mainly true for winter annuals. These annuals spend the winter as sturdy seedlings, and it makes sense that they must be sown as soon as their seeds can be harvested.

Examples include corncockle (*Agrostemma githago*), which produces a sturdy rosette of leaves by the time the first frosts arrive; angelica, whose seeds do not remain viable for long; and chervil. For corncockle and angelica, it is best to rely on self-seeding. Chervil seeds can be stored for two years, but if sown straightaway, fresh chervil can be harvested early the following spring.

The seeds of turnip-rooted chervil (*Chaerophyllum bulbosum*) lose their viability very quickly and are therefore not offered for sale. They must be harvested from one's own plants and immediately placed in the soil. This may explain why this tasty root vegetable is scarcely grown anymore.

The seeds of some well-known perennials should be sown immediately instead of being kept. These include bleeding heart (*Dicentra spectabilis*), winter aconite (*Eranthis hyemalis*), trumpet gentian (*Gentiana clusii*), Christmas rose (*Helleborus niger*), globeflower (*Trollius europaeus*), and sweet violet (*Viola odorata*).

So the most pressing task in the garden at this time of year is to collect the seeds of some plants while assisting others in their seasonal request, "Please sow me right away!"

July Harvest

One of my tasks in July is to convert unripe, green walnuts into black syrup nuts. It takes more than two weeks to prepare them, but in winter, they taste good with goose and red cabbage. At the beginning of the month, the fruits must be harvested while the nuts inside the fleshy hulls do not show the slightest trace of turning woody. First, use a knitting needle to pierce the fruits in several places. Soak them in water for a few days, which makes them lose part of their tannin-rich sap, and then cook the fruits until they are done. Soak them in water for a few more days, then steep them in hot syrup. Let the syrup come to a boil before pouring it into glass jars. It will take at least three months for the

Mahonia bealii has sulfur-yellow flowers, magnificent bunches of blue fruits covered in a white sheen, and devilishly prickly leaves.

nuts to soak up the sweetness. During that time, they turn as black as night, and the syrup is golden-brown. Black syrup nuts are indeed a delicacy, and some jars disappear somewhat before their contents reach maturity.

July is also the time to harvest mahonia fruits. Mahonias are commonly thought to be decorative shrubs, but they actually produce berries that are much too good to be left for the birds to enjoy on their own. Blue fruits with a whitish sheen can be eaten raw, straight from the bush. The taste is somewhat bitter and the acid is too strong, but the aroma is highly delicate.

Mahonia berry juice produces a jelly that can be saved to surprise guests on festive occasions, since the shrubs do not yield large amounts of fruit. My *Mahonia bealii* has produced just over a pound of fruit this year; harvests may be even lower for the common *Mahonia aquifolium*, widespread in gardens. Its shrubs and flower stands are smaller, but because its leaves are softer, the berries are easier to harvest. *Mahonia bealii* has hard, devilishly prickly leaves, and gathering a pound of berries inspires the gardener to howl out loud a few times.

Plants in Disguise

"Which fuchsia is this?" ask our garden guests. "None!" is the answer. True, the little red bells dangling from the branch look like the blossoms of a fuchsia, but its leaves immediately reveal that it is a currant. Its botanical name is *Ribes speciosum*, or the splendid one. This California native is not quite frost hardy in our area and is only rarely offered for sale.

Unfortunately the same holds true for another pretty plant, silver bindweed (*Convolvulus cneorum*),which grows like a shrub. Silvery hairs protect the plant from excessive water loss in its Mediterranean habitat. When kept in a tub, it is continuously decorated with white bindweedlike flowers, but its leaves are not at all similar to those of bindweed. They remind me of some species of willow.

One could plant an entire little forest of deceptions. Grow fern-leaf beech (*Fagus sylvatica* f. *laciniata*) next to oak-leaved hornbeam (*Carpinus betulus* 'Quercifolia') and willow oak (*Quercus phellos*), whose small and narrow leaves do not seem oaklike at all. Add hop hornbeam (*Ostrya carpinifolia*) to this group. Its leaves are similar to those of its relative, hornbeam, but its fruits are arranged in drooping cones similar to those of a female hop plant. In the semishade of this little forest, cut-leaved elder (*Sambucus nigra* f. *laciniata*) might do well. Its leaves are so deeply incised that at first sight one would never call it an elder.

Do not forget to include oak-leaved hydrangea, a North American native. Its white inflorescences are round and edged with large red flowers, and the red autumn color of its leaves is especially remarkable.

Columbine meadow rue (*Thalictrum aquilegifolium*) could be included among the woody plants in this forest of deception. This shade-loving herbaceous plant not only has the same leaf shape as the columbine, but it self-seeds just as freely.

For the hedge around my little forest, I would choose box-leaved barberry (*Berberis buxifolia*), one of the most beautiful evergreen barberries. It is densely covered in pretty little yellow bell-shaped flowers in March and has the advantage, when compared to boxwood, of being fast growing.

Behind this hedge, the gardener can then sit and think of other plants that will pull the legs of garden guests, for there are many more that grow in disguise.

Hop hornbeam disguises itself by borrowing its leaves from hornbeam and its fruit from the female hop plant.

The Tolerance of Plants

Many of our most popular garden perennials are prairie plants from North America, and they therefore need a lot of love and sunlight. The smooth-leaved Michaelmas daisy (*Aster novi-belgii*) is a good example. However, if one plants a bush in the shade, one is in for a pleasant surprise. The plant will thrive but will flower just a little later than usual, which allows you to extend the flowering time of Michaelmas daisies by quite a lot depending on where you put them.

This holds true for Michaelmas daisies, as well as for numerous other garden perennials whose flowering period can be extended to many weeks. Even sun-loving irises respond with delay rather than indignation at the unreasonable demand of being placed in a shady spot. Considering the short life of its flowers, this may suit us quite well. Oftentimes chance observations reveal what many plants can tolerate. For example, yellow corydalis (*Corydalis lutea*) self-seeds in the deepest shade where its yellow flowers seem to glow, even though nursery catalogs specify that it be grown only in indirect sunlight. Sanicle (*Sanicula europaea*) willingly can establish itself right in the middle of the fern garden even though it supposedly needs chalk. Sweet flag (*Acorus calamus*) and brooklime (*Veronica beccabunga*) can creep fearlessly out of the bog bed onto dry land. Turtlehead (*Chelone glabra*) can flourish in dry soil beneath the shade of a walnut tree, even though it supposedly requires sunlight to semishade and nothing at all is supposed to grow under walnuts.

I do not mean to suggest that we start torturing plants, but surely we may experiment a little to make best use of their tolerance.

All Right, Then, No Greenhouse

Initially, I could not remember the botanical name of *Trichosanthes kirilowii* until my wife came up with the mnemonic trick of calling it Saint Trichine. Now I can say it with ease, though to be precise I have to add var. *japonica*, which is the only variety that can withstand our winters. The plant, whose several species are all offered in Germany under the derogatory name of hair flower (known elsewhere as Chinese cucumber and snakegourd), does not start to grow until quite late in the season. Then it climbs with incredible speed up its wire frame to our roof gutters, faithful to a principle governing all plants in the cucumber family: after a reluctant start, they go off on full throttle, as if moved by a sudden decision. At the moment, the vine is covered with cream-colored flowers whose petals are so deeply incised that they look like bundles of string.

It is this boundless joy of living that makes me want these melons, exploding cucumbers, gourds, squashes, pumpkins, and every other kind of vine all around me. Most of them are worthwhile fruits or vegetables, and even the loofah can be useful as a massage sponge. However, one really needs a greenhouse to grow all these things. So far, I have managed to resist the temptation, but it is getting more difficult by the year. The prospect of tropical abundance is tempting, and I can picture myself sitting in a jungle under glass, melon juice dripping from my mouth. Yet a greenhouse demands even more work and creates even more obligations that must be met. Mr. Lower Back Pain smugly points out that a greenhouse requires a functioning gardener who does not constantly retire to his armchair, moaning about how he can neither stand nor walk. Ecologists reproach that a greenhouse uses as much energy per winter as a small apartment.

When the thumb-sized fruits are fully ripe—a rare thing at our latitudes—the black seeds of exploding cucumbers are flung out with a dry bang.

All right then, no greenhouse. A wave of emotions and thoughts and reasons rises up, all relating to gardens and work. What should I do instead?

The first possibility is diligent drudging in the garden, caring for a thousand edible and nonedible plants, clearing, digging, groaning, weeding, rejoicing, and harvesting in an immeasurable, never-ending area that permits everything. How about a pond? Yes, of course, a big one. How about two ponds? Sure, why not? Shall I create a strawberry meadow of *Fragaria* 'Florika'? Let's have it! Shall I collect varieties of ivy? No problem, I already have 19. And so on. An embarrassment of riches is what the French call it, and that it is. The sheer abundance of choices makes choosing impossible.

Then a depressing evening sets in. All those things left undone hang over me. Things I have not dealt with are throwing their long shadows ahead of me, and from this, another image emerges.

I conjure up a sheltered courtyard that is 7 by 7 meters. It is furnished with a bench, a burbling fountain, two small trees. Other than that, there is nothing but pots and troughs and pails. The plants growing in these containers are not arranged as in a garden, but rather as in a library, one next to the other, neatly archived, easy to see and easy to look after. Instead of a pond, there are three tubs. An apple tree grows in a big pot, and chives grow in a small one. It would be idyllic. I would simply have to do without the chickens and the blackberries, and there would only be enough potatoes in two or three pots for two or three meals.

But it would be idyllic. Mr. Lower Back Pain would agree, thinking of water consumption, which would be limited, and an orthopedically correct armchair, which would be placed next to the apple tree. In this chair, the gardener would sit and dream of a huge garden with a strawberry meadow and a collection of ivies.

Late Bee Fodder

For stinking ash (or bee tree), which starts to flower in late August in our area, one needs a big garden. This is a mighty big tree that grows mighty fast. It is perfect for impatient gardeners, who can order it as *Tetradium daniellii* from any tree nursery. The name of stinking ash has not become generally accepted, perhaps because it is simply a matter of individual taste whether one finds the spicy aroma of its crushed leaves quite as repellent as books suggest. After all, if one does not like the smell if its crushed leaves, one does not need to crush them.

The greatest virtue of *Tetradium daniellii* is that it goes on flowering for two entire months, and the large flower umbels are unusually rich in nectar. The flowers are visited by every sort of bee or bumblebee, particularly the honey bees that a beekeeper brought to Lindenhof because of the nearby field of buckwheat. Pure buckwheat honey tastes a little pungent, so a smidgen of *Tetradium* nectar is bound to be good for it.

I like showing this Chinese tree, which is almost under siege by bees just now, to those ecological gardeners who advocate planting only native species in our gardens, arguing that foreign species would yield nothing for our native animals. Where else can one find a woody plant that flowers profusely only in the months of August and September, offers a rich supply of nectar at the exact time when nectar from native plants is scarce, makes no demands on soil and position, and even develops its serene splendor on a north-facing wall in the shade? It even has the additional advantage of growing very quickly, so that one can spend less than five years—instead of decades—waiting for the new house tree.

Another worthy exotic that is native to Central Asia is buckwheat (*Fagopyrum esculentum*). It is a tender beauty, with heart-shaped leaves and innumerable white flowers. It warrants being sown in a garden (well after the last frost has passed!) as densely as possible, for one can harvest the leaves and turn them into delicious side dish like spinach. The leaves are soft, so they do not take long to be cooked; why the Japanese are the only ones to have discovered buckwheat as a vegetable remains a mystery.

Autumn

Large and Small Fruits

The gardener really does go to great lengths to collect reliable information for his readers, including facts about the fruits of ginkgo (*Ginkgo biloba*), which look like small yellow plums and are tough in every sense of the word. They are mature now, dropping from the trees far and wide. We will come to discuss their very special scent in "The Stinking Garden," which follows. However, as unappetizing as these fruits seem to be, botany books unanimously tell us that the seeds hidden inside are extremely tasty when roasted. In their East Asian homeland, ginkgo seeds are praised as a delicacy. Do they really have a taste? And if so, what is it like?

The gardener goes to great lengths indeed. Last year, I obtained some of these mushy fruits and removed their disgustingly stinking pulp under running water. My hands stank atrociously, but the seeds did not. I placed them in a hot frying pan with a generous layer of salt on the bottom.

After 10 minutes, the seeds burst open with a slight popping noise. I tested them 5 minutes later and found that the seeds, previously green, had turned brown and resembled roasted chestnuts. They tasted no worse than chestnuts, but no better either. They were somewhat mealy and blandly sweet, with a slight peppery aftertaste. I would not exactly call them a delicacy, but maybe a spicy snack.

If you want to try this yourself, you can plant a ginkgo and then wait many years for the fruits to appear. You will also need to have planted a female, fruit-bearing tree and make sure that a male is also planted close by, since ginkgoes can be either male or female and both trees are required. It would perhaps be easier to drive to Brucknerallee in Mönchengladbach and collect fruits there. The residents along this street are grateful for every single fruit that someone picks up and takes away. If there are no fruits to be found on Brucknerallee, you can go into the nearby botanical garden where they pile up as they fall. It so happens that Horst Busse, the manager of the garden, has collected many varieties of ginkgo with widely differing leaf shapes. The leaf shape variations are surprising and unexpected in a tree that is so ancient. Two-fold leaf blades split and dissolve, only vaguely hinting at their original contours. I find something distinctly playful in this, a description that naturally signifies a very human way of looking at the world but which always comes to mind when I see how a plant genus or species seems to try out all the possible variations that lie hidden in its basic form.

Sometimes playfulness is only a question of size. For example, a single puff-ball dares to grow to gigantic proportions and then to present itself as a giant puff-ball, a name that corresponds to its accepted scientific name. The white orbs are bigger than soccer balls and can appear overnight in a meadow, a limitless game that follows the principles governing the life of puff-balls.

Sliced and panfried, puff-balls taste delicious, and yet they usually just rot away quietly and remain unused. No better fate normally awaits cornelian cherries, which are ripening now. Too many garden owners just enjoy the early

Unfortunately, puff-balls are often underappreciated. Sliced and panfried, they really do taste delicious.

flowers of this common shrub, which are tiny, yellow umbels that bloom before the leaves appear. They are surprised to learn that its fruits can be turned into juice, into jam, and also into a liqueur that is almost equivalent to sloe gin. I consider these to be autumn cherries, and they provide a little compensation for the fact that all our other cherries are usually devoured by the birds.

Ornamental quinces are just another pleasant shrub whose fruits are naturally assumed to be of decorative value only. Totally wrong. These fruits are just as good for juices and jellies as real quinces are. They are rotting away by the ton—what am I saying?—by the trainload in German gardens, to say nothing of public parks, though there they are usually rendered inedible by car fumes and dog excrement.

Speaking of dog excrement, the last weeks of fall are also peak season for fly poop. At no other time can one find as many black dots on cups and tablecloths, on chairs and books, and even on butter. Single dots might be tolerable, but a curious fact makes matters worse if more interesting from a zoological standpoint. The later the season, the more one is likely to find many dots clustered or lined up in a row as though just dropped in passing instead of just one dot here and there.

What does this mean? How does it come about? Could the flies' metabolisms be so sluggish that they eat and eat and only get rid of the leftovers at the end of their lives? This is not likely, given that their digestive tract is just a small tube, starting at the mouth and ending at the anus, with very few bulges in between in which anything might collect. I believe that the flies are simply out to annoy us one last time before they say good-bye. If you watch them in order to catch them as they leave their traces, they merely rub their front legs together, washing their hands of any crime.

Tasty Things from South America

Yacon tubers in the frying pan, sweet *Stevia* leaves in tea—inventive gardeners have procured plants from remote regions of the world for everyone's benefit. Once we have them in our gardens, we would sorely miss them if we lost them, even if we have to make an effort to get them through our Central European winters.

The Latin name for the plant from which we get yacon tubers is *Polymnia sonchifolia*, a close relative of dahlias in the sunflower family. It is native to the eastern slopes of the Andes near Bogotá, Colombia, where it has always been valued as a foodstuff. It is a surprising addition to our own kitchen repertoire.

Unfortunately, yacon is not hardy in our area. Just as with dahlias, the rootstock must be dug up right after the first night frost. Around the rootstock, a whole nest of oblong tubers covered in brown bark store nutrients for the next year. These tubers have no buds, so they cannot develop into new plants and therefore do not need to be kept for propagation. They can end up in the kitchen, preferably via the basement because they taste even better after being stored in moist sand.

Yacon tubers develop their most delicious aroma in the frying pan. Simply blanche them, cut them into slices, and coat the slices in breadcrumbs. They can also be boiled like potatoes. Unlike the tubers of Jerusalem artichoke (*Helianthus tuberosus*), which are quite similar, they do not fall apart in the process. Their main content is inuline, a carbohydrate that the human body is unable to absorb. In addition, they contain many mineral and organic substances and something similar to glutamin. Yacon rootstock, which gets bigger year by year and gives you more and more divisions, can be planted back into the garden from mid-May onward. With some skill, it can be divided in such a way that every bud yields a new plant. Each plant needs just under a square meter of space, and every plant yields four pounds of tubers, so it does not take long to raise a small yacon plantation that will provide plenty of food for the winter.

Before harvesting, however, enjoy the plant outside. It is an imposing and robust beauty that grows to over a meter in height, with strikingly wide, arrow-shaped leaf blades joined to the stem. When harvesting the tubers, cut the stems and place them in a vase by a sunny window to enjoy the small yellow flowers indoors. They flower at around Christmas time. With luck, the stems will take root in the vase and can be potted up ready for the next year.

Stevia rebaudiana comes from South America, this time from Paraguay. Its flowers appear in the garden in June, after we have gotten the plant through the winter just like an indoor plant. Its leaves are of an extraordinary but pleasant sweetness. In Paraguay they are commonly used as a sweetener for maté tea, and one leaf is plenty for one cup. One can dry the leaves, pulverize them, and use them like sugar. For those with a sweet tooth or for those suffering from diabetes, a leaf may replace a candy bar. If you are growing a sweet garden in which children and adults may pick delicious things in passing, include a stevia, and next to it you might plant lemon verbena (*Aloysia triphylla*). It is not hardy either, but its leaves add a distinctive aroma to the stevia's sweetness that is only insufficiently described with the word *lemony*. *Aloysia* is also a South American native that comes from Uruguay.

Some More Things to Eat and Drink

By now my belated saffron flowers have wilted, though they did arrive just in time to harvest a small quantity of their red stamens, which produce the magnificent yellow color in rice or in Christmas baking. If you have ever harvested them yourself, you will know why saffron is so expensive and so widely adulterated. You get three measly strands from each flower of *Crocus sativus* and would need a few square meters just to meet your own needs.

In any case, saffron is not widely used in kitchens, though it is useful for dyeing and develops its own particular aroma, spicy and a little bitter, that induces the appetite.

Saffron crocus is rare in gardens and even rarer in gardening books, an inglorious end for a plant that was so highly esteemed in antiquity. According to Homer, the plant was responsible for scent and color in the bed of Zeus, and it was sought after both as a spice and as a medicinal herb during the Renaissance.

The culture of saffron is so ancient that nobody knows where it began as a native plant. Like so many other spices, it needs sun and warmth and therefore certainly came from the Mediterranean. But it does well here, unfolding its purple flowers with their yellow anthers and red stamens at the end of September and sometimes much later, when one has begun to think that there is not going to be a saffron harvest this year.

Unfortunately, only some very specialized nurseries offer saffron crocus bulbs for sale. One will never find it packed into those colorful bags in gardening supermarkets because it can only be bagged in July and has to be planted right away because it cannot survive storage.

Its upright, grasslike tufts of leaves are green in winter and disappear in spring, making it an anticyclical plant. In this (and only in this), it is similar to chickweed. The chickweed has been modest all through the summer, but now that vegetation in my beds is sparser, it is spreading like wildfire, covering all those bare patches with its thick, fleshy leaves and even flowering, as long as there are no real frosts.

Chickens are particularly fond of chickweed, chicken bite, or chicken spice, as its vernacular names imply. My silk chickens are totally mad about it. They attack it with enthusiasm normally reserved for the worms that my wife sometimes brings back from town.

We could eat the leaflets ourselves, of course. They are often recommended as a vegetable or salad, though they really taste only of green. However, we cannot be too choosy if we want to keep eating fresh things from the garden at this point. A reader once wrote to me, with a hint of reproach, that I talked rather too much about food. That is not so much my fault as the fault of the garden. It has more edible things growing in it than most gardeners realize, and I am tempted to explore them and try them out. As far as I am concerned, I like to regard edible plants as a reward for my toil, and time and again I find plants whose culinary usefulness had thus far escaped my notice.

Take sassafras, which has aromatic bark used in making perfume. It is a novelty from an old book. In its North American homeland, they dry sassafras leaves, pulverize them, and add the powder to soups as a spicy thickener, for not only do the leaves have a unique taste, they also contain mucous substances that swell up when cooked. I harvested a basket full of leaves, chewed on one or two of them (really, they do taste pleasant and a little sticky), and spread them out to dry. I will soon see how the powder performs in chervil soup.

Every year I await the flowers of the sassafras with great anticipation, but my tree, which is quite young, has failed to produce any to date. The flowers are supposed to yield a tasty tea called saloop. It is sweetened with milk and sugar and used to be sold "early in the morning on London street corners to the workers" right into the twentieth century. Now this really makes me curious. Why sassafras tea of all things, and why early in the morning for the workers? Does it lift one's spirits and make one want to work for a living? We shall see.

And now on to something besides food and drink. Until recently a subdued hawthorn hedge edged the driveway up to Lindenhof. We have now replanted the area with flowering shrubs: *Rosa glauca* with its plum-blue leaves, box-leaved barberry with its yellow bellflowers, and especially winter-flowering varieties that welcome visitors with splashes of color and do not need to be clipped twice yearly.

Guelder rose has long since covered itself in innumerable flower heads. Recently the first honeysuckle buds have appeared, creamy white and strongly

In addition to its aromatic bark and intense fall color, young sassafras has another claim to fame: leaves of different shapes grow on one and the same tree (heterophylly).

scented, too. Soon *Hamamelis*, or witch hazel, will emerge, and a little later we will see Japanese mahonia with its sulfur-yellow tufts of flowers. Finally, before the start of spring, snow forsythia (*Abeliophyllum*) will display its white flowers. Why are these winter comforters, magnificent presents from other areas of the world, not accorded a place in every garden as delicate and yet robust companions for the darker months? They are worth bearing in mind on one's next visit to a tree nursery.

Between all those winter-flowering things, I have one single currant, an unknown variety with giant clusters of especially large berries that was a gift from a gardening friend. After all, there has to be one thing in the hedge that is edible.

New Joys of Rhubarb

October is the right time to plant rhubarb and divide old rootstocks whose yield has diminished. More important, however, is choosing the right variety in the first place.

Year after year, the rhubarb roots pull the rootstocks deeper down into the soil while new buds form on their tuberous stems. I dig them out every few years in the fall and divide them with a sharp knife into fist-sized pieces that have two or three buds each. Then I plant those pieces again, giving away any extras as gifts (but only if they are of a good variety, such as 'Vierländer Blut' or 'Holsteiner Blut' with its red stems).

You might even look for a tastier variety now, and also try the following more unusual method of cultivation that has long been practiced in England's small gardens and large nurseries. In February, put a tall black plastic bucket over the rhubarb crown. Depending on the weather, you will find pale sticks with a small crown of leaves about six weeks later. The flesh will be very tender with a much milder taste than that of the later stalks.

If you fail to try this method, you will miss out on the tender side of rhubarb. And if you follow the advice of gardening books and pinch out all the flower stalks, you will miss out on a spectacular show that may be surpassed only by the look of the stalks later on in the season when their triple-winged seeds hang from them like greenish droplets. You can almost always find some mating tree bugs on them, too.

If the formation of flowers and seeds really weakens the rootstock and reduces its yield, as one often reads, there is a simple remedy: plant another one or divide an existing one. The latest time for this is now, in November.

Gray and Brown and New Plans

Oh, those autumn colors! But when all those colors have faded, when those yellow and red flames have vanished, there is brown and gray and in some places black and white, too. These are the colors of tranquility, of passing: brown for sleep, gray for calm, black for silence. Stalks and vessels, the supporting and protecting elements of plants, stand out within these shades like light or dark punctuation marks and remain visible for a long time while everything soft soon rots away.

These are not dead colors. Instead they are alive in their many shades and are produced by many different life forms. Bacteria, fungi, algae, worms, and insects are all going about their work of destruction and decomposition. Those who feel bored by shades of brown should take a closer look and discover the transitions represented by the variety of hues. For example, mold may sometimes create white or black accents. By taking a closer look, we can see vast ranges of color and discover what is colorful outside the color wheel.

As the garden withdraws into itself, it presents a background upon which imagination can sketch what shall be seen in the following season. Over there I can plant *Lonicera ×purpusii*, a cross between two shrubby Chinese species of honeysuckle. From January to March it regales us and the first premature bumblebees with creamy-white, scented flowers. Over there, a dyer's greenweed (*Genista tinctoria*) will light its yellow fire from June to August. Over in that newly dug bare patch I have already spread a handful of seeds from the wild herbs that are not capable of withstanding the competition of perennial herbs. These herbs—whitlow grass (*Erophila verna*), poppy (*Papaver rhoeas*), cornflower (*Centaurea cyanus*), and common scurvy grass (*Cochlearia officinalis*) to name but a few—must have a new seed bed every year.

A new dry-stone wall is being erected by the seat next to the pond for my growing collection of houseleeks, but it is being built against all regulations. The stones are joined with mortar, and each joint is nearly filled except for a thumb-deep gap at the very front.

There is a simple explanation for violating the rules. In a real dry-stone wall, seeds of dandelion, dead nettle, sorrel, or thistles all too often come in with the wind and germinate in the shelter of the houseleek rosettes. When you try to pull them up, they have long since anchored their roots in the depths of the wall, far beyond reach. From a human perspective, our new wall is easy to look after. From a houseleek perspective, it is paradise since the competition is barred from entry.

There will be a dense carpet of *Jovibarba sobolifera* at the foot of the wall if I keep the ground free. This species drops its offsets into the unknown in droves, and most of them miraculously survive.

Different Kinds of Horsetails

In my fight against tin weed, scrub weed, cattlestert, and scouring weed, I have been victorious.

Horsetail (*Equisetum arvense*) sneaked into the garden from where I do not know (probably with a gift of a gardening friend), and it was beginning to make a nuisance of itself between the thyme and the baldmoney. There is only one remedy: once a week, one has to rip out all new shoots that have come up. If possible, one has to keep doing this for two years, without so much as a summer break. It is tedious and time-consuming, but it works.

It is a blessing that horsetails do not grow quite as big nowadays as they did 370 million years ago in the swamps of the Carboniferous period. Even so, they are strong and tough enough to squeeze through any crack and can be starved into submission only by the method mentioned here. They simply laugh at herbicides and would have had to survive far worse things in their Carboniferous past.

If we were still eating from tin plates, horsetail would make a marvelous scourer (hence many of its vernacular names). Fine grains of silicone in the upper layers of its skin make it suitable for cleaning bathtubs, pots, and wooden tables. In the organic garden, of course, it can be used for making a strengthening and healing horsetail brew.

People mostly used robust, evergreen winter horsetail or scouring rush (*Equisetum hyemale*) for cleaning purposes, but caution is advised. This species of horsetail also mercilessly spreads by means of its steely rhizomes, so that it can be difficult to keep in check or to get rid of once it is established.

The only native horsetail that one may take into one's garden without regretting it later is variegated horsetail (*Equisetum variegatum*). Its stalks are very tender, as are its rhizomes and roots. If it is allowed to weave its straight, delicately etched, matchstick-thin shoots between other perennials in a moist, lime-rich bed, no harm is done.

Legend has it that in ancient Rome, the first shoots of horsetail were eaten as a spring vegetable. They are quite tough and do not taste like much of anything. Useful as a diuretic, however, is the tea that one can make from either fresh or dried plants, and the ashes of the burned plant can be used to treat heartburn and diarrhea.

The widely held belief that its German name, nested stalk, comes from its intertwined stalks is not true. The name is more likely derived from an older reference to shaft stem, relating to the shape of the unbranched stems.

The gardener's wife loves horsetail stalks, mainly in the spring. When they wither, their black stripes stand out in startling contrast to the pale white color they take on. In flower shops, they cost a lot of money.

Hidden Patterns

Much of the beauty that garden plants have to offer us is not easily visible and is sometimes revealed only by the cut of a knife or spade.

When we divide a rootstock, cut into a stalk, or halve an apple, forms and patterns emerge that we never even knew existed.

These forms and patterns often present bizarre and mysterious pictures that are open to many different interpretations. One simply needs to absorb the picture in its entirety without thinking of the three-dimensional object that yielded it.

Grotesque figures and fantastic ornaments suddenly become visible. The roots of orpine display new paintings as each layer is revealed, sections of fern fronds sort themselves into round mosaics with every slice, and longitudinal sections cut through red-stalked marigold roots remind us that plant colors not only attract insects but also can—for whatever reason—radiate from places that are completely concealed. These phenomena are visible only to those curious enough to go out into the garden with a sharp knife in order to investigate again and again where hidden pictures may be found.

Many of these pictures are quite fascinating. Not only do they serve as a source for abstract drawings and paintings, but they also provide insight into the inner structure of plants. We recognize the ornate architecture of the shoots, in which cavities and reinforcements provide reliable structure and bunches of vessels look after transporting water and nutrients.

How buds form, where a plant adds wooden fibers to its tissue, and the presence of annual growth rings on woody herbs as well as on trees are just a

The view justifies the sacrilege of making a longitudinal cut through a houseleek.

few of the discoveries waiting to be made. And once attention is focused on making discoveries, their abundance is overwhelming. Perhaps at some point, an advanced friend touched by the beauty of cross- and longitudinal sections will pick up a botany book to learn about the purpose of those structures and forms and will find that knowledge only enhances the enjoyment of the shapes.

Winter May Arrive Tomorrow

Most of the time, winter sets in overnight without any warning at all. Armed with a bundle of bamboo canes, I take a walk through the garden and mark all the plants that will need winter protection. One might otherwise be all too easily forgotten.

For example, the delicious pineapple-scented sage (*Salvia elegans* 'Scarlet Pineapple') flowers so late in the season that its magenta-red panicles have no time to wilt; they fall victim to the first night frost. Should I dig it up and let it winter in the basement? It is better to pick a bunch early in October for inside the house. A few shoots will produce roots in the water and, pinched back and potted up, can survive the winter on the windowsill.

There are many doubtful candidates among the inhabitants of the herb garden. Those that turn more or less woody, such as French lavender and some evergreen species of thyme, are not reliably hardy here. On the other hand, now that they are growing less vigorously, they do not take kindly to being dug up and stuck into a pot. Glass bowls or salad bowls can provide protection, but remember that the plants may either get too dry or too wet under their hoods. Check them every so often, even in winter. By the way, I have found that younger plants are sometimes more robust than older, woody specimens.

The same holds true for rosemary (*Rosmarinus officinalis*). I take cuttings by August at the latest. Two or three plants may spend the winter indoors, and the others—just as with the old rootstocks—take their chances of surviving the winter.

Some of the most beautiful species of mint are also somewhat sensitive when it comes to dry frost. I pot up at least one specimen of Moroccan mint and place it on the kitchen windowsill for the winter. It happily continues to grow and, just as in the summer, is available for a refreshing Mediterranean drink made from yogurt thinned with water, seasoned slightly with salt, and flavored with plucked mint leaves.

But what about those plants that are not hardy at all? Treacle clover (*Psoralea bituminosa*) must be taken into the house, for it would not be easy to replace. The same is true for lemon verbena—which has become just as indispensable for our teas as it is to the French, who call it verveine—and the tubers of our voodoo lily, which will produce hellishly stinking flowers for our enjoyment next year. Woolly lavender (*Lavandula lanata*), from southern Spain, is also better off inside. Its hairy coat, designed to protect it from the heat, makes it more susceptible to winter wet and frosts.

Many other things, however, we leave to their own devices and to their fate instead of forcing them through the winter indoors, risking molds, wilting, and stunted growth. This is not a throw-away mentality. It is instead a garden sacrifice, in keeping with life and death, and it is a tribute to our winter, which we do love after all.

Lost Ones

Some plants in our gardens are permanent guests. Others sooner or later say good-bye, and the gardener does not always know why.

I have a big pot full of name tags. It is a kind of catalog of lost plants. I use the tags to remember the victims, to caution me against repeating mistakes, and also as an aid to memory for my next spring sowing.

One tag reads *Mertensia maritima*, for example. This was the oyster plant from the Danish coast, its fleshy leaves tasting of anchovies and cucumber. It simply rotted away in the cold and wet of the winter, while my collection of hostas (seven tags!) owed their total disappearance to the slugs.

Rosularia sedoides, by contrast, was crowded out and suffocated in the dry stone wall by its own relatives, the houseleeks. My beautiful mountain laurel (*Kalmia*), whose flowers always make me think of children's spotted pajamas, has not survived the summer drought. Watering could have saved it, of course, but its first signs of thirst were overlooked and by then it was already too late.

Many tags in the pot are proof of my own negligence. More often, however, they serve as a reminder that not every plant can live in every place.

Take some field herbs, for example. They are nearly extinct in the wild, so we would like to conserve them in the garden at least. They need open soil and do not tolerate any competition. As long as they can have these conditions, cornflowers, poppies, and corncockles self-seed willingly and reliably. However, when sturdy perennials reign in the flower beds, they soon give up and can be coaxed into sticking around only through well-directed sowing.

Sometimes even this effort may be for nothing. The tag reading *Myosurus minimus* indicates that mouse tail, which is extremely rare and naturally unsteady, appeared out of the blue in the middle of the herb garden. It even set seed but then disappeared during the following year despite all the care bestowed upon it. Perhaps it will come back one day. Its tag, for one, is ready and waiting.

Winter

My Beloved Hay

Continuous frost—time for my herbarium. Adalbert von Chamisso once called his pressed plants "my beloved hay." He became curator of the Royal Herbarium in Berlin after having undertaken a strenuous trip around the world, and he remained in this position for the rest of his life.

It is easy to make fun of the hay and straw of herbaria, all colors faded, all life escaped from the dead, rustling archival material. Gardeners, however, appreciate herbaria for the same reasons that inspired their invention 400 years ago. Herbaria can create mental images of plants that do not live in the garden or maybe do not live anywhere anymore, driven out by frost or chewed up by mice. The pressed plants can be used to compare, recapitulate, exhibit, cross-check identifications, or refresh the memory. Inside my own herbarium box I keep my garden, some finds from my travels, and the leaves of around 40 different species of oak from my friend Günter's arboretum.

Now is the time to look through last year's treasures, glue them onto paper, label them, and add them to the collection. Narrow-leaved ragwort, for example, a plant native to South Africa, was sighted for the first time somewhere near Hannover about 100 years ago. It has since spread inexorably throughout Germany, following the country's main railway lines. In some areas, every station now has mats of this plant growing between the tracks well into November. Woe to those who get bewitched by the out-of-season sparkle of this African plant and collect it for their gardens. It spreads like wildfire, and one can never get rid of it again. It may only go into the herbarium.

In an herbarium, plants acquire a new lease on life, for they appear transformed when viewed in just two dimensions. Their leaf shape and structure become more obvious. What is picturesque in three dimensions gives way to austere graphics, and ethereal colors yield to earthy browns. Some plans and gestures of plant life are brought to life only on a flat plane; studying them increases awareness of hidden details that can be seen once one returns to the living plants.

It is true that many flowers lose their magic touch, and some plants are just too voluminous to press flat. They are obstinate and just will not give in. Tricks can sometimes help. The gardener's wife managed through careful cooking to prepare an entire leek in such a way that, after pressing, it turned into a magnificently transparent structure with delicate transitions from white to green. In former times, people would have used this kind of thing to decorate a lampshade.

Well, in former times there was also a more basic form of the herbarium. In diaries, poetry albums, and in any book at all, leaves and flowers were pressed simply because they were beautiful and symbolic, not for any botanical reason. In family registers, people pressed forget-me-nots or violets, which flower in secret; in a diary from a Swiss girl's boarding school, I found edelweiss and rhododendron; and in the last volume of my copy of *Die Fackel* (a reprint of a famous German satirical newspaper published by Karl Kraus), there is an ivy leaf from the author's grave.

These are all symbols that carry widely different meanings. Those who think this is nothing but teenage sentimentality should remember what Hermann Grimm had to say about what his father and uncle, the Brothers Grimm, used to do.

Both brothers would bring back flowers and leaves from their walks and place them into those books they most used. Once the leaves were dry, they would often carefully inscribe the date and place where they found them. Their entire lives are accompanied by these signs of remembrance. . . . I thus found a clover leaf which my father picked on the very day that my oldest brother, Jacob, who died in infancy, was buried next to his grandmother. In Jacob and Wilhelm's books, there are many leaves and flowers taken from their mother's grave. Under old writings, I found a dried rosebud wrapped in paper with these words on it: "From dear mother's grave. I took it on the 18th of June at eight o'clock for my dear brother so that he may remember me."

There were also the so-called Bible leaves taken from aromatic plants. People placed these leaves inside of Bibles and hymn books to prevent them from falling asleep in church. Some of these plants were given corresponding vernacular names: taster, tasting leaf, old wives' taster. Bible leaves represent an early form of aromatherapy and are, by the way, only mentioned in connection with women. Perhaps men simply did not fall asleep in church, or maybe they were allowed to do so. Or maybe it was considered unseemly for them to resort to such aids.

Sage and hyssop, lemon balm and feverfew, rosemary and santolina were traditionally used as Bible leaves. At a flea market I once found a hymn book with an ancient, brittle bay leaf in it. Such signs of life are touching in their simplicity. Behind these signs, images of people may sometimes take shape in one's mind, passing by and waving their greetings.

The most beautiful piece in my collection of sentimental botany is from Scotland. Three beech leaves and a rosebud are glued to a piece of cardboard with a piece of golden paper. Written underneath in faded English handwriting are the words "From Abergeldie, the residence of the Prince of Wales when in Scotland." This prince of Wales has long been dead and gone, but from out of the Scottish fog, I can see a royalist emerge. She is a retired teacher wearing sturdy shoes and a brownish-red headscarf. She picks the beech leaves and the rose at the foot of Abergeldie Castle and stores them in a worn leather bag. In the evening, back at her hotel, she glues them onto a piece of cardboard and notes in her most beautiful handwriting where she picked them for herself—and for me.

She died of influenza the following winter.

Some Things about Oaks

The producers of Glengoyne Single Highland Malt Whisky declare that it takes 111 years for the drink to be placed in front of us: 10 years for ageing, one year for drying the timber for the barrels, and 100 years for the timber to grow. The timber is the oak, and the advertisement for Glengoyne Single Highland Malt Whisky displays an oak leaf. Indeed, the oak is used as a logo for many companies and banks. It can be seen on Swiss francs, some small German coins, and who knows what else to symbolize maturity, steadfastness, and reliability. It exemplifies the power of money and the aroma of whisky. Or is it the other way around?

Once such a symbol has been devised or invented and its meaning agreed upon, it leads an adventurous life. In even the most disparate situations, it appears out of the blue. Oaks have been no luckier in this respect than many other symbols.

Symbols are simple images for compound things, tangibles for intangibles, small things for big ones, parts for a whole. Images can function as symbols because everyone understands them in the same way and, if possible, avoids examining them too closely. Really scrutinizing an image can reveal some surprises. Images can shatter to pieces and suddenly bear no relation to the original meaning. When it comes to oaks, things are the other way around. The more closely one looks at the oak, the more images one can find to serve as symbols in their own right.

I must immediately point out that there is no such thing as *the* oak. There are more than 500 different species of oak, and they are often vastly different in their habit, leaves, timber, and fruits. Some species can fool laypeople like us.

There are more than 500 species of oak in the world. Their leaf shapes are often very different from those with which we are familiar.

Willow oak (*Quercus phellos*) has long, small leaves; stone or holly-leaved oak (*Quercus ilex*) has spiny leaves similar to those of holly. Even the three species of oak that are or have become native to this region—German or English oak (*Quercus robur*), Turkish gall or downy oak (*Quercus pubescens*), and sessile oak (*Quercus petraea*)—make life difficult enough for us because not only are there immense internal variations within one and the same species, but they also hybridize most shamelessly and constantly produce new half-breeds.

Downy oak often grows into a large shrub. English and sessile oaks are trees with large, spreading crowns. They can attain a height of 30, 40, and even 50 meters and can grow in different soils under different climate conditions—but we will leave aside those insights of horticulture and forestry. Glancing quickly at the oak family in southeastern Europe, East Asia, and especially the New World, we note the existence of many different members, which are numerous indeed. We pay no attention to the differences among them, instead blending all of them together into an archetypal image of the oak with all its proverbial connotations. It is said to be strong and powerful and unshakeable, and in ancient times people believed that its timber would never rot. Never rotting and eternal life make this a tree that is truly worthy of the most powerful gods. The Greeks associated it with Zeus, whose oracle in Duodena was located in an oak forest. The Romans associated it with Jupiter, the Germans associated it with Thor, and enchanted oak branches were indispensable ingredients in the sacred rites of Celtic druids.

Oak timber really does have unusual properties. It is dense, solid, and heavy and withstands drought, heat, and fire. It is especially impervious to rot and simply scoffs at water. When placed in water, oak will last forever in terms of time measured on a human scale, though it may turn to dust as soon as it is taken out and dried.

The waters of the earth hold tons of oak timber. It can come from ancient bridges, but the main source is from boats sunk in storms or in battle. People have used oak to make ships and railway sleepers, furniture and houses, bridges and carts and barrels and many more things—even coffins, designed to last until Judgment Day.

Live oaks, too, have an incredibly long life span. There are innumerable and sometimes unreliable stories of oaks that are many hundreds or even thousands of years old. Given what we know with any degree of certainty, I must here point out that the life span of the more modest lime, famous for its soft wood, can be even longer than that of an oak. This is why there are so many individual specimens of both lime trees and oaks. Not only do they serve as memorials to their species, they also have, for good or ill, been dedicated to serve as memorials to people, too. A journey through Europe to visit all those trees that have been mentioned in books (and to check whether they still exist) would require quite a few weeks.

The most famous oak in Germany, marked in each and every history book, is the Danube oak near Geismar. To the ancient Germans, it was holy. In 725 it was felled single-handedly, as legend has it, by Saint Boniface, who was trying to spread the gospel by mercilessly destroying ancient holy sites. The villagers are said to have stood by and watched, speechless, waiting for their god Thor to retaliate and wipe the sinner off the face of the earth. They had to wait 30 years for this to happen, when Saint Boniface was finally killed by the Friesians.

Ever since, there have been two types of oak worship, one light and one dark. Light worship exists where people became obedient Christians and were negligent enough to simply swap their old gods for new ones and to let the Virgin Mary find a home in the hitherto heathen oak; many oaks are dedicated to the Virgin Mary. Dark worship exists in places where the Christian faith was understood in such a way that people started to fear oaks as the seat of heathen powers instead of transferring the oak's strength to newly held beliefs.

So, between holiness and heathendom, oak wreaths and oak leaves have since ancient times been used to bestow praise. They often serve as prizes for bravery and death and are awarded to those who fight in wars and to those who win athletic contests. It may seem strangely eclectic that the oak is associated with both victory and death and can be given for a handstand on the parallel bars as well as for a glorious death in battle. Bear in mind, however, that physical exercise goes hand in hand with preparation for military achievement.

Ancient oaks may have symbolized merit because Mediterranean oaks, such as cork oak and holly-leaved oak, are evergreen and could therefore represent glory that never fades. Our native oaks hold onto their wilted leaves all winter and often do not lose them until new leaves appear in spring.

The tenacity of oak leaves gave rise to a folktale that explains why oak leaves are shaped the way they are. Legend has it that the devil once made a pact with a farmer. The devil stipulated that he could snatch the poor man's soul in the fall, as soon as the oak had lost all its leaves, which were then rounded with a smooth edge. The devil was beginning to look forward to October. However, November came and went, and by December, all the trees were bare except for the oak. Its leaves, withered and brown, held fast to their stalks. Spring arrived and, one after another, the withered leaves dropped off the tree. When the last of the leaves had fallen, the devil thought the farmer's time had finally come. But when the devil appeared to collect his due, the farmer guided him very close to the tree and showed him that the tips of new leaves had long since started to appear. Upon seeing this, the devil flew into a terrible rage, venting his anger on the oak tree by attacking it with his claws. The leaves of the oak have had strangely lobed edges ever since.

So, we are still looking at the oak as an image of solidarity. It lasts for years and even centuries, it represents unassailable power, and it is used in incantations to summon other powers.

These powers must be why people believe that oaks are capable of lifting the burdens and relieving the infirmities of weak human beings like us. Near Frammersbach in the Spessart hills in Germany, there was (and may still be) an oak tree with a split stem. Children suffering from rickets used to be pulled through it so that their illness would somehow be scraped off and absorbed by the tree. In Petschuri, an Estonian place of pilgrimage, there are or were oaks with hardly any bark left on them because pilgrims had nibbled it off in the hope of curing their toothaches. Indeed, oak bark does work against inflammations in the mouth. This agreeable trait, still in use today, comes from the tannic acid that is abundant in oak bark. The tannic acid contracts the swollen tissues in the mouth; it also can relieve frostbite in the same way.

Tannic acid fits in well with the image of power and solidity, of pulling things together, of hardening and of hardened things. Tannic acid acts to harden and conserve animal hides, which were tanned with it to protect them from rot and decay. Oak skin helped animal skin become more durable. I can well remember the strange but not repulsive (to me, anyway) smell of a small tannery in my hometown; on my way to school, I used to take a shortcut across its yard. There, in large tubs in the open air, hides stewed in the tanning solution made of oak bark. (The word for tanning in Old German was the same as the word for cooking before it came to refer only to leather.)

Nowadays, other substances are used, but in former times, huge quantities of oak bark were harvested for tanning and for pharmacies. Bottle corks come from a special oak (*Quercus suber*), and large forests of it are cultivated mainly in Spain and Portugal. Cork oaks have to be 20 years old before the first unusable layer of bark can be cut from them. Only then do they yield the soft cork suitable for corking bottles. It can be harvested every 10 years. A corked bottle may be a highly metaphorical connection to the durability and stability that oaks represent, but it still fits, and it can serve as a springboard for thinking up new images.

Another example of how the oak evokes power and durability is its symbolic link to male and female fertility. The link to male fertility is derived from the shape of the acorns being similar to parts of the male anatomy, in keeping with the medieval belief that shape and function were related. The link to female fertility comes from the wealth of nourishing fruits that represent abundance and fullness.

These fruits may be rich, but like all other parts of the oak, they are bitter because of the tannins they contain. They were used to fatten pigs, who did not mind them at all, and thus were rendered edible. People also found ways to destroy the tannins by roasting the acorns or by grinding them up and rinsing them. This process produced a starchy flour that could at least be used to stretch other, finer flours, and roasted acorns made an acceptable substitute for coffee. So oaks are useful in many different ways and have thereby come to represent fertility itself. But the oak's fertility does not stop with its fruit. In addition to acorns, oaks produce another kind of special, even bizarre fruit that takes the idea of fertility to a totally different level, a level that is in stark contrast to the otherwise highly acidic toughness of the oak. For just at the point where toughness and acidity seem to reign supreme, the exact opposite comes into play, a subjugation, laissez-faire, and even a servility that one rarely finds in plants and certainly not in trees. In oaks, this dichotomy is tested and altered and executed time and again with a kind of playful imagination. I am speaking of oak galls, in which tannic acids are concentrated like nowhere else and where giving and devotion are combined in a most remarkable manner.

Most people recognize those round gall apples that perch on oak leaves like alien appendages, perfectly spherical balls with grayish bark. If one cuts a gall in half, one will find a tiny cavity in the soft, woody tissue. Inside this cavity, there may be a small, white larva if it has not already dug its way out through a narrow tunnel. Such a gall develops when an insect, a gall wasp, drills into the leaf and deposits one egg inside the oak tissue, you might say almost like a cuckoo's egg.

The oak, otherwise mercilessly tough and brimming with bitter tannins, does not respond to this imposition by rejecting it brusquely, as one might expect. It does not shut this leaf off or expel the intruder. Instead, it lets the egg tap into it. Moreover, from the very moment of arrival, it does its utmost to protect the egg from harm by building it a cover that is more than just a simple box for the egg. It is a gingerbread house, a land of milk and honey, an edible children's room with tasty wallpaper and nourishing floors for the larva that will soon emerge. Although its mother has long gone, the child is pampered and mollycoddled by the oak.

All of this is miraculous beyond measure for more than one reason. First, it does not seem natural for a being as substantial as an oak to stoop to the trouble of creating a home for such an unimportant insect. Secondly, the oak gains no visible advantage from this symbiosis, which is not really symbiosis at all. As an entomologist once said, it is a "usefulness serving another entity." This explanation does not solve the riddle; it merely restates it using specialized terminology. Thirdly, the hull that the oak produces appears in no other place within the plant. Its shape is a geometrically perfect sphere, created solely for this animal and its well-being. For itself, the oak does not know this shape at all. It is totally new and unique, produced only after a small insect has deposited its egg. By the way, this act in itself can take hours. The females of one special kind of gall wasp deposit their eggs in winter, and the process is interrupted when the female freezes at night. As soon as she thaws out in the morning, she continues about her business.

Biochemists have isolated the substances that gall wasps inject into the leaves when they lay their eggs to induce the formation of this strange shape. Curiously enough, when these substances (which have been identified beyond doubt) are artificially injected in an oak leaf, nothing happens at all. Oaks react only when they are injected by wasps and are not to be fooled by any artificial device.

With this, the secrets of oak galls are by no means exhausted. No other plants are willing to produce galls, but this does not mean that galls are found on most oaks, nor does it mean that oaks are not capable of producing different sorts of galls for different species of wasps. In addition to oak galls, there are wood galls, swollen leaf galls, potato galls, lentil galls, and oak roses. There is a kohlrabi gall, which really looks like the vegetable, and a silk button gall, which has a depression in the middle and has silky hairs spun around it, just like a silk button. In short, oaks produce more than 120 different shapes and sizes of houses for a correspondingly large number of species of gall wasp.

This is one of the symbols hidden within the symbol of the oak, like a doll within a doll: a strong and powerful tree makes a sacrifice that means nothing to it but means everything to the gall wasps. The oak gives something up, without any advantage to itself—disinterestedly, so to speak—in order to help someone very weak. And this gesture is not just made in passing; it is a constructive contribution to life, exacting nothing in return, not even a payback.

However, one cannot paint this beautiful picture of patronage without two caveats. First, biologists are always on the lookout for something useful. In other words, they like to find a return on the investment that any living being makes. To that end, they have speculated that oaks do not create galls out of pure altruism. By encapsulating the egg, they keep themselves from incurring greater damage. For various biological reasons, this is improbable, but I have to point it out to present a complete picture.

Secondly, the image of living well under the oak's patronage is seriously disrupted by the fact that even though no tree produces more galls than oaks do, no one in the animal kingdom is plagued by parasites as much as the inhabitants of oak galls are. No one faces quite as many highly specialized enemies, and it is possible for one and the same gall to host several dozen different species of parasite while the original larva of the gall wasp, which all these beneficiaries have to thank for their livelihood, is long gone. This, too, becomes part of the image. The oak does not speculate on repayment and profitability, and as a result, quite different beings get the advantage. This begs the question: Is there any harm in that? Instead, is this not cheerful proof that all animals want to live and should be allowed to live out of a large abundance, a generosity that cares about variety and not about purpose and usefulness?

However, there is something else that is very special about these galls that, in turn, reminds us of oaks as symbols for durability: for a long time, galls were the most important raw material for the production of ink, the very substance that helped people permanently to set down their thoughts, messages, bills, pacts, peace treaties, orders, and last but not least, their bookkeeping.

The durability of ink is due to a mixture of tannic acid from oak galls and some iron compounds. The resulting black dye eats itself so indelibly into the fibers of paper that it can always be made visible by dint of chemical methods long after it has faded.

Many hundreds of different recipes presented many different ways to overcome the shortcomings of oak gall ink: it tended to rot in its bottles, and it was also very runny. People added gum Arabic or other substances to give the ink a thicker consistency, and they added mercury as a preservative against rotting. So the durability of oaks takes the form of a liquid and, reinforced by the toughness of iron, makes numbers and words indestructible.

In a bitter and admonishing way, these lasting human efforts—writing bills, reigning, conquering—are the topic of this last chapter on the oak. They lead us back to ancient times, but they also lead us right up to the present day. In ancient times in European history (the most recent of times from a geological standpoint, however), the Mediterranean countries were covered in dense forests. In these forests, oaks, especially holly-leaved oaks, were common. Today one can find only modest remains of these forests, but oaks nevertheless make up about a fifth of the sparse forests of the Mediterranean. Just as with other tree species of antique forests, the very usefulness of the oak for civilization was its downfall. In antiquity, people cleared large tracts of land for agriculture. This much is certain. But what really doomed the forests was over exploitation for firewood and for building materials to supply an insatiable military apparatus that wanted to build boats and more boats. The countryside—whether in Greece, Italy, Lebanon, or wherever—turned to grassland, and fertile soils were washed away once and for all. Such large-scale operations are irreversible. And while all the ships and temple roofs withered away long ago, and the memory of all those conquests is long lost, the traces of destruction brought about by these things remain visible and will be felt for millennia by the people living in those areas.

At the time people did not know that using forests as they did would have such dramatic and, for ecological reasons, inevitable results. Therefore nobody was aware of the need to reforest. It also needs to be said that large tracts of the old forest were in those times preserved further inland and fell victim to the much more brutal and technologically sophisticated clear-cutting of the late nineteenth century. At least three things can be said in favor of the Greeks, the Romans, and the other Mediterranean people who undoubtedly cleared a tremendous number of trees. They were not aware of the consequences of their actions. They regarded the clearings, not entirely without reason, as great achievements, indispensable for civilization and growing populations. On their own, they would not have managed to accomplish the level of destruction that became possible only with the help of modern technological innovations. And now, we jump right into our own present time, into the budding third millennium. These days, oaks are named in federal reports on forest damage as being the latest victims of insidious poisoning by the exhaust fumes of human industry, in third place after firs and spruces.

At the moment, experts are still hemming and hawing, not wanting to rule out other factors that may also be contributing to oaks' becoming ill and weak. However, there is much evidence to support the suspicion that oaks, like other dying trees, cannot withstand the invisible damage done by atmospheric poisons or the invisible attack by pollutants in the ground. They cannot cope with such unreasonable demands, so they withdraw into themselves and just leave without saying good-bye.

One would have to be very thick-skinned indeed to accept this progress without becoming emotional or feeling depressed. Not only oaks but all trees seem to be larger than life—somewhere between humans and gods—because they live so much longer than we do. Their death makes us sad because it makes us aware that even though they comfort us by seeming to be untouchable and powerful, they are also mortal. Many a house tree has outlived the house next to which it was planted. Trees reveal other time spans that are much longer than our own. So the thought—or better, the knowledge—that begins to fill us with dread is that our lifestyle, our historically unique success, is defeating the oaks.

What is particularly touching about this image is the contrast between an oak's strength and the subtlety of the methods we use to kill it. This honest tree just cannot cope with the treachery of poison. Compared with it, Saint Boniface was an honest man and the Greeks were only naïve farmers and soldiers.

So, finally, the oak becomes a symbol for everything that we have ruined in this world through greed and the will to succeed and innocent or calculated adventurousness—cultures, peoples, landscapes, rivers, and sooner or later the sea and the air. We thought that the right to life of native groups and virgin forests counted very little when measured against our desire to be rich and powerful and to continue expanding our civilization. We thought the most noble task of rivers was to carry away our waste, and the task of the wind was to blow away our exhaust fumes. We were wrong, and our new eagerness to invent ever more modern filtering equipment will not be of any great use to us. Wantonness cannot be filtered away.

Of course, nobody did it, nobody wanted it, nobody knew anything about it. But the sentiment "To what end will we exploit the earth in future centuries? Just how far will our greed take us?" was not invented by us. It was written by Pliny the Elder in Rome nearly 2000 years ago when he was looking at bare hilltops. He, for one, along with some people who came after him and even before him, knew or at least felt something and pointed to the reasons behind it. In the face of this, there is a subtle, historical irony in the fact that we sometimes decorate our money symbolically with oak leaves to imprint the mark of durability on it while at the same time literally connecting it to what we were seeking (without taking into consideration nature's long memory) and to what we have deprived of durability and condemned to a slow death.

At the end of all the oak images we have now looked at, we are left with a dying tree stretching its branches up to heaven. To heaven? What kind of image is that? Stretching its branches to heaven and mourning, mourning and dying, without a sound. If there is still a course for us to take, this has to be its beginning. We must finally hear the silent cries of the oak and shudder when we do.

For the moment, we still have oaks. The image of dying oaks, which can be studied in statistical reports, is balanced by images of living, powerful trees whose parts yield flour, ink, coffee, and acorns for fodder; whose bark tans and heals; whose timber is still used for ships, houses, barrels, and warmth; whose sap feeds gall wasps and those that come after them; and in whose timber Glengoyne Single Highland Malt Whisky ages. This is the oak as a microcosm, an example of the interconnectedness and interdependence of the world's living things. A life of dignity is possible only where dependencies are not cynically exploited or simply annulled, but rather regarded in context and respected. The oak—its life, its gifts, and its endangerment—are only images, and these, in turn, are only parts of a larger image.

Winter Bulbs . . .

Garden soil yields many different types of lesser-known winter crops. As long as the ground is not frozen solid, we may now partake of the things that plants have stored up for next year.

Jerusalem artichoke stores its nutrients in tubers, and they do not mature until October. Once they are dug up, they shrivel up in no time, so it is best to get them fresh from the soil when you want a delicious salad made from grated bulbs. They have a peculiarly nutty taste. One can also boil the tubers like potatoes, panfry them, or turn them into a soup.

I must mention that these tubers may cause serious flatulence in some people, so they are really only recommended for singles and not for dinner parties.

Parsnips do not have this side effect, but they are not quite as tasty, either. They are best when mixed with other vegetables, such as carrots. Parsnip is biennial. In the first year, it produces a sturdy rosette of leaves and only in the second year does it produce its marvelous yellow-green inflorescences; in the meantime, its rootstock turns woody. In the winter between its first and second year, it is still edible and can be finely grated as a salad or steamed as a side dish for fish. It is a spicy variation to everyday carrots.

Parsnip and Jerusalem artichoke are at least familiar if not always sufficiently valued. By contrast, great pignut (*Bunium bulbocastanum*) is nearly forgotten, though during earlier, more modest times it was sold in markets. In some places (mainly in western Germany) one can still find it growing in the wild, left over from ancient cultures. Great pignut tubers taste a little like chestnuts. Their disadvantage, which is probably why their cultivation ceased, is that the tubers are no bigger than hazelnuts, and their hard, woody outer skin makes preparation difficult. When roasted in a pan, however, they develop such a pleasant scent that we should at least give this venerable vegetable a try, treating the task of peeling it as a fun activity for a winter evening.

. . . And Winter Stars

During these weeks, star symbols are everywhere, even in the garden. The star-shaped rosettes of stonecrops lightly shimmer at us and are sometimes decorated with an edging of ice. These winter jewels are a sight to behold, and a walk in the garden is worth it even in the cold season.

With houseleeks, it is the snow that changes the look of the rosettes and emphasizes their star-shape. Frost and snow can do little harm to these alpine plants, but wet and miserable weather is just as unhealthy for them as it is for us. Like us, they must not get wet feet. This is why they need free-draining soil.

Deep down on the ground cower the rosettes of those biennial plants that have finished the vegetative part of their life cycle this year and are waiting for the next year to develop their flower stalks. Among the most beautiful of these are the different species of thistle (*Carlina, Carduus, Cirsium*, and others), whose rosettes show us a star squashed flat on the ground. Shepherd's purse, foxglove, and evening primrose are beautiful, too, along with many others that one sometimes has to hunt for underneath the dead foliage. It is best to clear the

Star of Persia is an attraction in the garden, whether unfolding, in full flower, or in seed.

dead leaves away completely, for plants can easily rot underneath them. Winter stars are sensitive.

We can find a third group of winter stars among those plants whose seeds have managed to withstand the fall storms (and the desire for order), bizarre and at the same time graceful constructions such as the many-beamed ball of Star of Persia (*Allium christophii*), which is just as impressive dry as it is in flower. The winter stars of the carrot family are most beautifully expressed in those species whose umbel is composed of clusters of small umbels. Each small umbel repeats in a simplified and smaller form the plan of the larger one, creating stars within stars.

These are not spectacular images, but they are touching. Stars are symbols of light, and in them is the promise of its return. Soon the days will become longer again.

The
Stinking Garden
or a Fascination
with Opposites

The flower of dragon arum (*Dracunculus vulgaris*)
is as imposing as it is evil-smelling.

An Invitation to the Stinking Garden

The Stinking Garden that you are hereby invited to visit offers many scents that one never expected to find in a garden at all. There are odors of rotting fish, burned pork chops, carrion, and sweaty armpits. Most of the time it just plain smells bad.

When a gardener embarks on the search for stinking plants, the first thing he learns is that they are relatively rare among the flora of Europe.

Secondly, the gardener becomes acutely aware of the relativity of the word *stinking*. Every time he comes across a new stinking plant, he savors the success of the encounter with his nostrils wide open: the stench, sought after and finally found, turns into an enjoyable olfactory experience that is not annoying in the least.

"What's it good for?" the fans of more pleasant scents may somewhat reluctantly ask. "It is purely provocative," the gardener replies. Sniff out the unusual odors and then reflect on smells and smelling, on names and judgments, on the power of habit, and finally on the resulting questions about the history of life on earth.

The Stinking Garden often provokes general merriment, but even more often it causes arguments about what exactly makes a smell "bad." Black currant (*Ribes nigrum*) is a good example of this.

Some people—and I would tend to agree with them—describe the smell of black currant leaves as tangy but not unpleasant. Others, however, find it repulsive and are quick to cite Christian Schkuhr's *Botanical Manual of Plants Growing Wild in Germany*, published in 1791. This book refers to the black currant as the stinking tree and also as the bug berry because the peculiar aroma of the berries is said to be similar to the smell given off by bugs. This "bug odor" is one that is encountered again and again in the Stinking Garden.

We Do Not Smell Only with Our Noses

Now what does *smelly* actually mean? What exactly is a bad odor? The incredibly foul smell of blue cheese may whet one's appetite, but if one smeared just the tiniest bit of that same cheese behind one's ear, one would be avoided like a leper. Habit and other influences thus play a big role in how we evaluate odors.

Things are much easier for children, who are naturally curious, take delight in sensations and in sensory experiences that are outrageous and unusual, and are not yet constrained by the boundaries of "good taste." They are not nearly so receptive to the faint scent of a *Leucojum* as they are to the ghastly stench of a carrion flower, and when they shout "Yuck!" they really mean to say "Wow!" When adults are repulsed by a bad smell, their gut reaction is something that has been learned and practiced over many years and is largely conditioned by history and society. An unavoidable odor, such as that of a village dung heap, is tolerated by the villagers; newcomers call it a stench and demand that measures be taken.

What seemed impossible only decades ago has now happened: the world has been thoroughly deodorized. (This term is misleading, by the way; odors have not simply disappeared and left the world smelling of nothing. They have instead been replaced by different ones.) The bar has been raised so that many odors that used to bother absolutely no one are now considered vile. The smell of gasoline once represented freedom, the spirit of enterprise, and enjoyment in life, but no more.

Individual sensitivity also plays a role in the evaluation of smells. Memories are often triggered by particular odors—situations and the odors accompanying them tend to remain linked in a person's memory for life—and physiological characteristics may also be a factor. The sensory receptors in each person's nose are unique. What one person considers a distinct scent (or even stench) might go unnoticed by someone else. Anyone who wants to criticize the evaluations of smells in this book should bear this in mind and should also take into account that sensitivity to sensory experiences unfortunately diminishes with age.

Sensitive Botanists

When naming new plants, many botanists have cried out "Foetida!" or even "Foetidissima!" in plants that do not possess the faintest trace of an unpleasant smell. The great Linnaeus named a species of hellebore *Helleborus foetidus* and a species of iris *Iris foetidissima*, and these references to unpleasant smells have been incorporated into the common names of these plants: in English they are called stinking hellebore and stinking iris or roast beef plant. Many gardening books obstinately spread the rumor that these plants do indeed smell bad, but I have never found anyone to confirm it.

The same is true for a species of willow. The Swiss apothecary Johann Christoph Schleicher named it *Salix foetida* 200 years ago, but it has no odor at all.

All these plants belong in the Stinking Garden, however, because they are curious references to the overly sensitive noses of some botanists. It must have been one of these botanists who gave *Tetradium daniellii* its official German name, stinking ash. No part of this plant stinks. On the contrary, it has a huge number of scented flowers and is listed in many nursery catalogs as the thousand-flower tree, which is certainly better for sales. Bees (and therefore beekeepers, too) value this tree because it flowers in August and September when nectar and pollen are not widely available elsewhere.

True Stinkers and More Composites

Some plants do indeed live up to the expectations raised by their botanical names. One of these is *Aposeris foetida*, a composite closely related to the common dandelion. It grows in moist and shadowy forests in the Alps and contains a milky sap with a decidedly unpleasant smell. In spring, a rosette of leaves just like finely serrated jewelry sprouts at ground level, followed by a single flower stalk. After fertilization, the flower bends down to the ground so that the seeds, once mature, are not carried away by the wind but germinate right next to the mother plant. Consequently *Aposeris foetida* is usually encountered in dense stands.

Crepis foetida, stinking hawksbeard, is another composite that does credit to its scientific name. The revolting smell of its milky sap is said to be reminiscent of opium. As a wild plant, stinking hawksbeard has become rare in our country and needs to be regarded as endangered. Stinking hawksbeard is an annual, so that to cultivate this plant in the Stinking Garden, one needs to collect the little parachute-like fruits and re-sow them.

Speaking of composites, we should also add *Lactuca virosa*. It belongs to the same genus as our common lettuce but is not fit to be eaten. In English, it is called strong-scented lettuce or opium lettuce. Its milky sap is said to smell of opium, and indeed this plant has an ancient history as a narcotic: the Roman Emperor Augustus praised lactucarium as a medicine and erected an altar and a statue in its honor. A medicine with cooling, refreshing, and also narcotic

One can see from the flowers that *Helichrysum foetidum*, far from being dainty, is strong and built to last. Leaves and stems are covered in a web of fine white hairs.

properties was made by cutting off the leaves of the biennial plant and then collecting and drying the milky sap exuded by the cuts. The beneficial effect of these resinous granules was later forgotten. It was not until 1770 that a Viennese doctor rediscovered this old remedy, and in about 1850 the apothecary Alois Goeris grew the strong-scented lettuce in the Moselle Valley in order to produce lactucarium germanicum. This substance acquired great significance in surgery before the discovery of chloroform, and it was also used to treat cramps and heart conditions.

Another composite is *Helichrysum foetidum*, a biennial species of helichrysum native to South Africa and sometimes called stinking strawflower. At some point, this plant immigrated into Europe and now grows here, where the climate is very mild. It can occasionally be found on rocky screes, by the coast, or along roadsides. Visitors to the Stinking Garden have widely different opinions regarding the intense smell of its leaves; some find it "fruity" and "refreshing," whereas others (including me) find it slightly bitter, like vomit with just a hint of almonds.

Difficulty Finding Words and Bug Plants

The reader who is nauseated by the description of the smell of stinking strawflower should bear in mind that it is extremely difficult to define a smell in words that are meaningful and, more importantly, that mean the same thing to more than one person. There are thousands of words to describe colors, and many of them can be combined to describe nuances. Apart from a few very basic words for smells, however, there are only comparisons, and when it comes to smelly plants, these can sometimes be objectionable. Most of the time we must resort to using a word as imprecise as "unpleasant"; when we want to express something more strongly, we have to leave it at "disgusting" or "nauseating," which is just as vague.

The smell of bugs is a comparison often encountered in botanical books. One does not immediately think of bedbugs, which are now thankfully rare. Many other bugs found in every garden give off a foul-smelling secretion when they feel threatened. Stinking bugbane (*Cimicifuga europaea*) gets its name from the smell of its crushed leaves, which are faintly reminiscent of these secretions. Conversely, the leaves of this east European native are also said to be capable of repelling bugs. Initially, Linnaeus called this plant *Cimicifuga foetida*, but the somewhat musty smell of the leaves can hardly be termed "stench."

Much more impressive is the bug smell of wild bishop (*Bifora radians*), an umbellifer from the Mediterranean region that sometimes appears farther north as an uninvited guest on derelict land. It is an annual herb, as is the nearly identical-smelling coriander (*Coriandrum sativum*), which cannot be planted in the Stinking Garden until the last of the late frosts have passed. It is cultivated in western European herb gardens mainly for its sweetly aromatic fruits, which are used in baking at Christmas time. In southern Europe and South America, the bug smell of the leaves, which botanical books unanimously call "repug-

Many species of bugs that live in the garden give off foul-smelling secretions when they feel threatened.

nant," is valued as an indispensable spice in meat dishes. Actually, it does not take long at all to get used to its strange aroma.

Habits and traditions play a role in olfactory judgments. At first, outsiders and newcomers may instinctively reject unknown smells just in case— "instinctively" in the sense that one's sense of smell first assumes anything unknown to be dangerous. While only the nose actually does the smelling, the head assimilates the sensation, interprets it, and contributes from the brain's conscious and subconscious spheres to register a final opinion.

The smell of bugs will be encountered many more times. The black currant has already been mentioned; bug orchid (*Orchis coriophora*), bastard balm (*Melittis melissophylla*), and sea arrow grass (*Triglochin maritima*), a perennial of salty marshes, should not be forgotten either. This plant is easily established in the garden if given a boggy place and fertilized with a little common salt every so often, and its thin, tubelike leaves can easily pass as a substitute for coriander.

Finally, a bug smell with a fruity twist is present in common hogweed (*Heracleum sphondylium*) and in giant hogweed (*Heracleum mantegazzianum*). In both species, the seeds give off the characteristic smell. Long ago I asked a neighbor to smell the seeds several years in succession. I always hoped that he might become fond of the sweetish smell, but he found it repulsive every time.

Devil's Dung and the Scent of Wild Animals

Some people find the smell of an herb such as coriander to be really unpleasant while others find it aromatic enough to elevate it to culinary usage. Another example is *Ferula assa-foetida* from Iran, which has since ancient times been cultivated for its medicinal uses. Its leaves smell pleasantly like those of carrots, but if an older individual of this umbelliferous plant is cut just above soil level, a resinous sap is exuded. In dried form it can still be bought in pharmacies as asafetida or even as devil's dung, its old name. It does smell truly disgusting. In earlier times, it was used as a remedy for nervous excitement. Yet even its foul smell does not prevent it from being valued in southern countries as a seasoning for mutton and other foods.

Hyssop (*Hyssopus officinalis*) is a similarly ambiguous plant that is as strange as it is old and venerable. This perennial labiate from southern Europe no doubt belongs in every herb garden as a spice for meat, but it also belongs in the Stinking Garden since there are many people who would classify the pungent smell of the leaves as bestial and who find it too repulsive to imagine adding it to their food.

Like hyssop, tiger bell or bonnet bellflower (*Codonopsis clematidea*) smells of wet straw, like an animal cage in the zoo. It is widely used as a garden plant but has no culinary use. Neither has its distant relative, *Isotoma axillaris*, an Australian plant that is widespread in the horticultural trade but smells of rot.

Another garden perennial with a pungent and musty smell reminds us that sometimes an off-putting aroma is not enough to prevent a plant from being eaten. *Houttuynia cordata* is a plant from the family Saururaceae, native to the swamps of East Asia. Its leaves smell musty, though they do have a very faint fruity overtone and are a popular vegetable in Vietnam. However, even the Vietnamese seem to find the aroma somewhat disturbing: according to legend, the body of a drowned person lies buried in the swamp wherever *Houttuynia* grows, and the blood of this person gives the leaves their distinctive musty taste.

Being a semiclimbing plant, bonnet bellflower likes to scramble up inside other bushes. It is native to Central Asia and smells of the wet straw of animal cages.

The Ambiguous Madonna Lily

In an olfactory sense, nothing is as impressively ambiguous as the Madonna lily (*Lilium candidum*); its scent evokes no culinary connotations at all. The Madonna lily symbolizes purity and innocence. It is called the flower of the Virgin Mary and the rose of Juno, and the Archangel Gabriel carried it at the Annunciation. However, the bewitching scent of this flower can fill an entire room, particularly late at night; many people who enter a room with Madonna lilies in it find the scent unbearable or even indecent.

This smell impressively combines elements of flowery charm with the animal-physical world, and this is perhaps the key to the contrasting feelings it evokes. Perhaps the animal element is perceived as a threat and therefore the charming elements become a temptation to be fought against. Here we are probably groping in the darkness of our own tribal past, making interpretations and judgments according to primeval and entirely subconscious criteria that have everything to do with the search for partners—olfactory signals of lust—and with the more historic threats of punishment that lust is subject to.

This is yet another thread in the fine web that constitutes the experience of scents: the memory of those times in which scents were deeply important signals for our ancestors, signals that told of friend and foe, of strangers and relatives, of danger and security, and of the existence and disposition of a sexual partner. It is therefore logical that even today scent and how we experience it are linked to the most ancient parts of our brains.

The olfactory response to sweet flag (*Acorus calamus*) is similar to that of the Madonna lily but perhaps not quite so marked. When cut apart, the rhizomes give off a smell that is sometimes praised as aromatic and spicy, but is just as often reviled as musty and unpleasant. Those who praise sweet flag often add that its smell contains the memory of warm summer afternoons spent by a lake, with the smell of water that always contains a whiff of rot and decay. Perhaps those who find the smell of sweet flag repulsive associate lakes with uncertainty and fear because of their own inexperience.

Some plants keep their characteristic, more or less bad smells hidden away in their roots under the soil.

Quite unmistakably revolting is the smell of the roots of *Veronica gentianoides*, a native of the Crimean Republic that is sometimes offered in the horticultural trade. Even worse are the roots of false acacia (*Robinia pseudoacacia*). Anyone who digs up one of the lengthy runners to protect the garden from being taken over by this tough tree will remember its horrible smell of cat feces and rotten urine. Perhaps the bacteria in the root nodules, which convert atmospheric nitrogen, have a role to play both here and in the roots of dragon's teeth (*Tetragonolobus maritimus*), another plant in the pea family. By the way, a

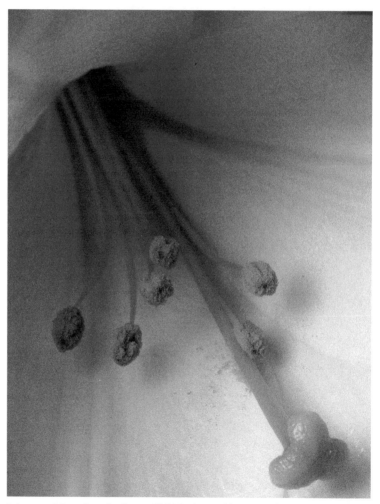

It is surprising that the beautiful Madonna lily is so often used to adorn altars and has been associated with the Annunciation. It has a very physical, sensual scent.

description of the smell of dragon's teeth roots illustrates how even obvious comparisons are only understandable to those who actually encounter a smell. Merely stating that dragon's teeth roots smell like a mixture of asparagus and rotting seaweed is hardly enough to conjure up the odor.

The tropical *Cardiospermum halicacabum* is grown as an ornamental house-plant in our climate. The leaves of this climbing plant are edible and are eaten as a vegetable in equatorial Africa and Malaysia. The foul-smelling root was used as a cure for stomachaches and as a laxative in traditional medicine.

In spring, when the crown imperial (*Fritillaria imperialis*) begins to grow, a mild scent of mouse urine wafts through the garden. Forget the smell of violets. This is indeed the first scent of spring. Much more impressive is its smell in late summer, when its big bulbs are on display in garden centers and can fill a whole room with their pungent smell. According to ancient gardening wisdom, even wood mice flee this smell, but all observations point to the contrary.

Similarly unpleasant is the smell of the bulbs of *Lilium hansonii*, a common garden lily of which there are many cultivars. Its flowers do not smell pleasant, either.

About Garlic

Does garlic (*Allium sativum*) belong in the Stinking Garden? A minority probably heartily agrees that it does, while the majority loudly objects. Only 30 years ago, when the smell of garlic was commonly considered repulsive, just the opposite would have been true. This is how fast public opinion can change.

Obviously there is a difference between smelling the aroma of a fresh clove of garlic and the breath of a garlic eater, or worse, of someone who has eaten garlic yesterday. Only where large parts of society are in sympathy is the garlic eater safe from being criticized. People who still criticize him, however, could point out that garlic was once famed for its powers in fending off demons, vampires, and even the devil himself, which obviously indicates that its smell was considered horribly repulsive.

By the way, a slightly modified version of this smell is present in *Tulbaghia violacea*, a member of the lily family that is native to the forests of South Africa. It is unfortunately not hardy in our climate. Its beautiful violet flowers and,

Travels to southern countries and an enjoyment of Mediterranean cooking have given garlic broad acceptance. Cultural influences affect how people judge smells.

above all, its wilting tubular leaves in autumn have the sharp, unpleasant edge of garlic mixed with something rotten and a faint whiff of animal excretions.

Rotten Cabbage

A treasure chest of bad smells, especially of rotten or bestial ones, characterizes the cabbage family. White cabbage that has been overfertilized and then prepared without due care can make an entire house reek so horribly that the smell has come to symbolize the staleness of lower middle-class life. It can affect one directly and even conjure up memories.

Often the odors of the cabbage family are just on that fine line between pungent and disgusting, as is the case with rocket salad or arugula (*Eruca sativa*), an annual from the Mediterranean region. In Central Europe, it was occasionally used as an oilseed plant, but the Italians always valued "ruccola" salad made from its leaves. They also used it as a vegetable despite its pungent smell, which many people would call a mild stench. It has only recently found a place in gardens, and many gardeners will use only a few leaves to spice up a salad, not daring to add more.

On one side of this line marked by arugula are the more appetizing species of cabbage along with its botanical relatives—mustard, horseradish, and cress—whereas on the other side are those cabbage plants whose smell tends to be slightly rotten. Examples are the North African annual *Biscutella lyrata* and lesser swinecress (*Coronopus didymus*), which comes from South America. Both smell disgusting in a way similar to the narrow-leaved pepperwort (*Lepidium ruderale*), which intrudes on derelict land rich in nitrogen. This plant actually loses its stench if transplanted into garden soil that is poor in nitrogen. In earlier times it could be bought as *Herba lepidii ruderalis* in Russian pharmacies and was valued as a good remedy for feverish conditions. In other places, such as in southern Europe, the dried herb was said to drive off vermin, particularly fleas. However, as with other smelly plants and their supposed effects, this naturally begs the question: did experience really back up the good advice, or were human feelings transferred to animals? After all, it was once believed that the best way to deal with bubonic plague was to use the worst possible smells against it.

Warty cabbage (*Bunias orientalis*) is native to eastern Europe and sometimes grows as a weed in garbage dumps and along roadsides. Its traditional name, which translates as little oriental toothed pod, sounds somewhat mysterious, though the plant itself is not mysterious at all. It is a robust perennial with overly rich inflorescences and decorative leaves. It proclaims itself as a member of the cabbage family by the pungent and slightly bitter horseradish taste of its leaves. It also has the faint smell of rotten cabbage, which is why it deserves a place in the Stinking Garden. In spite of the smell, the young leaves are considered a tasty spring vegetable in Poland, Turkey, and Russia. If one grows this plant in the garden, one might try blanching the first leaves under a black bucket as with chicory before trying to get used to the aroma.

The perennial wall rocket (*Diplotaxis tenuifolia*), an import from the Mediterranean region, is probably the most bizarre of the unpleasant-smelling cabbage plants. Without any doubt, its leaves smell of burned pork chops. This makes them a source of surprise and merriment in the Stinking Garden, even for the gardener himself upon returning to confirm this phenomenon after a long winter break.

The Scent of Tar and Diesel Oil

The smell of asphalt may be even more unsuitable for a garden than burned pork chops, and it can be found in the Stinking Garden if the gardener succeeds in getting hold of treacle clover (*Psoralea bituminosa*). This perennial grows throughout the Mediterranean region and on the Canary Islands, where it forms large clumps. Its shiny cloverlike leaves and pretty lilac papilionoid flowers make the unmistakable smell of tar seem even more astonishing. Unfortunately, this plant is not hardy in our climate, but it can easily spend the winter as a houseplant on a sunny windowsill.

With regard to its olfactory properties as well as to its history on earth, asphalt is related to petroleum. The smell of petroleum can be found in a plant called *Solanum giganteum*, which belongs to the same genus as potato and tomato. Its leaves are as soft as velvet and smell distinctly of diesel oil, with a sharp overtone that is reminiscent of fermentation. Its growth is truly gigantic even in our gardens, where it can be planted only after the last late frosts have passed, and it can grow to 30 meters in its native country. It has to spend the winter inside, but if it has grown too big, simply let the frost kill it. It produces seed in abundance, and new plants can easily be grown for the following season.

A Good Word for Sweat

Before civilized humanity began to get rid of their body odors (and viewed this achievement as the epitome of civilization), the smell of sweat was everywhere and was mostly tolerated. There were, however, some reservations: people could usually tolerate their own body odor but did not find it appealing in others. And there were exceptions: young lads at village dances would hold a sweat-soaked handkerchief under a girl's nose to entice and arouse her, and the sweat of a beloved woman was often said to have a stimulating effect on a man.

Today we know that sweat (and in particular, the sweat of male armpits) contains sexual pheromones that are, coincidentally, very similar to those of pigs. Thus our zoological past is at least partly conserved, and we should not turn away from it when we encounter its symbolic form in the garden.

Clary sage (*Salvia sclarea*) is a proud and beautiful biennial plant. In its first year, it displays a bunch of large, velvety leaves, and in the second year, an impressive six-foot flower spike. Its large labiate flowers stand in long racemes, and their color ranges from creamy white to pale lilac. Clary sage is one of the few plants whose flowers remain decorative—and scented—for weeks after they have wilted.

Most people initially find its scent slightly pungent and sharp but not unpleasant. When told that the smell is exactly the same as that of sweaty armpits, they are quite surprised and then readily agree. Perhaps this means that as long as people do not reflect on the smell, they remember it as something relating to themselves, something they do not have to fend off. Perhaps they even remember situations that were not unpleasant at all, and it is only the word *sweat* that makes them conscious of the smell and unleashes the socially conditioned reaction of disgust.

Clary sage, native to southern Europe, received its name from a type of oil that was distilled from it. The oil was used to add the taste of claret to an otherwise insipid wine.

Even More Body Odors

Smell receptors immediately signal one of the oldest parts of our brains and arouse instincts and feelings. However, reason then adds its two cents, so that a smell initially deemed good is later amended to be bad, just as an originally revolting smell can be redefined as highly appetizing. Remember the blue cheese.

Finally, it may happen—and the Stinking Garden with all its irritants may contribute to this—that we develop a greater sensitivity to a good scent when we have previously been insulted by a bad one. Stinking goosefoot is an example.

The smell of stinking goosefoot (*Chenopodium vulvaria*) corresponds to a very intimate area of all-too-human odors, though Linnaeus was unfair in imagining that this only occurs among the female gender. In truth, this odor is produced wherever urine is retained for some time in folds of human skin and begins to decompose under the influence of body heat.

Poetic justice came 50 years later when Heinrich Adolph Schrader, a botanist from Göttingen, named another, just as foul-reeking chenopod *Chenopodium hircinum*, buck's goosefoot or avian goosefoot. This plant is native to subtropical America and has been imported with wool, whereas the stinking goosefoot is native to the Mediterranean and has spread a little to the north.

The smell of both these plants is created by a substance called trimethylanin, which is produced in the decomposition of proteins. This substance can sometimes be found in old fish brine and occurs in the flowers of a whole series of plants, all smelling of rotting fish. Examples include native dogwood (*Cornus sanguinea*), the species of hawthorn (*Crataegus* spp.), to a lesser extent some species of pear and medlar, and the flowers of common ivy (*Hedera* spp.).

Biochemical scientists tell us that trimethylanin, in combination with other substances, is also responsible for the intense and disgusting smell of sperm that is given off by the male flowers of the sweet chestnut (*Castanea sativa*). All scents of this category work to entice flies and bugs to visit the flower and carry out its pollination.

The rancid smell of butyric acid is familiar partly because of humans (it is contained in sweat) and partly because of the breakfast table (before the invention of the refrigerator anyway). It is exuded by the mature fruits of ginkgo (*Ginkgo biloba*) for a short period every year. In Rheydt, a town near the lower reaches of the Rhine, there is a road on which a beautiful allée of ginkgo trees was planted many years ago. Every year in late autumn, people living on this road write letters to their local newspaper demanding that something be done about the unbearable stench.

Ginkgoes are dioecious, so only the female trees are dangerous to one's nose. Gardeners in public areas therefore try to obtain reliably male ginkgoes for parks and green spaces. However, in private spaces, female trees do have their charms; for the purpose of fertilization, they need to have at least one male nearby. Hidden underneath the pulp, which rots and reeks horribly of butyric acid and valerian acid—that is, of a neglected latrine in a pub—there is an oval pip with a thin shell. Inside it is a seed similar to an almond but immaculately smooth, rounded, and creamy white. Roasted, this seed is offered as a delicacy in Japan. If one can get hold of ginkgo fruits, they can be cleaned with a great deal of work. Roasted in a pan, the seeds taste very much like chestnuts—sweet and buttery with a slightly peppery aftertaste.

Scents of the Rue Family

The Stinking Garden would have to be rather large, more like a park, if we wanted to plant in it all those trees and shrubs that exude unpleasant scents from their leaves, fruits, or roots. A greenhouse would also be part of it since some of the plants do not survive our winters.

The rue family is particularly rich in scents, both pleasant and otherwise, its most important representatives being oranges and lemons. It is at home in the tropical and subtropical areas of the world and has dispatched only two of its members to Central Europe: burning bush (*Dictamnus albus*), which has a wonderfully fruity aroma, and rue (*Ruta graveolens*), which has a pungent aroma that is not to everyone's taste. For some people, this plant might merit a place if not in the Stinking Garden then at least along its edges.

Alleged to be truly smelly is bukkobush (*Barosma foetidissima*), native to South Africa and sometimes grown here as a houseplant. I have not been able to get hold of one yet, however, so I only know this from books.

Orixa japonica, a shrub from southern Japan, is also a member of the rue family, and its leaves smell repulsive (I would describe its smell as unhealthy sweat). There are three other plants of this same family that have often been described as foul-smelling, but these plants are slightly disappointing to the more demanding fan of plant stench. In the interest of being thorough, I will mention them here. Mexican orange blossom (*Choisya ternata*) is native to Mexico, Amur cork tree (*Phellodendron amurense*) is native to East Asia, and hop tree (*Ptelea trifoliata*) does indeed remotely smell of hop.

Moody Boxwood

There is a widespread opinion that boxwood (*Buxus sempervirens*) smells of cat pee, and for a long time I thought that was just a rumor. Initially I did not smell anything, and secondly, I once watched as one of our cats marked the boxwood by the terrace with its scent (and it was not even a tomcat).

"So that's why!" I thought. But I was far off the mark. Boxwood does smell, but not around the clock. Above all, it does not smell when I want a visitor in the Stinking Garden to smell it. Why it smells—and when—I have thus far been unable to detect. Temperature or humidity may be a factor, but I do not know. The theory that boxwood plants undergo mood swings is just as plausible. Regarding the cat, however, the animal probably did smell the plant and, sensing competition, was simply reinforcing her claim to the territory.

From Stinking Juniper to Stinking Rose

As an aside, I now mention stinking juniper (*Juniperus foetidissima*), a plant of the cypress family. Its nasty smell, though verified in the name of the plant, is so comparatively weak that one can even find people who call it pungent and spicy. The leaves were formerly used to induce abortion, which was potentially lethal to the woman. In addition, the branches were said to work against witches and their spells and were added to the palm bouquet on Palm Sunday. Once consecrated, the bouquet was said to protect the house, its people, and their animals from evil.

The tree of life (*Thuja occidentalis*), introduced into Europe from North America in the sixteenth century, belongs to the same family as the juniper and also has leaves that smell faintly disgusting.

Things are very different indeed when it comes to skunkbush sumac (*Rhus trilobata*) from North America. From a good many meters away one notices the awful stench of the leaves without even touching them, which is not recommended anyway because they are full of skin irritants (as are most species of this genus). People who are particularly sensitive to these irritants can get nasty and painful rashes from even minimal contact with these plants.

In milder areas, skunkbush sumac is hardy in our country, as are two other stinking shrubs: *Clerodendron bungei* and *Clerodendron trichotomum*. The German common name of this genus is tree of lots because the fruits of one of these two species, which are hard to tell apart by looks alone, contain a deadly poison, whereas those of the other species are perfectly harmless. In Indonesia, this fact was once used to mete out divine judgments. A suspected criminal was made to drink fruit juice from one of the plants. If he died, he was guilty; if not, he was free.

In contrast to its leaves, the flowers of *Clerodendron* are pleasantly fragrant. This cannot be said of the flowers of *Viburnum lantana*, which have a repugnant smell that is also governed by trimethylamin. On the other hand, the wood and

The flowers of the tree of lots smell sweet, but its leaves smell disgusting.

bark have a completely different stench that is reminiscent of bird excrement. The branches of this shrub are well suited to making switches and slings, which is why its common name was once excrement sling. This shrub is suitable for the Stinking Garden, being both smelly and decorative at the same time, with cream-colored inflorescences and berries that start off red and then turn black.

With alder buckthorn (*Rhamnus frangula*), the bark is what smells rotten. This has given the tree many different names that all relate to its smell, including rotten cherry in Austria, stinking tree in Westphalia, and stinking willow in Switzerland. In southwestern Germany, it is succinctly called stinker.

Bay leaves are highly aromatic and indispensable in cookery. However, this plant has a close relative—a half-brother, so to speak—whose leaves look very similar but give off a most pungent smell when rubbed. It is called Californian laurel or California bay (*Umbellularia californica*) and is native to North America. It was formerly used as a remedy for headache, colic, and diarrhea.

The pea family has two stinking shrubs to offer. The first one is bastard indigo (*Amorpha fruticosa*), which was used as a blue dye by the first settlers in North America and which can also be found as a decorative shrub in some nurseries in our country. Bright yellow anthers beautifully contrast with its purple flowers.

The second shrub in this family is *Anagyris foetida*, a plant from the Mediterranean region that is not hardy in our climate. In his book on herbs from 1687, Tabernaemontanus calls it the stinking tree. The leaves of both these shrubs smell musty and rotten.

The last shrub in the Stinking Garden once again has flowers that smell bad even though it is a rose, and roses are supposed to give off only the very sweetest and purest of scents. This is not so with *Rosa foetida*, the Austrian yellow rose, which is native to Asia Minor. It has been cultivated in Europe since the sixteenth century and has become the ancestor of all the yellow hybrid roses in our gardens. Only very few of them, however, have even a whiff of the original foul smell, which is like that of a fox in heat.

Two Types of Elder

Many people would probably like to plant elder (*Sambucus nigra*) in the Stinking Garden. This plant has a strange smell that some people find revolting and even positively nauseating. These people are not fond of tasty elderberry soup, elderflower biscuits, or elderflower wine.

Here we are probably looking at a purely physiological dislike caused by a difference in sensitivity in the nasal membranes of different people. The particular smell of elder can be found in another species, dwarf elder (*Sambucus ebulus*), where it is intensified into something quite horrible. Though dwarf elder has woody stems, the plant is herbaceous rather than woody, and the stems die down to ground level every winter.

A German common name for dwarf elder is stinkholler, a name fully vindicated by the plant, whose rotten smell is particularly long lasting. Many other bad smells from plants evaporate quite quickly, but even after 20 years in an herbarium, the dried leaves of this one still reek just like they did on the first day. The smell is said to drive off mice, probably because it is quite similar to that of a dead mouse. This again shows that the worst smells from the plant kingdom inescapably remind us of those given off by animals, especially those that develop when proteins decompose.

The Mint Family

Those who now want to recover from all these odors and are searching for more pleasant scents in the garden will certainly find something in the mint family. Almost no other plant family has developed the art of beautiful scents in as many variations as this one has. What would our kitchens be like without marjoram, rosemary, and sage, without oregano, basil, lemon balm, and thyme? We must also mention lavender here, even though only the most minute amounts of it may be used in cooking, for fish soup and herb butter.

However, revolting or at least ambivalent smells can even be found within this family. We have already encountered clary sage and hyssop in other places in the Stinking Garden. Two more native members of this family that deserve mention in this context are black horehound and hedge woundwort. Both smell muddy-grubby, and both are widespread perennials.

Black horehound (*Ballota nigra*), sometimes rightly called stinkandorn, is a village plant of dry, nitrogen-rich derelict patches and hedges. It belongs to the Archaeophytes, which are plants that were able to migrate into Europe and become resident here after the Central European forests were cleared. Black horehound looks similar to deadnettle, but its leaves are smaller and softly hairy. While not an obvious beauty, this plant does have a certain somber charm, with its murky-green leaves and pale lilac flowers.

Hedge woundwort (*Stachys sylvatica*), stenkerne in vernacular Suabian and called stinking nettle 250 years ago by Balthasar Ehrhardt in his *Economic History of Plants*, is a common plant of light forests and scrubland. It is also an ancient medicinal plant, *Herba lamii sylvatici foetidi*, once highly valued as a treatment for open wounds.

A member of the mint family that is native to southern Siberia and is quite similar to hedge woundwort in shape and smell is catmint (*Nepeta sibirica*). This plant can occasionally be found in nurseries as an herbaceous garden plant. A species of germander known as cat thyme, *Teucrium marum*, is similar to these two. Its piercing, even biting smell is said to attract cats and other wild animals. This germander is a woody little shrub of compact growth, with gray-green, pin-shaped leaves. It grows wild in southern Europe, but it was also widely grown in our climate because of its medicinal use as a treatment for nervous tension. A powder to relieve headaches was also prepared from its dried leaves.

Finally, dragonhead (*Dracocephalum ruyschiana*) is also a member of the mint family. Though native to northern and eastern Europe, it has established itself in some parts of our country as well. Because of its smell, the Swedes have given it the unambiguous name of märpissagras (horse pee grass). However, that does not stop it from being offered time and again in the horticultural trade because its inflorescence is truly impressive.

Pungent Smells

When trying to describe a smell that is almost a stench but not quite, we often use the word *pungent* simply because we do not have a descriptive word that is more precise.

Nearly rancid butter may smell pungent, as do goat's milk and urine and a whole list of plants, too. Some of these plants are inhabitants of the Stinking Garden that we have already encountered.

For me, a typically pungent smell is that of *Tagetes*, planted year after year as an inexhaustible summer annual in many gardens and public parks. Gardeners often call it students' flower. In the lower reaches of the Rhine, it is called stinking student, and in Hermann Hesse's books it is called stinking vanity. This is because many people find its intensive, bitter smell unpleasant. I cannot share this opinion, perhaps because memories come into play here, pleasant memories of childhood in which a whiff of *Tagetes* was an integral part of my garden experiences in summer. An herb gardener once assured me that to him the smell was both "penetrating" and "unpleasant." However, instead of the purely decorative (and supposedly anti-nematodal) species of *Tagetes*, this gardener grew pleasantly scented species that are cultivated for spices and teas in Mexico.

Tagetes is just one of many members of the daisy family represented in the Stinking Garden. Two species of *Tanacetum*, tansy (*Tanacetum vulgare*) and feverfew (*Tanacetum parthenium*), resemble each other in odor and certainly occupy the borderline between pungent and stinking. The pungent smell of the flowers of large garden daisies (*Chrysanthemum maximum*, or now *Leucanthemum maximum*) can definitely be classified as stinking, and the stinking chamomile (*Anthemis cotula*) is also aptly named.

Finally, the genus *Senecio* belongs to the daisy family, and this genus has produced two powerful stinkers. *Senecio rupestris*, the lime-loving rock ragwort, is native to the Tyrolean Alps and the Berchtesgaden area. However, for a pungent and distasteful whiff of it, one need not travel all that way because sticky ragwort (*Senecio viscosus*) smells quite similar. The smell is caused by a sticky secretion. In his *Flora of Central Europe*, the botanist Gustav Hegi associates this odor with the animal kingdom, calling it "unpleasantly muskrat-like."

Back again to the animal kingdom, we can add hemlock (*Conium maculatum*), also called mouse's mushroom because it reeks of mouse urine. Its German name, Schierling, also points in this direction. Its origin lies in the ancient Nordic word *skarn*, which means dung. The flowers of hemlock, however, have a gentle and pleasant fragrance, which makes it even more dangerous in the Stinking Garden. It is deadly poisonous, and if we bring it into the garden at all we should carry sufficient personal liability insurance.

The contrast between stinking leaves and pleasantly scented flowers is actually quite common. This is true of Caucasian crosswort (*Phuopsis stylosa*), a close relative of common aromatic woodruff that, like its common relative, forms rambling carpets. It is a native of the Caucasus and is very pleasant. It has light purple inflorescences with a delicate fragrance, making the animal-like smell of its leaves even more surprising. The odor is similar to musk, which has given the plant its English name, wet fox.

The same thing is true of *Patrinia scabiosifolia* and *Patrinia triloba* from Japan. Both are popular garden perennials because of their scented flowers. However, their leaves do smell truly disgusting, and their roots, with a different odor entirely, smell of valerian.

The smell of *Lantana camara*, a native of tropical America cultivated in Silesia as early as in the Renaissance, might well be called pungent. No matter how many new varieties of this plant gardeners may have bred, its leaves always retain their revolting smell and numerous small flowers in all shades of red and yellow always grow on the same plant.

Geranium macrorrhizum, the Balkan cranesbill from southeastern Europe, does well in the shadier areas of the Stinking Garden. It was first brought into gardens around 400 years ago as a robust groundcover. The fact that the disgusting smell keeps cats out of flower beds is likely to have played a role. Anyone who has ever dealt with the noiseless but thorough work of a cat's paws in the garden will know the value of this plant.

Our native herb Robert (*Geranium robertianum*) does not smell quite so unpleasant. It is an annual of derelict land and disused railway lines where it can form large stands, its bright crimson leaf color conspicuous in spring and autumn.

Carrion Smell

I have left the worst for last: the smell of carrion! For any human being, this is probably the worst smell imaginable, but for many species of fly, it is an irresistible temptation that calls them to table and, at the same time, entices them to do some useful work. Flies and other insects spread the spores of mushrooms that smell of carrion and help to pollinate other plants. The two groups of carrion plants are very difficult, if not impossible, to establish in the Stinking Garden.

With few exceptions and perfectly in keeping with the hint of secrecy surrounding their very being, mushrooms resist any attempt at domestication.

They appear out of the blue and are gone again just as quickly, and nobody knows why. Thus I have tried and failed to grow the incredibly foul-smelling stinkhorn, even though I kept collecting its juvenile form, the (edible!) witches' eggs, together with large amounts of mycelium and forest soil. Two centuries ago, the botanist Christian Hendrik Persoon christened this mushroom *Phallus impudicus*, or shameless phallus. The flies that spread its liquid mass of spores are attracted by the penetrating stench of carrion given off by the plant, so wherever the stinkhorn grows, large and dense colonies of it can be found.

The chemical reactions quietly and secretly carried out by mushrooms lead to a curious variety of bad smells in other species. Stinking coral and small fetid marasmius smell of garlic, and large fetid marasmius smells of rotting cabbage. These might be tolerable, but stinking parasol smells of coal gas, stinking toadstool smells of sulfuric acid, and yellow stainer mushroom smells of carbolic acid. Dog stinkhorn (*Mutinus caninus*) and devil's fingers (*Clathrus archeri*) spread a stench of carrion, as does stinkhorn; stinking ruscula first smells of rancid oil that later turns to rotting fish. All in all, this is an impressive collection of stinkers. Many more can be found in the tropics, and not only among mushrooms.

Three species from the arum family are examples of tropical and subtropical carrion plants. I can display them in the Stinking Garden only if they overwinter in a frost-free greenhouse.

Every nursery selling bulbs stocks dragon arum (*Dracunculus vulgaris*), which grows wild in the Mediterranean region and produces a flower that is as imposing as it is evil-smelling. Less often, one can find voodoo lily (*Sauromatum venosum*), which is a native of subtropical Asia and some countries of Africa. When its tuber is placed in the ground, it produces only a single, palmate leaf. Small tubers develop around the original one. To enjoy the experience of the stinking flower, which lasts only three days, one must take the tuber out of the ground in autumn, dry it off, keep it in the dark, and place it on a windowsill after Christmas.

The same goes for *Amorphophallus konjac*, another species from the arum family that is native to Southeast Asia and is only rarely found in cultivation. It is suitable for home use, so to speak, being the smaller edition of its relative *Amorphophallus titanum*, which can be translated as "clumsy giant phallus." It made headlines in 1996 when it produced a giant flower in the botanical garden in Bonn. It stank infernally for eight days. The plant is a native of Sumatra, and its tuber can weigh as much as 75 kilograms. The purple-lilac flower, produced at intervals of several years (the plant in Bonn had not bloomed since 1987), can grow more than 2 meters tall and, with a diameter of about 1.25 meters, it is the largest flower of the plant kingdom.

Finally, there are some more plants from the arum family whose flowers smell unpleasant, such as our native bog arum (*Calla palustris*) and the bog plant *Symplocarpus foetidus*, native to eastern North America where it is called skunk cabbage.

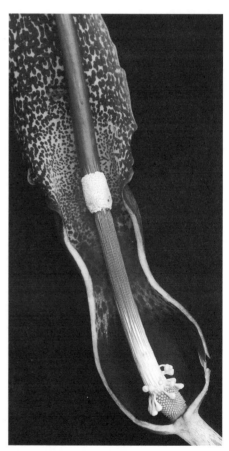

Wherever stinkhorn has established itself in loose forest soil, the air is filled with the stench of carrion that attracts innumerable flies.

The stinking flower of voodoo lily attracts carrion flies into its pitcher trap where they then carry out pollination.

The flowers of plants in the arum family consist of a spathe, a sheath-shaped leaf that surrounds the stinking spadix on which separate male and female flowers are positioned. Pollination is by insects who find the entry into the kettle trap but can leave only after fertilization has taken place and the plant hairs at the exit begin to wilt. Located between the male and female flowers, these hairs allow an insect to enter the flower but prevent it from leaving.

The Use of Stench

The smell of carrion is not exclusive to the arum family. Among the asclepiads, the imposing flowers of the succulent genus *Stapelia* give off a powerfully disgusting smell of carrion. It is valued by flies and other insects that are attracted to the plant and pollinate it. In the sense of evolutionary theory, there is a purpose at work here, or rather a usefulness, since nobody could determine such a purpose in advance. This usefulness has simply developed through the interaction of mutation and selection.

The idea of evolutionary theory should keep us on our guard when we look for or speculate about a purpose for every stench we encounter, be it to fend off grazing animals or to discourage other herbivores. Even a smell that is obviously useful has no true purpose. It is a useful and advantageous attribute that the plant has developed over time. It is not the result of planning ahead and may not with any certainty even play a role in selection.

Plants live by transforming substances from soil and air, by gaining energy in incredibly varied and complicated chemical reactions, and by synthesizing new matter for their tissues. Among the remains are leftovers and waste products. Whether they are important for the continued existence of the plant (or were at some point in its evolution) can only be assumed.

Much more interesting are the questions we can ask about our reactions to plant smells. These can lead to encounters with visitors to the Stinking Garden, and the results can sometimes be surprising. The Stinking Garden is a communicative place. Scents in general, and particularly the bad ones, entice people to spontaneous reactions, to carefree judgments, and to cheerful arguments over whose feelings are right. As though right and wrong feelings even exist! Feelings are always right for the one who has them.

So last but not least, the Stinking Garden can teach us that the more fundamental the experience we are subjected to, the more alone we are with our feelings. We cannot assume in the slightest that others feel the same way that we do, and we cannot even begin to imagine the effect of even a seemingly passive and straightforward sensory experience.

Thoughtful and pensive, we leave the Stinking Garden. Behind us we can still hear the laughter and arguments of visitors holding leaves and flowers under each other's noses. Perhaps tomorrow, we will begin to create a corner in our own garden, one that is not dedicated to the pleasant smells of this world but to their opposites, the smell of rotting fish, burned cabbage, and fermenting petroleum.

Postscript

According to everything I have heard, the stench of the durian tree or zibet (*Durio zibethinus*) has to be the most horrible smell of all. It cannot grow in our Stinking Garden because it needs tropical warmth. Under the right conditions,

The large fruit of the tropical durian tree has the most objectionable plant smell of all, yet its pulp is considered an unusual delicacy.

it grows to 30 meters high and bears fruits that weigh six pounds and are the size of a child's head. They look just like large lychees, but their color is dark yellow. Experts define its stench as a mixture of garlic, blue cheese, and skunk or, more simply, as that of a closet that has not been touched for years. In areas where durian is cultivated (Thailand, Malaysia, and Indonesia), carrying the fruits on public transportation is strictly forbidden. However, the sweet flesh of its fruit, which surrounds chestnut-brown seeds, is said to taste so exquisitely wonderful that it is a famous delicacy. In Singapore, there is a restaurant whose cooks prepare cakes, ice cream, and pancakes from durian fruits. The seeds, too, can be roasted and eaten.

So this might just be the highlight of a Stinking Garden gardener's life—a trip to Singapore to eat durian.

How to
Eat a Lily
The Latest News
from the Garden

Dried lily blossoms from China are commonly used as
a light, slightly bitter vegetable in soups.

Prologue

When we see lilies in flower, we think of purity, of love, and of death. Other cultures think of lunch. The Japanese and the Chinese, the Cossacks on the Volga, the Siberian Tartars, and—beyond the Bering Strait—some North American Indians all valued lily buds as a nourishing vegetable. Some still do.

Indeed, when the sweet and somewhat mealy-tasting bulbs are fried in hot butter, they develop a distinctive and pleasant aroma. Of course, one cannot use just any freshly bought bulbs for this purpose because they are usually drenched in poisonous fungicides, and the taste of lily bulbs is not quite irresistible enough to warrant digging up our own lilies and letting them end up in the frying pan. It is easier to spare a few lily buds or flowers and carefully dry them in the shade. They curl up lengthwise, and even though their water content evaporates, they remain leathery and fleshy. Their taste is slightly bitter with a hint of mushroom. If one adds them to soups (as the Chinese do), they swell up again and are sure to puzzle any guest trying to guess what exactly is floating around in the bowl.

The lily as a vegetable is just one example of the surprises that a garden has to offer, even if we sometimes presume to know everything important. For the curious gardener, gardening is not only about professionally building a pond, knowing 99 varieties of roses, and fastidiously obeying the strict rules of organic gardening. He is much more concerned with trying out old and new ways of doing things, with seeking out unknown plants, with perceiving the traces of life that often go unnoticed as they wind their way through the garden. He hunts in markets to find vegetables as yet unknown to him, he fishes in old and even older gardening books, and he is always on the alert when he enters a new garden where he is bound to find something new. If he does not, he just has not been looking closely enough.

This book is about such discoveries and experiences, and it is also about the everyday life of the gardener and his wife, about strawberries and snails, about chestnuts and parsnips. The writing gardener hopes that there may be many new things for the reader or, barring that, old things seen in a new light.

Just as in a garden, the chapters flow into one another, and their topics cannot be clearly delineated. The garden is alive, and therefore there is no order. Instead, there are several orders intertwined in many different layers.

The Gardener as Plant Hunter

The Library of Catalogs

The gardener's friends offered coffee and cake and loads of plant cuttings, two large baskets full of them. I really felt like Siebold the plant hunter.

Philipp Franz von Siebold—a doctor from Würzburg, Germany, and an employee of the Dutch East India Company—was one of those men who brought a wealth of the East Asian flora to Germany 150 years ago. He was not the first, but we have him to thank for our azaleas, camellias, and the ancestors of our hydrangeas.

One just has to imagine how those travelers must have felt. They were fairly well versed in their native botany, and suddenly they found all these plant species they had never seen before. The new species must have seemed like something out of a fairy tale or even paradise, especially since many of them had already undergone centuries of breeding and grafting.

The Japanese and the Chinese regarded these plants as their national property, so for centuries it remained very difficult for Europeans to get even a glimpse of them, let alone to take material abroad. They had to resort to trickery to accomplish this feat. To be precise, these plant hunters were nothing more than thieves and smugglers.

So like Siebold, I was blessed with new botanical treasures, but without the sneakiness. Most gardeners like to give each other gifts and feel proud when a visitor regards one thing or another as worth taking. It explicitly confirms their appreciation.

Later one walks about one's own garden, the basket full of plants in one hand and a spade in the other, looking for places to accommodate the newcomers without disturbing long-established neighborhoods. The smallest of gardens can be too big when it comes to the work that needs to be done in it, and yet the biggest garden is too small when one returns from a plant hunt and wants to provide for the prey: star allium with its captivating flower balls in bluish hues; licorice root, whose sweet roots we are not going to harvest but which nevertheless regales us with its flower stands; or a very strange meadow rue, with wilting petals that present us with its bizarre stamens as flowers.

In centuries gone by, plant hunting was a real profession akin to plundering other areas of the earth. Nowadays if we want to hunt for plants, we have to rely on our friends and on nurseries. However, since nurseries have been renamed garden centers, there are not many new discoveries to be made; the standard assortment does not vary from city to city.

So we are left with mail-order nurseries. Their packages in spring and fall are to the gardener what holiday presents are to other people. Wrapped in moist newspaper, carefully packaged in wood shavings, pot by pot, there are lots of green presents. They can be full of surprises, too, when the gardener has forgotten what he had ordered all those weeks or months ago.

The order was placed from a catalog. Of course, the gardener did not rely on those bright pictures from discount suppliers but instead used the far less bright and much more substantial catalogs of large perennial nurseries. He put ticks and question marks in the margins, consulted his garden plan, negotiated with his wife, and ended up yet again ordering much more than he had originally intended to.

This temptation is sweet and dangerous. But if one avoids it by simply not studying catalogs, one misses out on something and, of course, never receives those packets with the inscription "Caution, living plants!"—the prosaic password for a botanical poem in which *Edraianthus* rhymes with *Coreopsis*, and *Linum* rhymes with *Campanula*.

An advanced gardener has a whole arsenal of these catalogs at his disposal for a very good reason: they enable him at a glance to discover the availability and location of that plant he just read or heard about. A wealth of species and varieties spreads out in front of him, not in a dream world, but in a reliable list of what is available. There are still thousands of gardeners who rely on those garden centers with their standardized assortments as their only source and then ask themselves (or even me, paying for the return stamp) where on earth one can get hold of meadow knotweed or perennial honesty. They have no idea how easy it is to find plants.

Well, I will readily admit that sometimes it is not quite so easy. Bladder campion with its deceptive berries cannot be found in any catalog, nor can shrubby

Plantago, and I spent many years hunting for the magical mandrake until I finally found it. If those catalogs were nothing more than price lists, they would not be special at all. However, they are often much more than that. To varying degrees, they tell us the most important things about the looks and demands of these plants, including problematic traits (such as that a plant likes to wander) or remarkable features (such as decorative fruits).

A few examples are enough to give the idea. Many years ago, such a catalog of herbaceous perennials was my first gardening book. It served as both textbook and notebook and was the starting point for all my future garden dreams. This catalog exists to this day (it was already 50 years old when I got it), and there is none other like it.

It is produced by Kayser & Seibert, a nursery in the Odenwald forest (64380 Rossdorf, Germany), with a beautiful and rich assortment of herbaceous perennials from *Acaena* to *Zigadenus*. In addition, there are kitchen herbs, ferns and grasses, bog and water plants, and even a number of woody plants. One can obtain this catalog, as well as the others mentioned here, for a small prepayment.

In addition to all the necessary horticultural information, this catalog boasts another ingredient that one would otherwise have laboriously to dig out of many gardening books and the trial and error of one's own experiences. For every species, there is a comprehensive list of plants that it grows well with, both aesthetically and in relation to its demands regarding soil and light. It is compressed horticultural wisdom possessed of so many facets that there is only a very small danger of standardized combinations becoming the monotonous norm.

There is another speciality in the catalog from the perennial nursery Gräfin von Zeppelin in Baden (79295 Sulzburg-Laufen, Germany). For more than 50 years, it has been supplying, along with a huge assortment of herbaceous perennials, a large range of varieties of daylily (*Hemerocallis*). It offers the most noble rarities among them and quite distinctive types. With the help of this source, we can not only try all sorts of varieties in color and height, but we can also make use of their different flowering times, so that from the end of April through to the beginning of October we always have some representative of this noble plant in flower. If one has just started to explore this abundance, one will quickly come to understand that quite a few gardeners have dedicated themselves to collecting these plants alone.

A third source is the catalog of the alpine plant nursery F. Sündermann (88131 Lindau, Germany). More than 100 years ago, the economist Franz Sündermann started this alpine botanical garden and was raised to the rank of official supplier to the king. He had spent years traveling through the European Alps and the high mountains of all five continents in order to collect the peculiar, often low-growing and cushion-forming plants of these regions as guests for his garden. These are treasures, especially for gardeners wanting to collect many different things for very small spaces or who are more interested in small things than in large and decorative perennials.

Sündermann carries, among many other things, an imposing assortment of more than 80 varieties of *Sempervivum* and probably the largest collection of those captivating species of stonecrops. These grow best on pure lime and decorate the edges of their leaves with rows of minute lime pearls in both summer and in winter.

These are only three of many perennial nurseries, and each of them offers something that none of the others has got. This is reason enough to start or extend one's own library of plant catalogs to rummage around in any weather and in any season, memorizing names and dreaming colorful garden dreams, always with a pencil in hand and always with care. When a catalog says that *Physalis alkekengi* "rambles," it means that Chinese lanterns can easily turn into a plague, and when it says "plant for enthusiasts," one really is looking at a tender beauty and should think twice about whether it is worth inviting her into the garden; nothing is more exhausting than unrequited love.

One thing that those gardeners with their wealth of garden plants treat with contempt is scented and spicy herbs. How very exciting for the plant hunter that a small nursery that used to deliver only to two weekly markets in northern Germany now offers its treasures by post. The nursery is called Herbal Magic, and there really does seem to be a magician at work. His name is Daniel Rühlemann (27367 Horstedt), and he sends out a catalog worth reading. In it, one can find many scented and aromatic attractions whose names people like us had never even heard before: caraway thyme (*Thymus herba-barona*) from Corsica; American ginseng (*Panax quinquefolius*), the roots of which are said to be good against rheumatism; Siberian wallflower (*Erysimum ×marshallii*), which smells of roses; all kinds of mints, including those that do not rampage through all the beds. Two herbs that we so far have had to re-sow in the herb garden every year are offered as perennial varieties—a borage from Sardinia and a parsley from Japan.

There is also the decorative oyster plant, with its fleshy leaves and most unusual taste. The herbal magician describes it as tasting of "oysters or anchovies with a hint of champignons and borage." It is fitting that one has to feed this plant a little salt, since it is native to our Nordic seashores.

It is also fitting that the herbal magician offers the magic mandrake, or *Mandragora*. We have to clear entire beds to make room for the prey that our postman delivers.

It cannot be denied that modern plant hunters sometimes raid botanical gardens as well. This is immoral, and if everyone did it, our botanical gardens would indeed look terrible. But the temptation looms large, and humans are weak. Instead of preaching morals, I would rather admit that it has happened to me, too. I stole my first bulbs of bulbous meadow grass (*Poa bulbosa*) from a botanical garden. I am no less guilty for saying that I simply found them in my pockets when I returned home.

Bulbous meadow grass is a grass from the steppes of southeastern Europe. It has adapted to the dry summers of its native country by producing whole hosts of bulbs instead of flowers in April. The whole plant, bulbs and all, then wilts. In September it starts to grow again, and the bulbs develop into new plants. The whole family spends the winter dressed in green. In my garden, bulbous meadow grass is now doing very well indeed—contrary to the rule that goods unlawfully acquired never do well. Perhaps, sometimes, there are exceptions.

Buying a Tree Is Like Getting Married

Boxwood trees grow incredibly slowly. Anyone wishing to grow two strapping boxwood guardians on his doorstep has to spend a long time waiting, nearly as long as a garden's life, unless he was lucky enough to find trees of a dignified age already in place as the legacy of a gardener long gone.

Boxwood shoots, with their small, pointed, oval leaves, grow only a few centimeters per year, so one hardly notices one's little shrub increasing in volume. But boxwood is versatile and has produced some varieties with larger leaves that please the impatient gardener with their rapid growth.

Its leaves are dark green, large and shiny. Just when a cutting has more or less taken root, it starts shooting in all directions, starting at 10 centimeters per year and later increasing to perhaps 20 or more. A dense, tall boxwood hedge no longer remains a dream. The outline of a magnificent ball is visible in the front garden after a few summers instead of after two decades.

It is a never-ending dilemma that shrubs and trees reach the size we desire and dream of only after a long wait. Gardeners who, despite the cost, want to shorten the waiting time have to be prepared for disappointments. Grown trees often respond badly to being replanted. They can stop growing and fruiting and require years of pampering like sick people if they recover at all and do not simply say good-bye.

With all this in mind, we roam through tree nurseries and cast our greedy glances around. There is a young juniper, knee-high at most, no more than an infant if judged on a human time scale. We will have to spend a long time looking after it before it produces its first berries, and then they will take two years to mature before we can use them to refine our sauerkraut. I will not even mention oaks and walnuts, sweet chestnuts and tulip trees.

However, the opposite problem exists, too. Years ago a cedar (*Cedrus*) was planted much too close to our house. Looming large, it is now cutting off the light from our living room, and we will have to mutilate it most horribly every year if we allow it to stay. The exotic shrubs of Japanese bitter orange (*Poncirus trifoliata*) are beautiful to look at even in winter, and their long, green, spiny branches can withstand every frost. Over the years this much-loved treasure has turned into a thicket 6 feet high with scented flowers and yellow fruits that are tempting but bitter. It is such a pity to discover too late that this feast for our eyes should really have been planted in a completely different part of the garden.

Buying a tree is like getting married. One chooses, at least in principle, for life. A separation, if it does become necessary, entails considerable trouble, cost, and pain. The best prevention is a good nursery catalog, describing the final size of the plant and highlighting many other factors that influence our choice—such as demands on soil—and special traits—such as scented leaves and flowers, autumn color, edible fruits.

The hard October yellow of ginkgo, the abundant berries of *Callicarpa*, the lily-of-the-valley scent of *Elaeagnus*, the pungent aroma of the leaves of stinking ash (*Tetradium danielii*)—these are sensual, recurring experiences in the garden beyond mere decoration. People miss them if they see trees and shrubs as nothing but a backdrop and do not go to the trouble of hunting for rarer species not found in every nursery catalog. Our false quince (*Pseudocydonia sinensis*) is just now starting to flower. Its thorny twigs, just showing the tips of new leaves, are densely covered in flowers of various shades of red, according to the species, with one pure white one as well. One can plant them in dense hedges or individually in front of a backdrop that brings out the colors of their flowers and, later, the yellow color of their fruits, which have a strong quince smell. Just like the real thing, these can be made into juices and jellies; if left hanging, they rot away very slowly throughout the winter, and the birds then devour them. In terms of height, false quince is an easy shrub. It quickly reaches its final height, little more than one meter, and it never needs pruning.

So we are left with the problem of finding a tree that grows quickly but ceases once it has reached its desired height. Let's build it ourselves!

Join together a few sturdy metal poles or water pipes to form a small pyramid or simply drive them vertically into the soil. Wrap the poles with some close-meshed wire netting to form any sort of shape; 200 years ago it was that of the goddess of fertility, but it does not need to represent her now. Let any climbing plant that suits you wind its way up, arching back down when it cannot get any further and creating cascades of flowers, like waterfalls. You might choose clematis or a climbing rose or honeysuckle. *Lonicera japonica* 'Aureoreticulata' does not have a vernacular name and spends the cold season covered in many small, green winter leaves; in summer it decorates itself with yellow-veined leaves and cream-colored flowers.

In earlier times, people liked to use ivy for these climbing shapes, and it really is eminently suitable because it is evergreen and it does not mind the inevitable snipping. However, one should choose a small-leaved variety for this.

These are not trees for life, nor do they have to be. However, they are a pleasant way to help pass the time while waiting for the walnut tree to grow up and bear fruit, which can easily take 12 years.

Edible Botany

Blue Potatoes

One way or another people have always failed to appreciate potatoes. When Francisco Pizarro brought the first potato with its cheerful little star-shaped flowers to Europe 450 years ago, it was regarded as an ornamental plant and a botanical curiosity. It took people 200 years to discover that its tubers were edible. Once it became economically useful, everyone stopped caring about its beauty.

In the garden, we can do the potato justice and raise it as an ornamental without disregarding its usefulness—and vice versa—since there need not be an entire field of potatoes. Even the white shoots of a single potato left over from the kitchen can be carefully placed between some low perennials or kitchen herbs and covered with some compost. It will grow into a beautiful plant that will yield a modest harvest, a nest of yellow tubers with tender yellow skins. Harvest it when the leaves have died down in the fall or just before, when the tubers are still young and small and unbelievably tender. There may be enough for a small dinner, but there will certainly be enough for a plate of potatoes in their skins, eaten as a cold snack with salt and butter as a kind of savory praline.

Even a balcony gardener does not have forgo the enjoyment of this delicacy at least once. It takes only a large pot and a single sprouting potato. Simply bear in mind that new tubers grow above the old one and be sure to sink the sprouts at least 3 inches deep into the pot.

Of the more than 1000 varieties of potato that used to exist, some have survived and are doing well in a few gardens; in other places, Bintje and Hansa reign supreme in the potato kingdom. Last spring, a generous gardener let me have a dozen tubers of three ancient Austrian varieties, and in September, I had friends round for a multicolored potato dinner. I wanted them to be duly amazed, and they were. The bowl of yellow, red, and blue jacket potatoes looked like a nest of Easter eggs.

The yellow variety is called Kipferl or Bamberger Hörndl, the red one Linzer Rose, and the blue one Pongo. It became clear once more that the yield of a potato in no way depends on the size of the original tuber, as gardening books would have one believe. I received only tiny tubers and managed to harvest many large ones.

Linzer Rose is high-yielding. It produces large, round tubers that do not fall apart when boiled, and it is appetizing to look at. Kipferl is surprising, with its oblong shape that is similar to a horn. It also does not fall apart and is the traditional potato used in Viennese Heurigen pubs for their *pomme de terre* salads. Its flesh is as yellow as butter, and its taste is famous for being like bacon.

One of my guests commented that Pongo definitely made him think of poison and ink. I pointed out that blueberries are also blue and that this has never spoiled anyone's appetite, but to no avail. He stuck with the red and yellow ones, whose flesh had a more traditional potato color. One could turn Pongo into blue chips or, even better, into blue mash, for it falls apart easily when cooked. There could be some more dishes worth seeing: blue potato gnocchi with carrot salad, blue fried potatoes with spinach and fried egg, blue potato rostis.

By the way, a few blue or purple varieties were mentioned very early on in the history of the potato, but only two varieties retain their color when cooked—Pongo and French Truffle Potato, whose bluish-black tubers are said to be a delicacy for gourmets. In markets in large cities, they are sometimes offered at the exorbitant price of 8 euros per pound, and their buttery-nutty taste is not quite amazing enough to justify this kind of price. A clever gardener will buy two tubers but will not eat them. Instead, he will nurse them through to the spring and then place them into the soil to have his own harvest.

From this, one can see that the hunt for unknown varieties of potato is well worth it, both here and abroad, since they can be grown in the home garden.

Poison and Enjoyment and Enjoyable Poison

Where would we be without the nightshade family? Its family name sounds spooky, and some members of it are scary indeed. But how sweet are potatoes, how unique are tomatoes as delicious intermediaries between fruit and vegetable, and how fiery and bright are peppers (*Capsicum*). One could spend days cooking up new dishes using just these three plants. (I gladly do without egg-plants, which also belong to this family, but that is naturally a question of personal taste.)

For dessert, to stay within the family, serve bitter sweet cape gooseberries, decoratively covered in their papery husks. We have to pay exorbitant amounts of money for these in shops, but of course, we can grow them in our own garden.

And if we still belong to that group of people who smoke after dinner, we are making use of yet another member of the nightshade family.

All those plants arrived here only after America was discovered, and even then, some of them had to wait a long time before they were appreciated as vegetables. The smell of potatoes has only been wafting through European kitchens for some 200 years; tomatoes, until 100 years ago, were valued as decorative plants but mistakenly thought to be poisonous; and sweet pepper is a hybrid of the early twentieth century.

But this is only one part of the family, the decent, respectable part, useful in an honest and straightforward way. Another branch of the family consists of rather shady characters that produce poisons and are only beneficial when used very carefully indeed. Otherwise, they can lead to confusion of mind and body.

Henbane (*Hyoscyamus niger*), belladonna, thorn apple, and the not-quite-so-dangerous bitter nightshade (*Solanum dulcamara*) are the subject of some horrible stories. They date from times when this family's alkaloids were still used to numb pain; to enter hallucinatory worlds; to induce love and death with or without the help of wise women (surely, there must have been wise men, too); or simply to increase the toxic effects of beer. The seeds of henbane were sometimes added to beer, and etymologists still argue about whether the word *Pils* derives from Pilsen, the place, or from Bilsen, the German vernacular name for henbane.

Mandragora, too, belongs in this category. The roots of mandrake are shaped like human beings and have long been valued both as a versatile magic ingredient and as a real medicinal plant.

There is a certain attraction to planting such plants and then, with a mixture of respect for the many ancient traditions and a horror of so many deadly poisons, watching the magic herbs grow in one's own flower beds. And no one can stop us from imagining what we might do with them. It does not have to be murder. Belladonna roots, for example, are said to work against arthritis, but only if one has pure thoughts while digging them up.

Ornamental plants comprise yet a third branch of the nightshade family, though this division is only provisional. In reality, all useful nightshades are decorative, the poisonous ones are useful and the ornamental ones are sometimes useful and sometimes poisonous.

Among the ornamental nightshades are some species of tobacco that are useless for smoking but nice to look at; of these, the English, who are crazy about hybrids, have bred some of the most distinctive varieties. Poisonous thorn apple (*Datura*) has some beautiful species, and even petunias are actually members of the nightshade family. I might appreciate this so-called grateful (that is, totally undemanding) balcony plant more if I saw it less frequently. Some plants are used so much that they become fashion items, which degrades them.

Chinese lantern (*Physalis alkekengi*) is cleverer, if one may say so. It hides among the bushes, the semiprostrate branches doing acrobatics around other perennials, and only in the fall, when all other things are withering, does it

The dried seed capsule of a thorn apple is a natural, impressively filigreed work of art.

show its bright orange-red lanterns. It is a relative of cape gooseberry (*Physalis peruviana*), but while the latter hides its edible fruits in gray-green lanterns, the former bears less edible fruits more prominently displayed. The lanterns can be harvested and used as table decorations or for dried flower arrangements. The bright and sunny color lasts all through the winter.

Another member of the nightshade family wraps its fruit up in a slightly different way. The silvery-gray calyx of the shoo-fly closes around its fruit with rounded petals that are folded inward and delicately veined. These are papery treasures, lined up in abundance on a richly branched crown. Shoo-fly (*Nicandra physaloides*) is an annual. If planted in isolation, it can look like a miniature tree whose branches rapidly cover themselves in bell-shaped flowers with blue margins and white centers. In their place, the lantern will appear only two or three days later.

Shoo-fly (which is very poisonous indeed!) comes from Peru. It was initially grown only in botanical gardens. Later it was used as an ornamental, and then it escaped. Now it can simply appear out of the blue in some places, dubbed a garden fugitive by botanists, erratic and inclined to roam. The plant will settle only if re-sown every year by a gardener who, for mysterious motives, is drawn to this somewhat eccentric family in which poison is so close to good taste, lure so close to threat, darkness so close to light, magic so close to death.

Forgotten Spices

An herb garden is a museum. The plants we grow and harvest in it were discovered centuries ago and then passed on from one garden to the next. Their paths can be traced in ancient herbals back to Roman times.

Some spices have been lost along the way, particularly in our century. There are many treasures out there waiting to be rediscovered by the gardener. One rarely finds them mentioned even in books on old cottage gardens, let alone in garden centers.

Baldmoney is a good example. If it is planted in a warm, dry spot in the garden, one can start looking for its first filigree tips in spring. These later develop into large, more and more intricately divided fronds with leaflets as thin as pieces of string. It is an airy bush of the finest green and has many culinary uses.

Its strong, spicy aroma, not without a touch of sharpness, remains with the herb even when dried (in contrast to dill, which is otherwise quite similar), and it is as good with fish and quark (a soft European cheese) and eggs as it is with salads. It is best with cucumber salad and similar vegetables.

But this is not all. Its roots also have something to offer and possess yet a different scent. In the Scottish highlands, people used to boil it as a vegetable, and in other places, people used it to make an aromatic and bitter digestif.

Baldmoney is a perennial. Its botanical name is *Meum athamanticum*, and it belongs to the carrot family. This makes it a cousin of sweet cicely, whose botanical name, *Myrrhis odorata*, points twofold to its sweet smell. It also used to be a popular kitchen herb, and being perennial, it can often be found growing wild at ancient cultivation sites, in abandoned gardens, and next to derelict alpine huts.

Its leaves remind one of fern fronds, and their scent when crushed is similar to that of aniseed. The taste of its leaves is so mild that one can add large amounts of it to salads. Sweet cicely will do well even in the deepest shade and, like baldmoney, produces large, white umbels of flowers from March to July. Its mature seeds are deeply black and, when ground, are suitable as an individual spice, especially for meat sauces. Visitors will then be surprised and ask which spice produces such an unusual nuance, which reminds me that there are two motives for seasoning food. We either want to give a dish its own particular flavor (pizza is unthinkable without the scent of oregano), or we want to create a variation, so that a salad dressing can today taste more of baldmoney, tomorrow more of sweet cicely, and the day after of parsley and chives as usual.

The more often we go by the second principle, the more we will benefit from the fact that nearly all spices are also medicinal herbs; in earlier times, when pharmacology was nothing more than applied botany, they were mainly used as such. Baldmoney and sweet cicely, for example, activate the juices in one's stomach and thus help make a meal easier to digest. The same is true of sneezewort (*Achillea ptarmica*), a long-forgotten kitchen herb.

A double-flowered variety of this plant, called shirt buttons, has long been popular as a garden perennial. Whether it is this one or the original species, the tips of its young shoots with their delicately incised small leaves produce a spice of soft bitterness. According to a sign in the Hamburg botanical garden, they must go into the famous Hamburg eel soup. This, indeed, may have something to do with easing digestion. Sneezewort can be used cautiously in other ways, too, to create an unusual accent and, just as with baldmoney and sweet cicely, to give an old, dignified plant a new lease on life in the kitchen. The progression from medicinal herb to spice to decorative plant is a typical resumé for many plant species. Whether one sees this as reaching out to achieve higher goals or a decline into the category of "just beautiful" is up to each individual.

A Second Strawberry Harvest

Mrs. Jäger—known in Germany as Mrs. Dr. Jäger—could never, according to the customs of her time, have become a doctor herself but was allowed to share the title of doctor with her husband. In the middle of the First World War, she wrote a book on housekeeping in times of war, full of valuable hints on how to create a tasty meal out of nearly nothing and how to use native plants to substitute for the missing "colonial wares."

Her recipes were not necessarily brand new but recalled practices from former, less affluent times, in which people ate more native plants than imported goods. Tea made from strawberry leaves, for example, which Mrs. Jäger recommends as a nearly equivalent substitute for black tea, had been praised 150 years earlier by Johann Georg Künitz in his *Economical Encyclopedia*.

In late summer, we have the youngest and finest strawberry leaves available for making such a tea: the small leaves of the innumerable runners, which have developed in the rows of our strawberries and which we have to cut off now, to stop our rows from turning into a field.

The folded-up, fresh leaves, squashed a little with a rolling pin or in one's hands, undergo a magical transformation in a closed tin can in the oven at 50°C (122°F). After three or four hours, they have fermented and are now dark brown. They smell fruity rather than savory and can be dried. We regard this tea herb as a second strawberry harvest, especially since the first, real harvest left a lot to be desired this year, in quantity as well as in taste. Some gardeners take off not only the shoots but also most of the leaves of the stock plant. It is a kind of rejuvenation that supposedly extends the life span of strawberry plants by one or two years. For the first time this year, I have followed this advice. The bare rows look pitiable. But this is what it is like in the garden. For every harvest, we *also* have to mutilate, destroy, get rid of, exterminate, or kill something. We just call it by other names so as not to disturb the image of the gardener at peace with nature.

We call it harvesting when we cut those marvelous flowers that the garden now offers. Sunflowers (*Helianthus annuus*), for example, are cut before their flowers are fully open so that the buds, boiled and salted, can be put onto the table. The fleshy flower bases are similar to those of artichokes. Four centuries ago, John Gerard, an English herbalist, declared them to be preferable to artichokes. Instead of boiling the buds until they are done, one can grill them lightly and prepare them with oil, vinegar, and pepper. One has only to remove the green sepals as much as possible because these taste just as resinous as they feel. The small remains that are inevitably left add a whiff of bitterness to the dish, very becoming in an appetizer.

. . . And with It, Mustard

One should always have plenty of seeds of white mustard (*Sinapis alba*), also called yellow mustard, in the house. In summer, we can sow it wherever we need short-term groundcover, and it also gives us spicy leaves for salads and provides a good mulch. In winter, we can soak the yellow seeds in bowls of water and let them sprout on cotton wool like cress to then use the young plantlets in our sandwiches. Black mustard (*Brassica nigra*) is also suitable, but it is noticeably more pungent.

With the seeds of both types of mustard in stock, it is easy to make one's own homemade mustard from freshly ground seeds just as the English have always prepared it. Old German cookbooks have recipes for this, but they often contain mistakes. Ground mustard seeds, so they tell us, should be mixed into a paste with vinegar, salt, and hot water. How horrible! Each of these three ingredients by itself is capable of blocking the enzymes that make mustard pungent. The mustard seeds will be mild and bitter if abused in this way. Instead, one should prepare the broth with cold water and then wait for 15 minutes before adding vinegar and salt and maybe a little pepper and cloves. Heat will damage this mustard. If mustard sauce is to taste of mustard, it should never be boiled with food, but only stirred in at the end.

Black mustard is more pungent than white mustard. In preparing one's own mustard, one can try out different mixtures and create a personalized, domestic brand. And instead of the hot mustard of the Dusseldorf region, create a mild, sweet southern German one with lots of sugar, or a French one with onions, thyme, cinnamon, cloves, and bay leaves. Actually this would be more of an herb paste than a true mustard.

Lots of False Capers

A few small green balls can totally change a dish. Capers are a spicy addition to many egg dishes and salads. They can spice up sauces and add that special taste to pizzas. They are absolutely indispensable in meatballs, and those who have not gotten too lazy to prepare their own party snacks probably value them for decorative purposes.

Capers are the flower buds of a thorny shrub (*Capparis spinosa*) that grows only in the warmer regions of the Mediterranean. Even so, we can harvest our

Buds and very young fruits of nasturtium can be used as capers.

own capers from the garden; people have always used the buds of some native species to substitute for the real thing. It is even possible to find a nuance in the substitute that is indeed preferable to the original.

The pleasantly pungent, mustard-tasting buds of nasturtium (*Tropaeolum majus*) are commonly recommended for the purpose, but beware. The inside can be rock-hard when the outer skin is still fresh and green, so harvest them when they are very young. The buds are better suited when they are still closed, though they are not quite as crunchy.

Other buds that substitute for capers are those of marsh marigold (*Caltha palustris*), broom (*Cytisus scoparius*), and some species of thistle. With the latter, make sure to pick them before their sepals have hardened into thorns. The ones I like best are dandelion buds; they taste a little bitter, just like real capers. Daisy buds, by contrast, are milder.

One can often read that celandine buds make good capers. However, when in flower, this plant produces a poison somewhat less than harmless (this is why its leaves, too, should only be used in spring salads, before the plant flowers). Perhaps it would be better to avoid these altogether.

To preserve caperlike buds of any kind, cover them in tepid salt water and leave them to stand overnight. Then, after adding a generous amount of vinegar, bring them to a boil. After they have cooled down, puts the capers into a resealable jar and add enough of the vinegar (brought again to a boil) to cover them well. A splash of oil spread across the surface forms an airtight seal to make them last.

Weeds for the Kitchen

Anyone who happens to have ground elder (*Aegopodium podagraria*) in the garden will agree that it is a weed and will not object to calling it that. Wherever ground elder grows, nothing else stands a chance, and it extends its realm every year. To drive it out is hard work, and just when it seems to be gone, it lifts its head in some corner or other.

It is quite probable that the ground elder in our gardens is a relic from former times, when people used to cultivate it. It was considered a remedy for arthritis and gout, but people also used it as a vegetable. Its very young leaves, which look freshly lacquered, are slightly bitter, but they can be added to mixed salads. For those who like bitter things, they can also serve as a vegetable, boiled and seasoned like spinach. And this is by no means the only edible garden weed.

If we want to harvest and eat wild herbs, it is best to rely on the garden. Outside the garden one can never be sure that the herbs have not been polluted by fertilizers or exhaust fumes, not to mention the ubiquitous dog turd.

This warning, by the way, can be found in the small print of most wild plant cookbooks, which aim to entice us, at least occasionally, to swap lettuce for dandelion, spinach for ground elder.

They say that we should get the herbs from "unfertilized, dust-free locations, not polluted by pesticides and detrimental environmental influences."

For most of us, finding such a location is just wishful thinking. And if we did find it, we would still need to justify carting off bags full of the plants that grow there. Small amounts just will not do if we are going to use them for cooking, and hordes of plant gatherers digging up dandelions and plucking leaves off plantains is not what I would consider a desirable scenario.

So, any wild plants we might want to use in the kitchen must first be established in our own gardens. This way, we may not altogether escape all those detrimental environmental influences, but at least we can avoid the worst poisons. And the seeds for our cultures can be collected from roadsides, parks, and fields without worrying about it.

It is obvious that all the weeds in the garden will not be edible, nor would we wish to cultivate them in amounts sufficient for kitchen use. We must be selective, and in doing so, bear in mind that ground elder is not the only edible weed that can make a nuisance of itself in the garden. Quite a large amount of space is required for a sufficiently large thicket of stinging nettles to develop without having them become annoying, or to tolerate ground ivy, which simply cannot be tamed and chokes everything around it under its thick carpet of leaves.

By the way, when it comes to stinging nettles (and some other nitrogen-loving species of plants), we should ask ourselves where we stand on the issue of nitrates. One cannot bemoan the nitrate poisoning of drinking water and over-fertilized lettuce and in the same breath recommend eating "healthy" wild plants that contain more nitrate in a single portion than 10 liters of heavily polluted water and at least as much as a head of the lettuce.

I do not mean to sound negative, but I do want to point out that the enjoyment of wild plants should not make one blindly enthusiastic about them. In wild plants, we can find many useful substances that garden vegetables lack—especially store-bought ones. But our knowledge of the substances wild plants contain is usually sketchy at best, and we therefore need to be prepared for nasty surprises. Pyrrolicidin alkaloids, which are found in germander (see the list), are only one example of this.

Dandelion is a weed that is easy to cultivate. It is not rampant. It is a perennial, so it does not have to be re-sown. Once cut, it simply produces new leaves without sulking. Ten to fourteen days after one has put an upturned bucket over a dandelion, new, bleached (and less bitter) leaves that have formed in the darkness can be harvested. Advanced dandelion growers dig out the rootstocks in the winter and force them in the basement, just like chicory. The leaves make a tasty vegetable and nice salads.

The different species of willow herb (*Epilobium*) are just as easy as dandelions because they thrive on a most refined cultivation method. If you do not grow willow herbs already, get hold of a few seeds and let several plants flower and set seed in different parts of the garden. The seeds will come up in the same year, and early the next spring, small seedlings, which look like field salad, will cover the beds. They can be harvested right away, roots and all. Leave a few rosettes to ensure a supply for the following year. The new leaves are very tasty, slightly bitter, and can be used in the kitchen for salads, on sandwiches, and as a vegetable at a time when there are not many other things to be had from the garden.

So much for my favorites. Other gardeners may prefer different vegetables. For them, I have compiled a list of the most important edible plants that can be found in the garden or that are at least suitable for cultivation. I have left out species that are common in cultivation (such as sorrel, burlap, and parsnip); I have also left out spices, for they would merit a chapter to themselves.

A List of Choices with Some Hints on Cultivation

Bugle (*Ajuga reptans*): Perennial. Bugle produces runners, so one constantly has very young rosettes, and it is evergreen, so it can be harvested even in the winter. The leaves are quite bitter and therefore should not be used on their own. Its red-leaved variety, common as a garden perennial, can also be used. In moist semishade, bugle can be cultivated as a groundcover.

Burdock (*Arctium lappa*) and lesser burdock (*Arctium minus*): Biennial. The young shoots and leaves can be used in salad, and in its first year the root makes a moderately tasty vegetable. Burdock likes light and nitrogen, and therefore it does contain nitrates.

Chickweed (*Stellaria media*): Annual. Chickweed spreads on bare patches mainly in the fall and can be harvested all through the winter. In nitrogen-rich soils, one can find lasting colonies and try to maintain them. Depending on the amount, it can be used as a vegetable or added to salads.

Chicory (*Cichorium intybus*): Perennial. Its leaves, always a little bitter, can be harvested young or all through the year. Its root, which used to be roasted as a substitute for coffee, makes a very bitter vegetable. With cultivated chicory, the bitterness has been removed by breeding, and I prefer it to the wild form.

Comfrey (*Symphytum officinale*): Perennial. Unfortunately comfrey contains pyrrolicidin alkaloids, which are damaging to the liver. So although it is very tasty (especially if dipped in pancake batter and then panfried), one should eat it only on rare occasions. In the garden, it needs a lot of space and nutrient-rich soil.

Daisy (*Bellis perennis*): Perennial. For use as a vegetable or in salads, one needs large patches, which are not that easy to maintain. However, it is worth a try in a suitable place, especially since the leaves can be harvested all year round. It requires compacted soil and lots of light but is otherwise not demanding.

Dead nettle (*Lamium album*): Perennial. Like all other species of dead nettle (such as the common ornamental plant *Lamium galeobdolon*, yellow dead nettle), this often evergreen variety is a good, high-yield vegetable, said to be particularly rich in minerals. However, it, too, likes nitrogen!

Dwarf mallow (*Malva neglecta*): Annual to perennial. As with all species of mallow, the leaves make a good vegetable and are nice in salads; they taste wild and a little slimy. The plant is an indicator for nitrogen and is not well suited to cultivation.

Gallant soldier (*Galinsoga parviflora*): Annual. Its mild leaves are suitable as a vegetable and in salads, but it is not recommended for cultivation. If shaggy soldier (or Frenchman's weed) does appear in the garden, one can use the leaves in mixed salads. If it does not return, it is no great loss.

Garlic mustard (*Alliaria petiolata*): Biennial. Raising this plant is not worthwhile, considering the yield, and as an indicator of nitrogen, it is rich in nitrates.

Goat's beard (*Tragopogon pratensis*): Biennial. The leaves can be used in salads or as a vegetable, and the roots can also be used as a vegetable. If one likes it, one should try to get hold of the seeds of salsify, the cultivated variety (*Tragopogon porrifolius*), imported from the Mediterranean region 500 years ago. However, people do not prefer cultivated varieties for nothing. Those who eat the wild forms for principle's sake merely punish themselves.

Great burnet (*Sanguisorba officinalis*) and **small burnet** (*Sanguisorba minor*): Perennial. This undemanding, often evergreen plant with a mild, spicy taste used to be popular in cottage gardens.

Ground ivy (*Glechoma hederacea*): Perennial. This plant is rampant, so be careful when taking it into the garden! Its leaves, which can be harvested all through the year, have a strong, spicy taste and are suitable as a vegetable and in salads.

Hogweed (*Heracleum sphondylium*): Biennial to perennial. Its new leaves and shoots make a tasty though not very strong vegetable. Grows in rich soil in sunlight or partial shade.

Lady's smock or **meadow bittercress** (*Cardamine pratensis*): Perennial. If one manages to establish this beautiful plant in one's garden, one might understandably hesitate to use its leaves in salads. Its cresslike taste is common to many other plants, including, from this list, wild mustard, dead nettle, chickweed, plantain, chicory, and burnet.

Lesser celandine (*Ranunculus ficaria*): Perennial. This likes to establish itself in the shade of woody plants and produces spring leaves with a high content of vitamin C. It has to be harvested before flowering; when the plant flowers, a poisonous substance develops. It can be used with other vegetables or in salads.

Orach and **goosefoot** (*Atriplex* and *Chenopodium*): The many different species are nearly all edible. However, because of the substances they contain, they are not altogether safe and should be used sparingly when they appear, for example, in the potato patch. For cultivation, garden orach (*Atriplex hortensis*) is more suitable and can be obtained through the trade.

Plantain (*Plantago*): Perennial. Several species of plantain are desirable, but all have a disadvantage in that the veins in their leaves are quite tough and have to be either removed or chopped up into very small pieces. For an attempt at a plantain salad, I would recommend ribwort plantain. It has the tenderest leaves and is easy to harvest because it grows upright. Young plants that are mown down will grow back, and it does well in poor soil.

Shepherd's purse (*Capsella bursa-pastoris*): Annual to biennial. This plant is typical of those growing in places outside the garden where one cannot harvest them safely. It is not suitable for cultivation, and any plants appearing by chance are usually inadequate for kitchen use.

Stinging nettle (*Urtica dioica*): Perennial. The problem of nitrates has already been mentioned, and it may be true that the younger leaves do not have high concentrations. At any rate, only the youngest leaves should be used for nettle soup, for salads, or as a vegetable. In the garden, it needs a lot of space and nutrient-rich soil.

Wild mustard (*Sinapis arvensis*): Annual. The wild variety is tastier and higher-yielding than its relative *Sinapis alba* (white mustard). Seeds are easy to get hold of and one can have several sowings per year. Its young leaves make a spicy vegetable and quite a good salad, either on their own or mixed.

Yarrow (*Achillea millefolium*): Perennial. Even the young, mostly evergreen leaves are bitter and can therefore be used only in small quantities with other vegetables or in salads. Yarrow needs sunlight but is otherwise undemanding.

Things in the Garden

Crafted Walls

One of my first gardens was in the middle of a large city. It dated back to the times when people enclosed their backyards with walls over 6 feet tall. Old gardens like this one have something magical about them. They make one think of monasteries or castles, of pious paradise gardens or less pious gardens of love.

But—so we are cautioned—walls close us in. They take away the light and the views and the space. This may be true, but in taking away, they do give us something in return. They protect us from being seen as well as from the wind; they store up and give off warmth; and, the most curious thing of all, they enlarge the space that they enclose.

A 100-square-meter garden enclosed by walls makes a gigantic garden room, whereas the same space, if open, seems somewhat measly.

These days, garden walls, especially those that are 6 feet high, come only as a gift of fate. One is lucky to find them, for building them is possible only in exceptional cases. Our housing authorities are touchy about walls, and the costs are disproportionately high. This is why people often resort to planting hedges, which undoubtedly have their charms but lack the particular fascination of built walls.

Really tall walls enclosing a garden are only one aspect of the walls issue. Another one is the hint of an architectural gesture that brings what is attractive about walls into the garden. Whether it is a low border between a pathway and plantings or a single wall chunk that makes a room behind a screen, creating suspense by shielding something from sight entices us further into the depths of the garden room.

The reason so many small gardens fail is that people do not make use of such design elements because they fear feeling cramped. They try to turn the area into a wide open landscape instead of creating the illusion of space by dividing it.

165

Low walls and partial walls, however, need to be carefully integrated into the garden as a whole. They have to correspond to the logic of the overall plan as well as to their immediate surroundings. They can be linked to woody plants, make a terrace, or delineate the boundary of a seating area; they can create a surprising accent or a focal point, or they can blend into the background; they can make a lively vertical gesture or accentuate a horizontal line—or both.

Such walls, large and small, do not even need to be built. That is, they do not require mortar but can simply be stacked-up bricks or natural stone or even rubble and concrete blocks. In England, the traditional art of building a dry stone wall has become so popular that people can take weekend courses where they learn how to stack up stones so that the wall is held in place by its own weight.

There are also some far easier methods for making a stable wall. A few years ago, I discovered a long, three-foot-high terrace in a small garden near Bern in Switzerland. The wall was built of stacked-up old roof tiles with soil in between —a surprising idea! The clay ribs quickly turn green, and the gaps between the tiles, whether horizontal or vertical, made an ideal ground for wall plants such as stonecrop, sempervivums, and Kenilworth ivy (*Cymbalaria muralis*).

I have no doubt that a roof tile wall could safely be stacked up to 6 feet high if it is solid enough. Care must be taken to make all mortarless walls good and solid. Even when one really leans against them, they must not yield even the tiniest bit.

Breeze blocks made from pumice, available in many shapes and sizes, are very useful for building stable walls. They soak up a lot of moisture (which also makes them heavier), which then provides a good base for mosses and lichens that soon appear of their own accord. One can speed this up by watering the wall with liquid manure as soon as it is finished. Do not worry—any bad smell will simply evaporate in the space of just a few days!

Breeze blocks are handy. They are just like toy building blocks, and one never wants to stop playing with them, piling them up to create niches or even benches and towers. If built on ground that is perfectly level and compacted, these walls can last for decades. A frost may sometimes take out a corner, and the wall begins to integrate itself into the garden. If one wants to speed up this process, one needs merely to plant an ivy or a climbing hydrangea against it.

Another rather unusual building material for walls arrives at our house every day, and we sometimes have trouble getting rid of it. It is newspapers.

Piled up in solid stacks, newspapers have their very own aesthetic value; they look their best when completely covered in algae and mosses, and one has to look very closely indeed to realize that one is not looking at old flagstones.

Perhaps I can impress the skeptics by mentioning that the most beautiful (and the biggest) newspaper wall I ever saw was an attraction outside the paper museum in Düren. So why should it not have a place in the garden?

On the inside, newspaper walls take decades to rot because there is no oxygen. Newspapers do not contain any substances that can damage the environment, and when one has had enough of the wall, one can simply recycle it on the compost heap. This method can even be used to first create a model and test out its visual impact before building the real wall.

A newspaper wall can be crowned with a layer of turf or some low-growing groundcovers or even a board to sit on. The wall will quickly become a part of the garden once it grows in and its contours soften. Perhaps it can hide the compost bin or shield the iris bed from view, and the plants will shine out all the more once we have walked around it. Walls are like bends in a hiking path. They hide and reveal a change of scene.

Finally, timber walls can be very nice and are reminiscent of those piles of firewood outside some country houses with their patchwork of stems. There is nothing to stop us from piling up shorter or longer pieces of timber. A wall like this should be quite long to keep it from looking like a mere pile of firewood. It is particularly good for terracing slopes; one can put boards on top of it to sit on, and fill the gaps with loamy soil. Then such a wall will come alive, either by itself or through some intelligent planting.

When we talk about walls piled up from dead wood, we are only one step away from talking about green walls made from living hedges. These can be loosely stacked from the branches, twigs, and leaves we end up with when pruning. At the edge of a plot of land (if the land is not too small) or as a kind of bolt across a garden, they enliven the picture of a garden in a variable way. In time, they sink into themselves. New branches are placed on top of them, and a host of different herbs establishes itself in the meantime. One could also plant a clematis against this wall or, in summer, pumpkins. If one allows and encourages this living wall, it will soon be covered in greenery and flowers—an ideal refuge for toads, hedgehogs, and birds.

In fairy tales, walls often have to do with protection and magic, offering a glimpse into an enchanted world. A wall, even a small one, can always add this mystery to a garden.

Eggshells and Rubble

We often unthinkingly speak of the times and customs of our grandmothers, when in reality, times and customs are changing so quickly that we are actually talking about our great grandmothers. At any rate, our grandmothers knew all about pots made of compressed peat used for sowing vegetables and herbs, while our great grandmothers had to use other things.

Some great grandmother had an ingenious idea while separating her eggs for a cake. After letting the egg white drain away and energetically dropping the yolk into a bowl, she was holding the two empty halves of the shell in her

Eggshells make ideal seed pots. To make them more stable, place them in the egg carton they came in.

hands. It was just about time to sow pumpkins, and it occurred to her that the shells would make ideal seed pots. She tried it out, and lo and behold, the seedlings did magnificently well. When it came time to plant, one needed only to crack the pot—the eggshell—very lightly and then plant the entire thing, container and all, without damaging the roots of the plantlet.

Great grandmother passed this trick on to her daughters and daughters-in-law, and even though they too are long gone, nothing stops us today from taking special care when cracking open our own eggs. Wash out the halves with hot water (or put them out in the rain for a while), place them in their cardboard containers, and use them instead of those expensive peat pots. *Probatum est!* I can hear my great grandmother call.

The lime surrounding the seedling roots partly dissolves and helps to nourish the plant while it grows. It is a shame that all this lovely lime from eggshells just ends up in the bin. We could use bags full of shells—on the compost heap, where they promote rotting; for feeding to our chickens and geese so that they can produce new eggshells; and, time and again, to feed those plants that are native to chalky mountain screes. Among them is scented burning bush (*Dictamnus albus*), German pink (*Dianthus carthusianorum*), and some species of stonecrop that love lime enough to decorate the edges of their leaves with very fine pearly chains of lime droplets. These members of the genus *Saxifraga* are evergreen and easily survive our winters. In June they show us the magnificence of their many splendid white flowers on high, wiry stems.

The little rosettes producing these flower spikes completely wear themselves out in the process and die off afterward, but not before forming a whole host of little rosettes around themselves, which extend the stonecrop cushion in all directions and take care of propagation; the seeds, light as dust, germinate only with difficulty.

One can often see stonecrops planted in gardens, slack and watery; our rich soils really do not do them any good. What they need is sheer chalk, so the best thing for them is a pile of rubble full of nooks and crannies into which they can spread their roots to draw out the moisture from deep within the stones and thus to nourish the beautiful rosettes. They require nothing but rubble, cement, mortar, and bricks, no fertilizer and, above all, no peat, and never even the smallest puddle, which immediately leads to rot!

If only some front gardens had such hills instead of dwarf conifers and

ranks of tulips. If only there were small, compact rosettes of stonecrops growing on them, those with broader leaves and those with leaves as narrow as
matchsticks. It would be a pleasure to walk past such a garden at flowering
time, and for the whole rest of the year, even in winter, they would present a
treasure chest full of little gems. Anyway, there are some special beauties
among lime-loving plants. The dryness, heat, and burning nature of lime find
meaningful expression in the stature, colors, and scents of these plants. They
have a rigidity of form, shining colors, and ethereal scents in which warmth
seems condensed into oils.

We can often approach the essence of a plant if we see it in combination
with the soil it grows in, since a plant is a kind of response to the conditions of
its surroundings. Beyond all purposeful adaptations, there are harmonies that
can be captured only in images. And this is one of the most beautiful experiences in the garden, learning to understand shapes and how they interconnect.

At the bottom of my little chalk hill, some species of hellebore have found
their place: Christmas rose (*Helleborus niger*) with its white flowers, of course;
some hybrids with red flowers; and, above all, stinking hellebore (*Helleborus
foetidus*). This last one is my favorite because in early spring it decorates the garden with its shining flowers, yellow-green and bell-shaped, when no other
plant is yet out.

Not only are its flowers of this light green shade, but also its entire, richly
branched inflorescence, including the petals, rising up above a dense, evergreen bush of finely incised leaves. When it is still almost winter, here is a bright
example of life starting over; the first bumblebees, woken up precociously
from hibernation, appreciate it. They naturally are not at all disturbed by the
strange smell of these flowers, which is not exactly pleasant but is not unpleasant enough to justify this plant's name. Shining hellebore would certainly be
more fitting.

Something About Garden Tools

There is a garden sprinkler that shoots off to one side like a rocket when one
turns on the tap. It gets stopped short by the hosepipe, twitches around a few
times, and then remains flat on the ground on two of its legs, pointing its third

one into the air. It is unbelievable what havoc such a twitching sprinkler can wreak in only a few seconds. Its ergonomically wonderful but otherwise rather fragile adjustment has broken off. One could perhaps order another one, but one must first think up and construct a counterweight to keep the thing in place for the future. And, as soon as it has been built and installed, one of the legs snaps off as though it were made of very thin plastic—which indeed it is. No doubt qualified engineers, ergonomists, designers, and marketing experts have worked on this sprinkler, and perhaps it has even been tried out on the testing ground of—well, no names! A simple gardener does not know anything about ergonomics and design and marketing, but he does notice whether a thing works or not. So his awe at what engineers and ergonomists and designers and marketing experts do is always mixed with a dose of skepticism. Does this thing do what it is supposed to do? Is it supposed to do what it does?

There are many things to marvel at besides sprinklers with rocket effects. Above all, there are motorized things.

An electric lawnmower with a box for the grass, seven levels of depth adjustments, and a soft-lifting mechanism is one of the cheaper offerings. At the other end of the range, one can find a remote-controlled lawnmower by an Italian tractor company that does 2.6 kilometers per hour and can mow 1200 square meters of lawn per hour. Even on slopes.

Thus the transition between gardening implements and cars is not clearly delineated. There are many lawnmowers that could be used equally well for driving one's children to school. And there are edge cutters that sound like secondhand cars. And if one is annoyed about the fact that it is now illegal to saw off one's exhaust pipe, a shredder will more than compensate for any enjoyment one feels one has lost.

Strangely enough, the motorization of gardening is inversely proportional to the decrease in the average size of building plots. The smaller the gardens became, the more motorized the kit. An explanation for this may be that people's lawn mowing is a kind of displacement behavior for driving, without traffic jams and oncoming traffic, or maybe people can only bear to look after a garden if it at least sounds as though they are really driving.

Taken to extremes, the garden itself is regarded as a type of car. For a long time now, the equivalent of the car-washing ritual, usually carried out on Saturday mornings, has been the lawn-mowing ritual, undertaken on Saturday afternoons. In some areas, people mow on Friday evenings while their children are being bathed, and one can readily see that cleanliness is the strongest connection between gardens and cars.

The process of irrigating one's garden with drinking water can be mostly automated, with moisture sensors and sprinklers that push themselves out of the soil when needed just as intercontinental rockets push themselves out of their silos. However, there is inexplicably a gaping hole in the range of products available. The empty space falls between fully automated irrigation systems on the one hand and those mangy sprinklers and their stands that one has to weigh down with stones to stop them dancing around on the other. There is no middle ground, not even some kind of tripod that can lift the legs of some sprinklers high enough to make them rain on the whole garden, as the manual promises us they will.

And, speaking of water, we are still lacking a watering can that we can leave outside without our eyes being offended by the most vile shades of green. It can be made of plastic, because of the weight, but why is it never made of that black plastic, for example, that water tubs are made out of? Then it would not clang so cheaply and break quite so easily. And perhaps even its sieve could be constructed so that it only comes apart when one wants to take it off for cleaning and does not burst off just as one is gently watering some tender seedlings.

It is simply inconceivable that watering cans should be too mundane a topic for designers and ergonomists, for they incessantly deal with far more mundane objects. After all, we are constantly provided with new hoes and new diggers, large ones and small ones, even though the basic shape and the range of these implements was developed centuries ago. They are totally natural and untouched by the science of ergonomics, with simple, round handles and without those comfortable grips that for a gardening layperson are the most visible traces of ergonomic labor. It would be over the top to say that those molds always fit the gardener's hands. In any case, gardeners are often plagued by the suspicion that these manifold changes to classic shapes have nothing whatsoever to do with ergonomics but are simply there because their producers must innovate under pain of death.

Otherwise, it would be difficult to explain why one can find such things as detachable plastic spade handles, oozing ergonomics out of their welds. Touching one of these handles is a testament to the total futility of trying to improve on something that has as many centuries of thought and experience behind it as a spade handle has.

Some time ago, a new spade was designed in England. Its handle is most bizarrely bent according to the latest discoveries of ergonomic science. It will probably vanish without a trace, not only because gardeners are too stupid, but because ergonomists are too clever.

Until the last days of spades, people are going to debate the question whether those with T-shaped handles are preferable to those with D-shaped handles or even to those with buttons. In a sixty-year-old book on domestic garden implements, I can read that "the question of the best spade handle has not yet been finally solved." Seeing that it has not been solved in the intervening years, one can safely assume that it cannot be solved at all. There is a simple reason for this. It is a not a question of ergonomics but a question of habit.

I know what I am talking about. It was not until late in my gardening career that I painstakingly changed from a T-handle to a D-handle. This was because the single improvement on spades, for which we have the English to thank, only comes with a D-handle. It is a stainless steel spade in which bar and blade are welded from a single piece of metal, and the plastic handle is attached so well that it only breaks if one uses the spade to lever tree roots out of the ground—and there are other implements to do that.

Of course, the simplest garden implement is one's hand, but often this is just not hard enough. One would need the iron hand of the legendary Götz von Berlichingen, but that would lack the necessary sensitivity. So we need a little trowel (also available in stainless steel) and a narrower and therefore more important weeder and thistle-cutter, which one can also use for getting off-shoots and crushing slugs and loosening up the soil between perennials.

Near the far end of the range of garden implements, we find horrible equipment such as shredders, noisy monsters that inspire so many neighborly disputes and are, in fact, totally superfluous, a sign of our modern impatience. We cannot wait for branches and twigs and leaves to rot into fertile humus on the compost heap in their own time with the help of animals and microorganisms that neither need electricity nor make any noise.

We are going to do some shredding this summer, but only because we received an old, beautiful implement from a friend—an old straw shredder with a large flywheel. A broad camshaft first squeezes the straw, and only then chops it up with its rotating blades. The whole thing, as I have said before, is not really necessary, but who could resist the temptation of a functioning flywheel?

It is very rare for revolutionary innovations to be forgotten again once they have been rediscovered. As a precious example of this type, I keep a pair of angled shears with handles elongated to such an extent that one can operate them from a standing position.

At the back of these shears, there is a small wheel, so one can run them in front of oneself and effortlessly cut not only lawn edges but, even more remarkable, the tall grass of our meadow. For this job, salespeople in garden centers can normally only offer lawnmowers or those weed whackers with their nylon strings, their name raising hopes that their weak mechanisms simply cannot live up to. Unfortunately, nobody has ever bothered to rebuild my ingenious wheely shears.

Instead, toolmakers are mad about creating ever new varieties of hoes and cultivators, most of which are superfluous, especially the ones that run on wheels and want us to believe that hoeing with them is child's play. Dignified, old, and simple things are always the best. Take the one-pronged fork, which

Blades of trowels in different shapes.

one needs no force to use, but which uproots any weed and loosens up the soil without turning it over. Its only disadvantage is that it has no more scope for modifications by ergonomists and engineers and that it does not lend itself to representing a company's image in a snazzy marketing campaign. It is a simple implement and will never cause any great sensation, and so it disappears, modest and industrious, behind masses of implements pushing themselves to the front with their ever-changing colors and designs.

This arsenal of garden implements, made ergonomic, designed and colored attractively, often quietly amuses a simple gardening soul. Let them invent hoes on wheels, he thinks, or framed hoes with replaceable steel blades or those star rototillers that, instead of rototilling, merely dance across the field and deliver the gentlest of pokes to the ground. Let them put easy-grip moulds on every handle and spruce them all up with engines. Spade in hand, he turns to the garden and serenely smiles to himself. The latest piece of news he has heard is that in England they have just designed the prototype of a new spade and handed it over to the marketing department for an expert opinion. The spade has one side turned into a saw, so that when the gardener encounters a root while digging, he can saw right through it without having to exchange one tool for another one. Perhaps, so the gardener thinks, this really is the peak, the glorious end of the evolution in garden implements. However, he thinks that for only a very brief moment, because in reality he obviously knows that this will go on and on, and there will be no end to innovations. But still, the best garden implements will remain the best-kept secrets—such as bread knives with their wavy edges, or possibly stainless steel knives with pointed tips. Keeping one handy in the garden can help in many sticky situations. It can be used to divide perennials, saw off small branches, cut down chives in the summer, and many more things. However, experience teaches us that one has to buy such a knife especially for the garden. Getting it from the kitchen means asking for trouble.

Things and Opposites

When the real gnomes had stopped cleaning stairwells and digging beds at night, people made images of them from burnt clay, painted them, and put them into the garden. When wooden cartwheels were replaced with rubber tires, the wooden ones went into the garden. The same thing happened to wheelbarrows, wooden barrels, harrows, and similar implements. At some point, even satellite dishes are going to end up in the garden. Who knows, people might turn them into wetland biotopes.

It is easy to joke about this. However, in the first place, people can do whatever they want in their garden. In the second place, there have always been things in gardens, and gnomes and cartwheels are just what anthropologists call "depreciated cultural goods." They are trivial imitations of a feudal way of portraying oneself; they give us more to contemplate than to ridicule. At all times, people have put things other than plants in the garden, things made of iron, timber, and stone. The gardens of medieval monasteries, Goethe's garden on the Ilm, eighteenth- and nineteenth-century parks—all of these contained different types. They host sundials, gravestones, mighty carafes, climbing frames, crosses, glass balls, small and large memorials, grottoes, and fountains. In fact, when I think back to the palace garden that I used to cross decades ago on my way to school, I see not only trees and shrubs but, right next to them, Hector's endless good-bye to Andromache. From October to May, the two of them were hidden inside a shed to keep from catching cold. Yet I always knew that they were continuing to kiss inside.

A particularly beautiful garden ornament has unfortunately remained only a design. Bernhard Palissy, a French ceramic artist and builder of grottoes, described it 400 years ago in his book on the ideal garden. It is a beautiful lady on a pedestal, holding a letter in one hand and a jug of water in the other. Anyone who stepped in closer to read the letter would get a jug of water poured over his head, aided by a complicated mechanism of levers.

Palissy does not say whether he intended to educate people by punishing them for their nosiness. It is certainly possible. Many garden ornaments have a deeper meaning and something to communicate, while some are only stage props and backdrops, but they all have one thing in common. Their shape and material form a striking contrast to the freer, softer tones of the plants.

Growing things stand out against manufactured ones and vice versa, and both benefit from the sharp contrasts. In the middle of the rose garden at the botanical garden in Linz on the Danube, there is a captivatingly beautiful statue made from scrap metal that depicts a fabulous bird. There can hardly be a more striking contrast than that between roses and rusty iron—and none that could display both rust and roses to better mutual advantage.

No less impressive than the contrasts between them are the transitions from living things to dead ones. Just as rust can grow the most bizarre crusts that are reminiscent of plants, sometimes the bark of old trees looks just as if the trees are turning into stones.

Traces of age can make objects become part of the garden. Old gates embody their own history as well as that of the people who lived behind them. If we fall silent in the face of such traces to better hear their quiet tales, it is not for sentimental reasons, but for a real sense for the spirit of objects.

Stones get covered in mosses and lichens; some timbers, when ageing, take on a shiny gray hue, just like silk; a shiny glass ball becomes cloudy over the course of the years. All objects that at first may seem strange in the garden become assimilated. We can see and touch with our own hands how nature eats things up, using the wind, the sun, and the rain, and we can see that tran-

Sun, rain, and wind leave their traces on driftwood from the river Rhine and make it part of the garden with wonderful, ever-changing shapes and colors.

sience does not only stand for disappearance, but also for a procedure in which every stage has its own form and its own charm.

Anyone who wants to may help himself. He can find clay pots, stone benches, brittle figures, and many more things. They may be antiquities, melancholy from remembering days gone by, or replicas, which are not cheap either. But integrating different objects into the garden, regardless of their immediate decorative value, means getting them in tune with one's plants, just like a musical chord. One does not need antiquities for this. There are worn-out stones, rotting boards, bleached stumps displaying the traces of time that can lie between our plants in the garden as though they are resting; they can yet pass some time along with us.

So the garden can become a heavenly museum of the gardener and his wife. They are the only ones to know that the little pile of rubble next to the lavender is stones once taken from Provence, or that a black oak beam came from a ship loaded with dynamite that exploded 100 years ago in a nearby river; every now and then when it is dry, pieces still drift up.

These are traces of one's own life and the lives of others that inwardly enrich the garden. Perhaps, one day, someone will come and try to discover all those secrets. Then again, maybe not.

All Over the Garden

Unexpected Arrivals, Arriving Daily

Exploding cucumber (*Cyclanthera brachystachya*) is a strange plant. In the space of only a few days, its spiraling shoots climb up its tall frame and decorate themselves first with elegantly folded leaves and a little later with innumerable male and a few female flowers. From the female flowers will grow spongy, inflated, yellowy-green, sometimes spiny cucumbers, each one as long as a thumb. Inside are bizarrely shaped black seeds. When these mature, the casing becomes brittle, bursts open with a dry bang, and ejects the seeds. Exploding cucumbers are native to South America, however, so in our climate, this rarely happens. The plant is simply used to better weather.

This year, my exploding cucumber did not turn out well. It was yellowy and listless, climbing slowly on slack stems. It hardly flowered and only produced three or four fruits instead of its normal ten or twelve. It was impossible to discern the reason for its reticence. There had been no lack of warmth or water, the soil was as rich as ever, and the slugs that normally like to attack its fleshy stems also stayed away.

The gardener has to put up with such mishaps, as well as with never finding out why they happened. On such occasions he becomes acutely aware of something that he often tends to forget. That is, while he can initiate and enhance growth in the garden, the real work is not up to him. The plants, the soil, and the weather make their own arrangements among themselves. The gardener can only watch and sometimes lend a helping hand, supply some water, murmur some encouraging words, or add a bamboo cane for support, but nothing more.

Apart from these gestures, the gardener has to accept that what is happening is the fulfilment of laws and rules and life structures, is the result of connections and dependencies, and can be chalked up to pure chance. He thinks that he is in charge of his garden. Instead, he is faced with its independence in success as well as in failure.

By the way, the gardener naturally likes to attribute any success to his green thumb. But why oh why has his dainty birthwort, which has contented itself with flowering for years, decided to choose this year to produce for the first time a single big, green, spherical fruit? This has nothing to do with having a green thumb, and no one knows what else it might depend on.

In this, the garden is different from the rest of the world, where everything either works or can be repaired by an expert. Trains are on time (mostly), cars start up (nearly always), my fax spits out its paper, and the postman comes at half past nine. In a garden, things do not work, they happen—maybe. Every walk in the garden shows us what is going on and whether our toils have been rewarded or our offers taken up.

There is something else comparatively incalculable that the garden shows us if we take it seriously as a space in which things happen. In it, totally unexpected plants and other beings appear. Lettuce is sprouting out of gaps in the paving beneath an east-facing window where we feed birds in winter. Its seeds must have been in the bird feed, for right next to it, we can also find canary grass (*Phalaris canariensis*), which comes from the Canary Islands and is not native here at all. Its seeds are common in bird feed. As if out of nowhere, a clump of bulrush (*Typha*) is pushing up its pipe-cleaners at the edge of the pond. Nobody ever planted it. Its delicate seeds must have been blown in by the wind.

Insects are even less predictable than plants. They suddenly appear and just as suddenly are gone again. Only some of them have fixed dates, such as glow worms in June. Even if we do not know their names, after a while we come to recognize them as old acquaintances or as new guests: the little butterfly with the red dots that habitually copulates on my mints in July and that I have not yet found in any book; the four or five different species of bumblebee that love to accumulate on the flowers of our Welsh onions, as if they knew how good they look there; those flies with their greenish, shining bodies that appear by the hundreds as soon as our peppermint is in flower; those bugs and caterpillars. Some of these bugs annoy us by gobbling up our lilies or gnawing holes in our cabbages. In May, dragonflies with their wings like glass emerge from dark-brown larvae in a process that takes hours. In August, we may see some grasshoppers making large jumps in flight, though they are becoming more and more rare because our meadows and fields are poisoned. September is the month of spiders. They put up their webs and catch tired flies, and shining out from every little place are the yellowish cocoons of cross spiders. In these, hundreds of tiny spiders will have matured by the spring when their mother is long gone.

We can be part of this life if we patiently take the time to notice it and do not think of it only as a backdrop or as something to harvest or as some kind of "success." There is suspense in all this, originating from the tension between what is available and what is not and between what we do and what happens by itself if we let it be instead of stopping it in our quest for an arbitrarily defined order.

There are other orders, relationships, and patterns that seem rather bland in contrast to our own designs. The idea of a garden comes to mean more than spring flowers and summer magnificence. Above all it comes to mean unexpected arrivals on a daily basis, even in winter, by the way.

Ninfa Is Everywhere

If ivy sometimes seems sinister and depressed, it is mourning the better times it once enjoyed. It was once sacred to Bacchus and was used to make wreaths that crowned the gods' companions, drinkers, poets, and sometimes heroes, too.

This was long ago. Today ivy is mostly doomed to whisper in cemeteries of the immortality of the soul and to prove its own immortality in dreary backyards, not because of any symbolism, but because it is so easy to look after. It does not drop annoying leaves; it climbs up any wall unaided; when it cannot climb any more, it starts to flower and to fruit. Such daring should merit more attention than ivy normally gets, and it certainly should merit a closer look. Right away one would notice that it is ivies, not ivy, for there are several species and numerous varieties.

Furthermore, every single shoot can display diverse leaf shapes—lobed and round, narrow and broad, small and large.

When ivy becomes old and treelike, it dispenses with showing off such variation. It produces only oval-shaped, complete leaves and dedicates itself to the serious business of generative reproduction through flowers and fruits. The gardener, however, does not grow ivies from seed; instead, he makes use of the ability of every small cutting, at any time, to take root in moist soil.

Ivies have special climbing roots. Word has now got out that these are not at all damaging to plaster and joints. Once they have dug in their claws, they dry up and stop growing. Ivy leaves, however, form a thick, protective layer that keeps off any rain. The wall is bone dry beneath its ivy coat, and wrens, in particular, like to build their nests there. Ivy can protect buildings for centuries. Southeast of Rome, in the foothills of the Lepini mountains, is the ruined city of Ninfa. It used to be called Nympha because when it originated in Roman times, it was dedicated to the cult of nymphs. In his Italian travel tales of 100 years ago, the writer Ferdinand Gregorovius said, "This bewitching Nympha is the most attractive fairy tale of history and of nature that I have ever seen." He called Nympha the "city of ivy."

In medieval times, the city must have been very important—a pope was consecrated there—but nobody knows why it was later abandoned. "Many a

Ivy plants show enormous variety in the shapes and sizes of their leaves.

square and many a road are still there. At their sides are derelict houses spun in ivy; some are like palaces, with semigothic architecture, once abodes of rich noblemen. Walls, towers, churches, and monasteries—dark ivy flows over all the ruins, pouring down walls in green cascades. There is so much ivy here that it seems to me as though Nympha must be Italy's stock of ivy, as if from here the ivy ghosts of history could supply all the ruins of this magnificent country with its shoots."

Ivy as a beautiful protection, as a softly flowing carpet, can gently cover everything derelict and hide the wrinkles of old buildings in Ninfa and elsewhere. It can also cover trees, and they have nothing to fear from it, even if its stems become as thick as arms in the course of time. The German poet Theodor Körner knew this when he wrote of the woman "who weaves her love's tender ivy around a bold hero's oak."

Years ago in the dead of night in Romberg Park in Dusseldorf, some concerned friends of trees sawed off many old ivy trunks to "save" the trees they were caring for. These people were really barking up the wrong tree. If they had only trusted their eyes, they would have seen that the trees did not need their help in any way. (In parts of the United States *Hedera helix* or English ivy is classified as an invasive noxious weed.—Ed.)

Anyone who does not like the fact that a wall planted with Himalayan vines is bare in the winter should plant an ivy. Walls and ivy complement each other well. When it comes to species and varieties, however, the nomenclature is a matter for specialists, who by no means always agree. For us, it is enough to know that our native *Hedera helix* is the most common and most variable species. It even boasts a creeping variety that grows stiffly upward. The triangular leaves grow up the stem in two precise rows as if the ivy wanted to see what would happen if it tamed its tendency to vary.

Hedera colchica, sometimes called Persian ivy, is from southeastern Europe and has nearly egg-shaped leaves. This species is fast-growing, but in rugged areas it is not quite hardy. This, by the way, is also true of some varieties of *Hedera helix*; its hardiness may depend on the microclimate.

One simply should try out every ivy that one comes across. The smallest cuttings suffice to put together a whole collection that can cover up many walls, columns, fences, and pyramids with shoots that overflow at the edges. In three or four years, the dullest fences can be turned into dense, green walls.

Ninfa is everywhere. Everywhere, ivy finds something to spin itself around in order to enhance, to cover up mercifully, to frame effectively, or to crown proudly, showing off its variability and enchanting those who take the time to look.

The Meadow Does Not Exist

The first meadow I can remember was right next to our house. It was used for grazing horses and was, in fact, only a thin carpet on dry, sandy ground. In the nibbled-down grass were patterns of pale purple thyme flowers, the shiny brown ears of wood rush (*Luzula*), which we called rabbit's bread, and innumerable gray pills left behind by rabbits.

So, no picture-book meadow, with its abundance of tall grass and all kinds of bright flowers in between. In other words, *the* meadow does not exist. There are only meadows, and a variety of very different ones at that.

Another misconception about meadows is that they are the epitome of a natural landscape, paragons of unspoiled freshness, ideals of perfect ecology. They are none of those things. Except for a few types of meadows in remote locations, all meadows have developed through human intervention, injuring and destroying natural orders. Moreover, without continuous care—that is, without continuous and sustained intervention in their natural development—these meadows would not be alive at all. They are all aiming to get back to their natural state, which are forests like the ones that used to cover Central Europe before humans started to clear large tracts of land to make space for houses and for fields and for meadows to use as pastures.

Well, nature has always had a say in this. Nature was and continues to be the one to determine what grasses and other plants can prosper in a given location. For example, dry, warm slopes with lime-rich soils that were formerly grazed and deforested by sheep have a totally different plant cover than the more or less damp meadows in low-lying areas. The former would turn into chalk meadows with thyme, cowslip (*Primula*), and orchids; the latter would turn into a rich meadow with tufted vetch (*Vicia cracca*), cow parsley, and meadow sage (*Salvia pratensis*), with white campion (*Silene latifolia*) and meadow knotgrass. In between, there are at least a dozen intermediate types, carefully classified by plant sociologists and ordered and named according to their individual qualities.

Nevertheless, the soil and the climate are not the only things that determine the character of a meadow. The most important factor in determining what grows in a meadow is its use.

A primary example are meadows in extensively used orchards. These have become more and more rare with the automation of agriculture and should now almost be a protected species in themselves. They were once used for making hay and were mown only once a year, in the fall, when the grasses had already withered. Such a meadow can support only plants that grow at least as tall as the grasses or that can survive in the semishade of the green thicket at ground level. In addition, the fauna of such an undisturbed meadow is entirely different from that of a meadow mowed more often or used for grazing.

On meadows that are mown two or three times a year, one can find specialists whose life cycles correspond to the mowing dates. The tubers of autumn crocus (*Colchicum autumnale*), for example, produce rich foliage in spring. In June (just before it would die down naturally, anyway), the foliage falls victim to the first cut; autumn crocuses spend the second and third mowing underground and only then do the flowers appear. They often wilt when the meadow is mown for the last time in October. With dandelions it is the other way around. They go through their flowering and fruiting phase before the first cut and then continue to pass the rest of the season as a low rosette.

Such life cycles, their rhythms exactly corresponding to the cycles of human interference, have often been destroyed by the intensive use of meadows in modern times. As a result, the plants themselves have disappeared or have become the last relics of a diversity long gone. Instead of the mowing cycle, meadows are now often grazed intensively or are partly grazed and then mown once they have recovered. Meadow flowers do not have much of an opportunity to survive, especially in competition with ever-richer, ever-more-nourishing grasses. Meadows are grazed short and also overfertilized (which kills many plants). In between the grasses, only two types of plants remain: those such as dandelions and white clover that can withstand the hooves of the animals, and those at which animals turn up their noses, such as thistles and sorrel. Both groups must take into account that the farmer might be out to get them with his herbicides.

From the early days of the first meadows until the present, dramas have played out with victories and defeats, conquests and expulsions. Plants that previously had not existed in Central Europe immigrated into the open meadows, especially from the south. With them, by the way, came many of our butterflies, which needed the meadows for a place to live and food for their caterpillars. Now this wildlife is in retreat, driven to extinction by agricultural technology that launches ever more brutal attacks. Fertilization and overgrazing leave hardly any of those brightly flowering meadow plants, and their importance as medicinal plants for cattle is almost forgotten. From formerly damp meadows, characteristic plants (such as bittercress) have disappeared through drainage, and people have damaged the chalk meadows by trying to increase their yield through fertilization. This has almost never worked, but the plant community, centuries old, has been destroyed once and for all in the process. So our meadows are becoming ever poorer in species, making the dream of meadows all the more enticing.

Lady's smock holds its own not only through propagation by seed but also by offsets that form on its leaves and then put down roots.

Upon seeing an alpine meadow, a friend called out, "I would like to be a cow here!" I could have responded, "And I a grand beetle!" for to really experience a meadow, it is not enough merely to look at it from above. One needs to squat down or, even better, to lie down on one's stomach to see which animals live on the ground or in it; one needs to lie on one's back to see the meadow as bugs and beetles and wood lice and spiders see it and to smell the thyme (if it is still there). And then, closing one's eyes, one can listen to the sounds of the meadow, the humming and chirping and the quiet rasping of leaves and stems as they rub against one another. There is warmth in this dream, perhaps a soft breeze, and birds, some of which really live and breed in the meadow, such as lapwing, skylark, whinchat, and meadow pipit. But where can one still find them? One is more likely to find crickets and, of course, moles, whose hills remind us that the meadow was once like a big house, inhabited from the basement to the rafters.

When we observe our ill-treated and impoverished meadows carefully, even here we can find other signs of life besides moles. We can find plants and animals that have so far managed to withstand the onslaught of chemical and motorized agriculture. But beware of false hopes: the dying continues. That today's farmers can collect a premium for leaving small strips at the edges of their fields as refuges is just one indication of how mercilessly our ancient cultural landscape is being devastated.

Faced with this, many people want to fulfil their dream of a meadow in their own gardens. Seed packets with their colorful pictures give them the illusion that this will be easy. But if the seeding was at all successful and if the meadow gardener has learned before how to use a scythe (lawnmowers capitulate when faced with tall grass), a meadow in a garden is like a bird in a cage, an isolated piece of land with a few colorful flowers.

Not to mention that a meadow is certainly not colorful all year round, as the pictures on those seed packets promise. A meadow has peak flowering times and periods of rest, which belong to the grasses.

Grasses. Well, they are not an easy chapter of botany. Cock's foot (*Dactylis glomerata*) is easy to recognize because it has no close relatives that we might confuse it with. Foxtail grass (*Alopecurus pratensis*), perennial ryegrass (*Lolium perenne*), and crested dog's tail (*Cynosurus cristatus*) can be identified with the help of a book and without going to any particular trouble. After that, things get difficult, and one needs a magnifying glass and a lot of patience to explore the detailed structure of ears, spikelets, scales, and awns and then to distinguish the species—the sweet grasses of soils with a medium level of ground water, the sour grasses of damp and wet soils.

Grasses would soon appear in our garden meadow even if we did not sow them because their seeds are always carried by the winds. Apart from that, life on this small patch will always remain artificial and limited. The meadow of our dreams *also* exists because of its sheer size, not only because the gentle rippling of grasses in the wind (as on water) cannot otherwise appear, but mainly because meadow life needs space. It needs room for expansion and refuge and for interchange with neighboring habitats such as hedges and forest edges and shores. If one shrinks it down to a few square meters, only a pitiable lot remains, a kind of model at best, a scale shrunk 1000 times. We can neither expect a blue butterfly to find its way here, nor can we expect to encounter more than a few ubiquitous species of the innumerable different insects, spiders, and other small animals.

So we must continue to rely on finding meadows, perhaps on holiday in the mountains where protected areas are still mown and grazed extensively, according to old traditions—that is, gently.

In such places, in the midst of chrysanthemums, yarrow, and ground elder, the dream of our meadow may come true, if only for a few hours or days, while we are suspended between heaven and earth, watching the clouds move, breathing in the scent of the grasses while bumblebees hum and mosquitoes bite relentlessly. There is peace and tranquility in this dream, though some people might feel abandoned and lost in the middle of a meadow; suddenly the moving clouds seem to stop and they are swept away, not knowing where to turn.

Upon closer examination, the cliché of *the* meadow shatters to reveal a number of different images: images of forest destruction to which meadows owe their very existence; images of colorful mountain pastures in summer; images of brown meadows in the fall, spiders hanging their cocoons from stalks, oblivious to the fact that one last cut is yet to come; images of jubilant felicity; and images of the melancholy of death, which the soul can only bear when it looks at trees and hedges as trustworthy companions in the winter months. Meadows can be feasts and many other things, too. There is no such thing as *the* meadow.

Angelica Around the Neck

In an enchanting manner, East Asians manage to make something distinctly far eastern out of the most ordinary things. Among their best treasures are tokos, the East Asian food shops of many larger cities.

In tokos can be found dried vegetables in picturesque packaging; teas in see-through bags that are suitable for framing; and the "Racine de Angelique" of the Wah Long company from Hong Kong, a little chest full of thumb-sized,

Dried pieces of angelica root seem secretive and bizarre.
It is no surprise that they were used as amulets.

secretive, and bizarre pieces of root, sculptures that have noses and eyes and mouths and that remind us of the magical mandrakes. The healing power of these roots seems to be expressed in their shape, and they call earth spirits into being without themselves being altered. A few side roots have been trimmed off, and the fragments have then been straightened out a little and dried.

This simple but effective preparation would be fitting if the roots of angelica were also used as amulets in China, as was once the case in Europe. To wear such a root around one's neck was to be loved by everybody and to be immune to the evil power of witches, to the plague, and to cholera.

The belief in the magical power of angelica has quite a tangible origin. Angelica (*Angelica archangelica*) has for centuries been used as a reliable medicinal plant. Teas and ointments from its root induce appetite, help digestion, and loosen coughs and bronchitis. As the alchemist Leonhard Thurneysser wrote 400 years ago, they work by "warming, dividing, expelling." The gardener who does not yet have angelica should not hesitate to establish it in his garden if only to convince himself that this highest praise is indeed justified.

The plant really only has one disadvantage, but it may be why it is so rarely found in gardens. It is biennial, which means that it dies after flowering, and its seeds only remain viable for a very short time, so that they need to be sown right after maturing. In the garden, angelicas do this by themselves. Just the other day I had to mercilessly reduce my army of little seedlings that had sprung up in the angelica's usual place since each plant needs one square meter to itself. It grows 6 feet tall and has a majestic, spreading habit, an impression that is softened later on in the spring when it presents us with its flower heads. The flowers are arranged in a star shape at the ends of rigid stalks as long as a finger, originating from one center. Thus a ball of stars develops, a picture of beaming cheerfulness in shades of yellow and green.

As a member of the carrot family, angelica is a close relative of many familiar spices such as lovage, celery, and chervil. The aroma of its leaves, stems, and roots is similar to that of these spices, with an undertone of refined sweetness and watery freshness. There is some bitterness in its taste, too. For this reason, its leaves are suitable only as a spice, but its stems, which are less bitter, can be used like celery. One can even make a sweet dessert out of it. As the anthropologist Fridtjof Nansen tells us, the Eskimos chew on pieces of bacon, spit them on mashed angelica stems, and let the whole mixture stew.

Surely more appetizing is the idea used by Mr. Robertson from Chelsea to earn his jams lasting fame: he added some angelica as surprising spice. In France, bakers invented (or perfected) the art of making candied stems that were then sold as sweets. They were also sold in pharmacies as remedies for stomach upsets, thereby mixing enjoyment with medical benefits. The same is true of angelica liqueurs. Some kinds of schnapps contain the plant only because of its taste, while in others it is an indispensable ingredient, warming and calming to the drinker's stomach.

We have a long way to go before we can pull off the outer skin of the hollow, juicy angelica stems and then eat them raw, as Laplanders do. For now we will content ourselves with dried roots from the East Asian shop to ease our bronchitis and soothe our stomachs.

When they drop their seeds in the fall, the flower heads of angelica resemble silver stars covered with ice.

If some of the scented shrinking heads are left over, we incorporate them into our collection of natural things, our unsystematic collection of garden things that are beautiful or bizarre, colorful or remarkable in any number of ways. It is an anti-museum with displays on window sills, on shelves, and in drawers in protest and counterbalance to today's museums, which are styled through to the last label. One can learn a lot in them and in the right order, but they are becoming ever emptier for all their precision and structure; the old natural history museums often had just that charm of chaos that stimulates one's curiosity.

Even if covered in dust, such a collection evokes the fascination with chaos and the joy of touching. It is naturally only for those who create their own cabinet of natural things—bones and stones, skins and timber, snails' houses and the case of a dragonfly larva, owl pellets, infructescences and wasps' nests, and a few angelica heads from Hong Kong. When we go out we wear one to make everybody love us.

The Mice Have to Go

My fingernails have black rims. It is hardly worth cleaning them, for now is the peak season for weeding. Everything is growing like mad, including those plants one does not want—at least not quite so many or in that particular spot.

Sarcastic and strict, organic gardeners point out that one does not need to pull out every herb and every blade of grass and that the very term *weed* is a testimony of arrogance and a brutal attitude toward the garden. It does not impress them that the term was coined hundreds of years ago.

To be sure, the advocates of undisturbed growing are not totally wrong. But what they fail to mention is that a large plot of grass can grow out of every modest little tuft, and the most delicate herb can turn into a huge bush. The patch of grass can become so large and the bush so huge that, if left to their own devices, soon nothing would grow next to them. Diversity, which is ecologically desirable, would quickly give way to the supremacy of knotgrass and bindweed (*Calystegia sepium*).

Oh yes, bindweed. It is a beauty, a beauty in a good mood, with elegant, lovingly encircling movements. The famous poet Goethe, who certainly had no problems with being called a male chauvinist, described it as the embodiment of the female principle of need.

Need! Ha! And ha again! The strings of its stems entwine to form real ropes, suffocating any low plant under a dense carpet of leaves and easily defeating anything upright by mercilessly bending it down or climbing on it, weaving curtains, heavy screens, behind which entire shrubs are silently choked to death. Goethe overlooked this unsavory demise of the male principle of growing upright when he interpreted the "spiral tendencies of vegetation" as gender-specific.

There is little consolation in the fact that bindweed tea has a diuretic effect. There is no way I could eat enough to use anything like the amount of bindweed I have in my garden.

Weeding and pulling out does not harm bindweed. It merely responds by growing twice as fast. In this, it is similar to the diabolical ground elder and equisetum and also to the innocuous ground ivy that seems so tender and delicate and yet is so mercilessly tough. Some nurseries sell it as a groundcover, with no signs to warn those gullible customers.

I should not really be complaining. It is better to have a piece of land on which to fight with ground ivy and that female bindweed than to have to grow one's ground ivy in a balcony flower pot for one's cough tea.

Nurseries do offer among their assortments quite a few things that a clever and lazy gardener would do well to avoid. Casual remarks such as "likes to roam" are surely euphemisms in the face of the toil that will be required two or three years after planting. Chinese lanterns, for example, whose beautiful orange-red seed heads serve to embellish any dull dried-flower arrangement, has a network of roots just like bindweed that enables it to roam for meters. Nothing can stop it, and it inadvertently appears in all sorts of places. One will never get rid of it again, unless one digs up the thick strings of its roots down to every tiny last piece.

The most tenacious plant I have ever seen, however, is earth chestnut (*Lathyrus tuberosus*), a delicate, magically scented being from western Asia. It was brought into Europe either by mistake or as a food plant because it grows from edible underground tubers.

Its tubers are surrounded by black bark and are white on the inside and the size of a thumb. With their root system, they look like little mice, which is why they are sometimes called earth mice or Dutch mice. The Dutch used to grow this plant on a large scale, take the tubers to market, and eat them fried in butter. The Tartars and the Kalmyks, in whose native country earth chestnuts grow in the wild, used to boil it in salt water.

Such facts naturally arouse one's curiosity, and we enthusiastically welcomed the first shoots creeping across neighboring plants. We admired the flowers and ate our first year's modest harvest. The following year, despite the harvest, our small stock had multiplied. In the third year, we were positive that the mice had to go, and that as soon as possible, for nothing could be seen other than its shoots, spinning their way along like the lianas in a jungle nightmare.

It took us two years to finally dig out all those black mice. If only some of the more tasty vegetables were this powerful and energetic! But with most of them, we have to take care to weed them, water them, and collect caterpillars

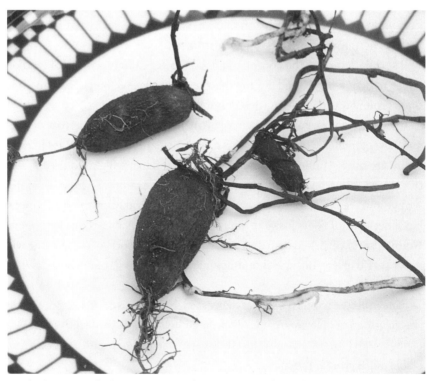

Earth chestnut is far less innocuous than its mouse-shaped tubers suggest. It spreads like wildfire and can become a nightmare for any gardener.

off them as we dream of rampant tomatoes, indestructible pumpkins, tough broccoli. A spinach tree would be nice, too.

Thoughts at Bedtime

Who worries about us when, in desperation, we scrunch up our pillows and just cannot get any sleep? The writers of books on sleeping disorders certainly do. They advise hot and cold foot baths, hop tea, and light meals. They also suggest mental journeys through our own bodies or along a never-ending sandy beach or through a garden.

Entering through a gate, one is immediately enveloped by silence and scents and soothing greenery. Birds are singing, panicles of flowers quietly sway in the breeze, a whiff of lavender calms the senses, and somewhere there is a babbling brook. One sits down on a bench and simply falls asleep.

It works for me. And even if sleep does not come straightaway, one can pass the time until it does in a most agreeable fashion. The one caveat, of course, is to use an invented garden for this bedtime journey rather than one's own garden. If one's own garden is used, one will see that the hellebore seedlings need water, that the comfrey needs relocating because it has become too large, and that it is time to prune back the oregano to prevent it from self-seeding in the strawberry patch quite so lavishly as it did last year. Mine is no garden to help me fall asleep. On the contrary, my hands start to jerk, my legs start to ache, and my diaphragm vibrates. When this happens to me, I turn on the light and write everything down to stop it from bothering me quite so much.

Plant out sage seedlings.

This is not the common kitchen sage. It is a perennial and can be propagated by cuttings if need be. These seedlings are from a different, biennial species that I raise indoors from seed. It is called clary sage. It does not smell of claret as its common name might suggest, but rather like a whole troop of sweating mountaineers, which is why it is also called sweat sage. I do not grow it for its smell, but for its magnificent flower heads and the transparent beauty of its individual flowers towering high above its big leaves that feel scarred and soft at the same time ("Just like Eddie Constantine," says the gardener's wife. How does she know that?)

Cut down the chives that have tipped over.

Cut them totally, right down to the ground, to make the new shoots even fresher and more tender. At Lindenhof, I have 16 meters of chives next to the pathways, so I use—no, not the lawnmower—a bread knife with a serrated edge, which is more useful for many garden jobs than any pair of scissors. Of course, one can also let the seeds mature. But then, sooner or later, one will end up with more chives in the garden than one could ever feed to one's vitamin-hungry guests.

By the way, the purple flower heads of chives, when harvested very young, make a racy-spicy salad all by themselves; one need only pluck them apart, removing every last bit of the stem, which is hard and impossible to chew—another reason for chopping down the entire row now.

Harvest the chervil seeds.

The seeds are ripening just now and need to be sown right away so that there is no break or only a very short break in the chervil supply. Depending on the weather, one has to re-sow in August so that sturdy new plants can grow by next February.

In late winter, chervil is one of the first herbs that we can use to satisfy our craving for fresh things, and when we harvest the seeds ourselves, the plant also presents us with a curious color show. While its seeds, clustered closely together in small umbels, get blacker and blacker, the color of the wilting stems and leaves changes into a whole range of violet and whitish hues. Chervil plants die as pale beauties, sink to the ground, and then have to be taken indoors for threshing and harvesting.

Closely related to chervil, what might be called an elephantine version of it, is giant hogweed (*Heracleum mantegazzianum*), which is unfolding the umbrellas of its flowers just now. It immigrated 100 years ago from southern Europe and is rightfully considered dangerous. If one touches it, at least in the sunshine, one can suffer painful skin irritations. Where the plant is happy, it can turn into a powerful weed by self-seeding freely, suffocating all other plants under its large leaves.

Still, I do not want to yield to the current, very common demand to banish this plant from gardens. Its shape is too magnificent, the wealth of beautiful details is too fascinating (its burgundy leaf sheaths, its slowly unfolding leaves and flowers, its hollow stems that are sometimes as thick as an arm) for me to want to dispense with it for the higher ecological good.

When it comes to skin irritations, these are easily avoided by using gloves when working with giant hogweed. And the danger of the plant spreading and causing ecological mayhem in the neighborhood can be avoided by cutting down its flower stalk before the seeds mature. It will last much better inside and remind us, bizarre and brittle though it is, of the heady magnificence of summer.

Suggestions for Front Yards

Sometimes it just gets to be too much. When there has not been so much as a drop of rain for two weeks and two dozen newly planted trees have to be watered by hand day in and day out; when elders and beans and tomatoes and blackberries are all ripe at the same time and the abundance becomes a nightmare; when stinging nettles are advancing on the goose pasture, almost howling with joy because there is no one to put a stop to them—then it can happen that the gardener and his wife lose their faith. Alone and in secret, they start to dream of a minute garden, about as big as the garden squares of the Beginenhof in Breda in Germany, where each Begin grew his own healing herbs and spices on his own 40 square meters. These plots are still looked after today—not by the Begins, who have ceased to exist, but by a municipal gardener.

I would happily make do with a front yard.

It would be easy to deride most existing front yards and to enumerate the inventory of their desolation: a much-too-large cedar of Lebanon, a much-too-small lawn, kitschy tulips, brave pansies, and all the other things that one might see as twisted images of horticultural skill in any given place at any given time.

But this cheap mockery will not get us anywhere. Just because a garden owner has certain responsibilities, he is certainly not obliged to create his front yard in such a way as to please us, the passers-by.

I am not even speaking of the fact that millions of front yards, through the brutalization of traffic and through mercilessly peeing dogs, have become all but unusable. But the other million yards in quiet residential areas, in terraced estates, in the suburbs—what might they look like if only the gardener had his way? A road might easily become a horticultural exhibition. But how?

Probably not by trying to achieve a decorative effect in the entrance and choosing a harmonic design of one tree, three shrubs, and several groundcovers. Instead, one might take plants as a starting point, or those hundreds or thousands of words that can tempt us to start a limited topic in a limited space. Somebody, for example, might express a fondness for the tender lines of grasses, with a collection built up, bit by bit, from nurseries. (The very popular pampas grass, however, is already present in far too many front yards.) Some representatives of these plant families like it hot and dry, and others like it moist and shady. For every front garden climate there is something that will look good next to the paving or reflected in a small pond.

In places where the toxic fumes of cars can be held at bay, a small herb garden containing everything needed in the kitchen can also be aesthetically pleasing—magnificent lovage, an alley of chives, and as a last flower in the year, the melancholy purple of oregano. In between, in a pot that can be taken indoors for the winter, old-fashioned lemon verbena (*Aloysia triphylla*); in France, its leaves are used to make verveine tea.

Another front gardener might take up strawberries as a topic, with several varieties on the ground as well as cascading down from several pots. They are nearly evergreen, flower benevolently, and produce fruit for months if they have had our native forest strawberry crossed in.

In dry and sunny places where the gardener shuns any kind of work, even in the front garden, there could be a roughly piled-up dry stone wall, or piles of stones with 20 or 30 different species of houseleek sprouting from them. They hunger only for light, making no other demands. The yellow and red star-shaped flowers are just as nice as the sinister leaf colors in winter.

These are only four of the innumerable front yard gardens possible. By focusing on one topic, they can tell us something about it in passing, instead of shouting at us with a cacophony of colors or boring us, the passers-by, with meaningless props.

Where it is still possible for a front garden to be a zone of contact to the life of the neighbors instead of just a buffer against a hostile road, there might also be a bench. On this bench, the front gardener can sometimes sit and answer questions—whether the basil has turned out all right this time, if an admiral has appeared in the butterfly front garden, and if it might be possible to get an offshoot of the Welsh onion. Gathered on its creamy-white flower balls are all species of bumblebee and wild bee that still exist in the area.

Of course he can have the offshoot. And a bunch of basil, too.

In Honor of Vita

When penny plant is itself nearly dying, the seeds for its new generation mature. On wilting bushes, the walls separating the seeds dry up into silvery skins. These are a popular addition to dried flower arrangements. The grand Linnaeus did not think of money when he named this plant. He thought of the moon and named it *Lunaria annua*. It is sometimes also called honesty.

One can commonly find the purple variety of honesty in gardens. There is also a white-flowering variant that bears the name of 'Sissinghurst', in honor of the famous garden of Sissinghurst Castle in the English county of Kent. In this place, the famous gardener and garden writer Vita Sackville-West, together with her husband, Harold G. Nicholson, created a great piece of horticultural art. Part of it is the white garden. In the four decades of its existence, it has been copied hundreds of times, though usually with one crucial modification.

Vita's white garden is impressive because its exclusively white-flowering perennials are surrounded by boxwood quarters and placed within a green framework. Imitators simply jumble white-flowering things together, and the result seems somehow self-righteous, and besides that, it looks boring.

Another idea from Sissinghurst is much easier to put into practice. They cut long twigs from the hazelnut tree in the spring and then shape them into arches set into the soil to support perennials or rose bushes that do not have a compact growth habit. This is a practical alternative to all the ugly support structures sold in the horticultural trade. Two or three such arches, placed at angles, make a supporting framework, and this usually saves us the trouble of tying the plants up. And even if one puts them in place very early in the season, the arches look unobtrusive and natural.

Of all the ways of paying homage by imitation to the great gardener of Sissinghurst, this is a modest and yet practical way, and it is much more becoming than those fraught attempts at imitating the prayer of the white garden.

The Many Uses of Blackberries

Everything is suddenly ripening at once. Baskets full of elderberries need processing; the plums still have their agreeable bitterness but are getting sweeter by the day; the potato sacks are filling up (alas, not by themselves); the carrots are sunk into the sandbox so that maggots cannot get to them; and, with all that, it is time to pick the blackberries, too.

Blackberries look like fabric samples by William Morris—a thousand black dots on the backdrop of their green leaves. A bowl full of picked fruit cannot even be left overnight without getting covered in a fine, gray carpet of mold. And all the people one could invite round for the harvest are on holiday.

One can always hear good things about harvest time, and yes, it is true that one feels like it is one's birthday. But the thing is that the seasons are, after all, somewhat impractical. Overwhelming abundance comes just when it is hottest and one would like nothing more than to sit by the pond with a glass of cider. Then, in the winter, one can harvest a few sloe berries at most or dig up a few tubers of Jerusalem artichoke with freezing-cold hands. All right, blackberries first. Perhaps I would not have needed 20 meters of hedge; 10 would have done, seeing as the hedge bears fruit on both sides and thus is really 40 meters long and easily 6 feet high, for we do not grow it along metal frames as the rules prescribe but instead let it grow freely. So the new shoots clamber over the old ones and create an embankment, its crown now beyond reach. We will really have to prune it soon.

Once the shoots get long enough, they bend back down to earth in long arches, and the shoot tips immediately send out thick bundles of white roots. Hobbling along, the hedge tries to enlarge itself in all directions, but we stop it by cutting off the shoots in the fall.

In earlier times, particularly in England, blackberry arches were considered a foolproof magic remedy for all sorts of ills. One needed only to creep underneath them to magically get rid of boils or a cough, and in Saxony, this was said to be effective against domestic quarrels as well. It is a beautiful image, the spiny arch sort of scraping the ills off people creeping underneath it.

Blackberry jams and jellies are not at all magical but are really tasty. Even a tea made from its leaves tastes much better than those who have yet to try it might surmise, as long as one goes to the trouble of fermenting the leaves first.

As with black tea, it is through this process that aromatic substances are formed. The easiest method is to let the leaves wilt for half a day and then roll them between the palms of one's hands or with a rolling pin and pack the rolls tightly into a tin can. Set the can in the oven at 50°C for three or four hours. The leaves of raspberries and strawberries, as we have already mentioned, can also be turned into an evening tea in this way, and it is worth taking seriously.

Of Wind and Threshing

In former times, people fed the wind flour and crumbs on the windowsill, which they allowed to be blown away. In doing so, they wanted to stop the wind from taking off the roof. By contrast, seafarers who wanted wind attracted it by beating up the cabin boys. If storms around here continue to increase, we might try out the feeding method.

Our guests at Lindenhof, particularly those who stay here overnight, can hear the comforting rustling of poplars and of two lime trees. But the limes are too close to the house, and the poplars are so high that they would hit the roof if they fell. So when the rustling gets louder and louder, it sounds somewhat menacing; right now, while it is still rustling, I will go out and use a stake to protect the newly planted medlar.

We have also installed a kind of defensive magic. It is a Balinese wind chime on a high pole. It has a double wing that turns on a long axis. Once the wind chime gets going, little clappers on the axis strike three bamboo plates tuned to different pitches. It is a kind of xylophone that strikes three or four single notes or emits a constant chord, depending on the force of the wind. To my ears, at least, it sounds much more tender and less dangerous than the rustling of the poplar leaves. With this beautiful bamboo creation, I defy the wind, I take the threat away from it, I force it to be cheerful, and then, perhaps, it will spare the roof and the medlar.

The wind does have its merits. No one else would be capable of blowing all that dry and wilted stuff into such neat piles; to loosen everything that is not nailed down; and to spread seeds all through the garden so that there are always some in a place where they feel happy enough to germinate. In the spring, they are welcomed as permanent residents newly relocated—marigolds (*Calendula officinalis*), parsnips, borage, yellow rocket (*Barbarea vulgaris*). Its leaves (as even sober botany books remark) smell of totally burned pork chops, and frankly, they stink. Evolutionary biologists habitually interpret this as protection. I like to imagine that yellow rocket has a problem with being eaten by humans and therefore uses an olfactory camouflage.

Anyway, its ruse is of little use. In Mediterranean countries, where yellow rocket grows in the wild, people worked out 3000 years ago that it tastes excellent, whether as a vegetable or as an addition to lettuce that seems rather bland by comparison. The Italians value it, and the Swiss eat their "Rickelsalat." Two thousand years ago, when horticultural books were still written in rhyme, the agricultural writer Columella wrote *Excitat ad venerem tardos maritos!* (It excites lethargic couples to lovemaking!) So it is an aphrodisiac, a love salad, a vegetable of passion. This cannot be the reason for its disappearance from today's gardening books.

In our garden, it grows everywhere, spreading like a common weed, so that we always have a few plants from which to harvest young leaves. Its leaves are

This wind chime is from a totally different culture, but its construction and its sound fit harmoniously into our garden.

lobed, and its flowers, a murky yellow, reveal their beauty only upon close inspection. They have four spoon-shaped petals that are criss-crossed by delicate purple veins.

We cannot rely on the wind to distribute the seeds of many other plants. We have to take off the pods and capsules at the right time, dry them carefully, thresh them, and remove the seeds. We have just finished doing this work. This fall's seed harvest is ready for next year, cleaned of all those bits of chaff that so often cause rot among the seeds.

Threshing is a matter of feeling and is best done between the palms of one's hands. Then the cleaning is a wind-game. If the seeds are heavy and the remains of their capsules are light, one needs only to blow into the mixture and anything light drifts away. In a similar manner, people in former times cleaned their grains by throwing them up into the air and letting the wind carry away the chaff.

The lighter the seeds, the more difficult things get. One has to try to make use of any minimal difference in weight, placing the seeds on a tray or a piece of paper, slightly tilting it and rocking it gently until the seeds collect on one side and the chaff on the other. With some valuable seeds, one has no choice but to pick out each individual seed with a pair of tweezers or a little piece of wood.

Harvesting, threshing, cleaning—these ancient tasks are not surprisingly surrounded by a lot of superstitions. They represent a sequence in the rhythm of life, and their ritualization guaranteed their durability. When collecting our own seeds, we should pay attention to the mechanical and aerodynamic problems that are posed. At the same time, we should see that we are preserving a benefit passed on to us as custodians of their continued existence. In doing so, as with so many tasks in the garden, we have once again directly experienced an element of reciprocity and safe keeping.

A Failure to Appreciate Rushes

Chinese health teas are special because their ingredients are not hacked to pieces like the contents of our tea mixtures; they instead come out of the packet whole. Sung Shans Children's Medical Tea, for example, contains many different types of leaves, along with flowers and seed capsules and several chitin hulls of large beetles that seem somewhat spooky. Upon seeing this, most children probably recover very quickly indeed to avoid having to drink a brew from this mixture. There are also some pretty and artfully wrapped parcels of rush marrow that at a glance look like bundles of spaghetti. (In fact, one can find the same sort of bundles made from rice noodles in packages of Chinese soup.)

Now what effect rush marrow has in a medicinal tea, I do not know. In Europe, it was used only for candle wicks, not medicine. Its marrow feels like a thin string of foamy rubber. It is a labor-intensive, typically East Asian skill to peel the skin off the round leaves precisely so that only a clean strand of marrow is left in the end, with an inflorescence at its tip, revealing that the specimen is a soft rush.

In gardening circles, rushes (*Juncus*) are widely regarded as having no decorative value, so that a few next to a pond are the most that people will accept. I like the powerful, rigid bundles, annually increasing in size, tolerating no com-

The mixture of Chinese health tea seems quite adventurous to us. It contains bundles of rush marrow and the chitin hulls of beetles.

petition, and green even in the winter. Their rigidity forms a striking contrast to most other plant shapes, which makes them stand out even more. It is very pleasing to the eye to have some rigid lines next to all the variety of other plants. Lawns are made up of nothing but green lines but the blades are rarely seen so that even grasses are not so severe.

Some rushes are almost abstractions of plants. Their leaves and stems are indistinguishably round with inconspicuous balls of flowers. The business of fertilization sometimes occurs in total secrecy while the flowers remain closed. It is a minimal shape, yet powerful and sturdy.

Rushes like boggy, wet soils but will do well in other places as long as they do not have to cope with sustained periods of drought. Young rushes are easy to transplant, but with older stands one may need to get out a pickaxe to shift the enormous root balls.

All in all, there are more than two dozen different species of rushes, and some are very tender. I have a number of them already, and all others are welcome, even if they have no decorative value and are no longer used for mats and baskets and floor coverings.

And when it comes to Sung Shans Children's Medical Tea, we sieved out all the seeds it contained. We are now waiting to see if anything germinates and, if so, what. There truly is no end to a gardener's curiosity.

Long Live Pumpkin Seeds

I can understand why seed companies do not indicate how long the seeds in their bright packets will remain viable. They would prefer us to buy fresh seeds every spring just to be on the safe side. However, they could at least indicate the year in which the seeds were packed. However, since they keep silent about that as well, the clever gardener writes the year of purchase on every packet he buys, and any seeds that remain after sowing do not get thrown away. They get put back into a (well-aired!) storage box.

The gardener then takes out his gardening books to look up which seeds he can expect to sow successfully after how many years. And what does he find in his gardening books? Nothing. It would seem that the writers of gardening books are in league with the seed producers and that they all have agreed to keep silent about this fact: among all the miracles of seed formation and germination, even the most minute grains containing the entire plan for the structure and life of a carnation or a lavender can keep their viability, often for years.

To be one up on the books and seed sellers, I want to publish how long at

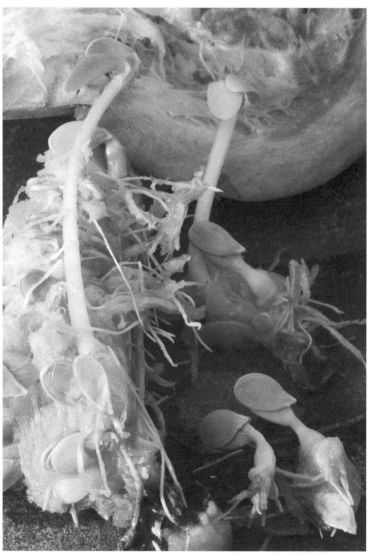

The seeds of all plants in the pumpkin family are long-lived. They remain viable for five to six years.

least the most important seeds in the kitchen garden remain viable, always calculating from the year of their harvest.

The seeds of all plants in the pumpkin family (that is, not only pumpkins, but also cucumbers, melons, and marrows) remain viable for five to six years. Some other seeds last nearly as long—say, four or five years—in their packets: all species of cabbage, radish, horseradish, celery, and endive. The seeds of ordinary lettuce give up the ghost after three years, which is also how long carrots, parsley, and mangold seeds last. Our stock of peas and beans remains viable for at least two years, as do the seeds of leek and onions and black salsify.

The one who knows these dates can save some money. However, I hasten to add that there are also many seeds, including savory and dill, that must be sown in the year following the harvest. Other seeds do not even last this long but need to get into the soil as soon as they are ripe. By no means do they germinate immediately; they simply build up their strength for germination the following spring.

This is the reason why, for example, one can never buy seeds of the delicious chervil. The small seeds expire before any seed seller can harvest them, bag them, and send them off. This is especially sad because turnip-rooted chervil (*Chaerophyllum bulbosum*) has a thumb-sized root that is a real delicacy either boiled or fried; it tastes like sweet chestnuts. Dusseldorf gourmets have the advantage here. They can buy turnip-rooted chervil, albeit at horrendous prices, in Karlsplatz market, though it may also be offered in other places. If one finds fresh chervil anywhere, one can get one's own seeds. It is enough to plant the tubers (no matter what season one buys them) and wait. From the little beets, a plant that is similar to parsley will grow. It flowers in July; let its seeds ripen in September. Then follow the drill: sow the seeds immediately and, above all, mark the spot well so that you know where your chervil will come up in the following year.

The Berry That Is Really an Apple

Creating a stir is part of their business, but in some mail-order nurseries, there is rather too much of it. In the catalog of such an enterprise, I once found a "world sensation from the U.S." touted as a "sensational, brand new breed."

Hiding behind the fantastic name of "Black Colorado Berry" was nothing but good old red chokeberry (*Aronia*). It was introduced to Europe from North America as early as the 1700s and rightfully counts as an excellent hedging plant and richly fruiting bush for feeding birds.

Red chokeberry gets its name from its "berries," which look like pea-sized apples and also have a similar internal structure, including pulp and core. In fact, just like apples, pears, plums, cherries, and blackberries, *Aronia* belongs to the rose family (Rosaceae).

In autumn, this shrub surprises us with magnificent shades of magenta and vermilion. Whether alone or in a hedge, it irresistibly stages the last act of a play featuring bright colors after having been covered in white or pale pink flowers in May. In July, its red or black fruits (depending on the variety) ripen. They grow in bunches, like grapes, so that one can easily pick a handful in passing. The little apples taste pleasantly sweet and sour and a little spicy; like all plants in the rose family, they combine sweetness and delicacy with the principle of tannic contraction. How boring pure, unmitigated sweetness can be. We can taste it in those tropical fruits that do not contain even a hint of bitterness.

Well, red chokeberries are a little mealy, but they are good in preserves and jams. In their native country, the Indians would squash all fruits of this type between two stones and, from the moist pulp, form small balls which they then dried in the sun to boil up in the winter. Nothing other than the fact that we are too comfortable and spoiled stops us from imitating the Indians. It may be only an ethnological game, but bear in mind that many of the Indians (who did not play it but lived it) have ceased to exist because the Europeans believed they had the right to abolish such uncultured half-humans. The garden is entwined with the wider world and its history much more closely than we realize.

A Fern Path

A big shower of rain, welcome anyway after a long period of drought, came just in time to prepare the ground for a new fern path. The path is 30 steps long, planted on both sides with different types of fern. They look somewhat lost, standing at attention right now, but in a few years they will have grown into a veritable jungle, the light shades of green set off by shrubs that provide a dark backdrop and the necessary shade at the same time.

Our fern path is a "teaching path" that should finally help us, through continuous observation, know the different species better. Ferns are all too similar to one another with their finely incised fronds and feathers. The differences only stick in one's mind if one sees the plants next to one another: male fern (*Dryopteris filix-mas*) with its long, doubly pinnate leaves; lady fern (*Athyrium filix-femina*), which is very similar at first sight; bracken (*Pteridium aquilinum*), which can grow 6 feet high; ostrich fern (*Matteuccia struthiopteris*), whose fronds form a narrow, tall funnel; and, in addition, all those smaller ferns with their delicate stems and sometimes wafer-thin leaves, sprouting from cracks in the rock or gaps in the wood.

In contrast to flowering plants, I always regard ferns as being mute and dignified; according to their age, they really are. Three hundred million years ago in the swamps of the Carboniferous, they grew into giant trees, along with species of burlap and equisetum that were just as tall. My fern path is there to impart an element of this jungle atmosphere, with the help of a hidden pipe from the house drain that continuously moistens the ground with seeping water.

The never-ending invitation to create a sample of the world from scratch, to make an image of a piece of nature as only a rough sketch and yet filled with real life, is one of the grand liberties of the gardener, even if the scale has to be adjusted to the space available. Here a sketch of a dark carboniferous forest, there a memory of a path along a riverbank or a citation from the southern slopes of a chalk mountain, a few tones from the chord of a landscape. Those much-maligned lawns backed by a group of conifers are, after all, nothing more than attempts at creating the essence of a forest clearing.

Two Kinds of Mushrooms

It is still totally uncertain whether our puff-ball will return this fall. Mushrooms in the garden are restless and capricious guests. One can invite them, but whether they come and how long they stay is up to them. It always depends on whether all their demands regarding soil and temperature and moisture have been met to the letter.

Then they suddenly appear out of the blue, literally overnight. For a long time, sometimes for years, their underground mycelium has been growing, spreading, and strengthening itself, and now it sends up fruiting bodies that let their spores ripen to ensure propagation.

Mushrooms can be expected in places where we leave an old tree trunk or pile up chopped wood in the shade. Wood sponges and other specialists should appear quite soon, taking over the dead matter and working it into fine mulch. Our thick layers of newspaper, too, which we use to suppress pernicious weeds, attract certain kinds of mushrooms, such as common dung cup (*Peziza vesiculosa*) with its leathery caps.

It seems to be an immutable law of nature that any mushrooms that deign to appear in the garden are not edible, as if edible ones know that their life is in danger when they get too close to humans. Exceptions to this rule are rare.

Bushy ink cap and wrinkly ink cap sometimes appear at the base of a compost heap. If they do, they have to be harvested immediately because they can mature in the course of a single day. For them, maturity means dissolving into black, inky mush. Both are edible; however, one must not drink alcohol for one day before and after eating wrinkled ink cap. Otherwise, sickness and dizziness threaten, though wrinkled ink cap is not known to cause death.

When it comes to nonedible mushrooms turning up in the garden, at least they have the advantage of being beautiful to look at. The shape of common dung cup is bizarre and immutable, rather reminiscent of animal shapes. Verdigris agraric is of a poisonous blue-green color, but after a few days, it calms down to a harmless gray-brown, as though the exertion of turning blue had exhausted it; big laughing gym shines in a magnificent orange on rotting stumps of fruit trees. These are only a few examples of many surprising encounters.

Mushrooms in the garden are like goblins. They can even be a bit spooky, like earth spirits, living off dead matter, familiar with poison, incalculable and deceptive, tempting and dangerous. If one aims to know their names, one needs expert instruction and rather a lot of patience. In some cases, the color of the spores, which are situated between the lamellas of cap-forming mushrooms, can be helpful. To determine the color, place the cap on a sheet of paper and wait for a few hours. The dry spores then drop out and create a delicate pattern on the paper, an exact drawing of the lamellas; only where a breeze has moved the spores do they burst apart and alight as if it they have been painted. It is hard to believe that a new mycelium can grow out of each and every little spore the size of a dust particle.

The small ground-dwelling mushrooms reveal themselves only to attentive gardeners. White bird's nest, whose caps make large colonies, produces spores in round capsules; in earlier times farmers used the number to predict the level of grain prices.

Champignons—beings from another world, a moon world with pale light and moist shades—have always been grown in dark basements. Other mushrooms, too, have been tried out in cultivation, but most species resist the human desire to make them grow under prescribed conditions. Only in the last 30 years have people found at least a few species that lend themselves to domestication—oyster mushroom, brown hay cap, shiitake, velvet foot, and two-toned wood tuft.

A mushroom was lying here. Its spores are so light that the slightest breeze would destroy its image.

There is a second category of garden mushroom if the gardener has space for a bale of straw or a few pieces of wood. He can order mushroom stock, inoculate the timber or the straw (depending on the species), and let the mycelium grow through the base. One day the mushrooms will unfold in large batches like flowers. One will have to invite guests to use such a large harvest while it is still fresh.

A mushroom corner in the garden, shaded by a tree or under the roof of a shed, has something of an alchemist's workshop about it. Dead plant matter rots away and is changed according to secret recipes. It finally gives birth to bursting, boisterous shapes of the most delicate scent and taste. The earth spirits have been tamed; willingly they now deliver the finest of the fine.

No wonder that there is so much imaginative superstition surrounding these spirits and their products. In Silesia, popular belief held that a meal of mushrooms at Christmas would ensure that one would wear only well-suited clothes in the following year. I am all for putting this superstition to the test at some point.

Love, Death, and Animals

Where Love Shines

A moment of glory for the gardener is when, late in the evening, he goes into his garden and finds a glowing glowworm in the grass (zoologically speaking, a shining shiny bug) which he then can place, still glowing, at the feet of his wife with a few fitting comments—not the stars from the sky, but the glowworms from the garden, and so on.

He keeps a crucial bit of information secret until the following morning: the female glowworm is easy to catch. They are unable to fly and instead just lie around and glow for three hours, "waving their backsides in the air" (according to Jacobs and Renner in their fascinating handbook, *Biology and Ecology of Insects*). It is understandable that the females glow, for they somehow have to draw attention to themselves. However, people do not know why the males, flying around, sometimes switch on their lights as well. The substances that contribute to this "cold" light are D-luciferin, luciferase, and adenosine triphosphate. The chemistry of love is always somewhat sobering (except in *The Elective Affinities*, a book by the famous German author Goethe).

The Garden as a Place for Courtship Displays

A gardening friend once wrote that she had read with pleasure that I had a male parsnip in my garden. In her garden she had a female parsnip, and one should really find out what would happen if the two were brought together.

Of course, this was a dig at me. What she really meant was that I did not know that parsnips are female. All right, out with the dictionary!

The origin of *parsnip* is the Latin *Pastinaca*, a clear score for femininity. But then things get unruly. In Old High German there was pastinaga as well as pas-

213

tinac (one female, one male), in Middle High German there was pasternacke and pasternack (again, one female and one male), and so on up until the present day. There are many different German vernacular forms, some male and some female, such as palsternach and pestnache, pinsternache and pastenade. Somewhere near Leipzig, people even pronounce it as "basternade" (with a soft b), male and female jumbled up, promiscuity crying out to the heavens, lascivious disorder.

I have nothing against the combined form, but out of habit I will stick to saying pastinak and not pastinake for parsnip. And this year I will allow far fewer of these strapping lads to grow than I did last year. Despite all those rumors spread by organic gardeners, parsnip roots are far less tasty than carrots, and five or six plants are enough for decorative purposes. The yellowy-green umbels are unique, and in combination with sunflowers they look wonderful in a vase that lasts long after the flowers have wilted.

When it comes to maleness and femaleness, however, the garden has always been a place of encounters. Long before people in the cold occident began to appreciate the sensuality of a garden, people in the orient had been celebrating its never-ending feasts—the garden as a symbol for woman, as a symbol for love and the pleasure of it in a very real sense, as a place of sexual encounters (confirmed by the Bible in The Song of Solomon 4—look it up and read it to your partner!).

Later, in a gently wayward manner, the tempting idea of gardens of love established itself in the Christian occident, even though the church sometimes suspected the garden to be a place of the sins of the flesh. Saint Hieronymus lashed out against gardens that tempted people to sin, and a hermit at heaven's gate is said to have slid down a few rungs on the ladder of virtue because he turned around for one last glance at his beloved garden. However, on the lower Rhine, an anonymous copperplate engraver engraved so many gardens of love that he entered the history of art as Master of Gardens of Love, and in Manesse's medieval writings people even take baths in the garden—that is, the lord takes a bath and three ladies look after him.

There is no bathtub in our garden, but there are many benches and chairs on which the male element, the gardener, finds the female element, his wife, and they keep each other company. Sometimes. We actually have two gardens, and we each work in our own. The gardener's wife grows vegetables and quite a few flowers, while the gardener is responsible for botany, be it edible or decorative or neither of these.

Separate gardens are at least as beneficial for harmony as separate bedrooms are, and not only because of the inevitable conflicts when two people work in the same garden (commonly kept at bay because one person is responsible for the trees and the lawn and the other for the flowers). Not only are negative things avoided, but positive things become possible. For example, the gardener's wife can give in to her love for zinnias, which the gardener could not care less about. The pair can invite each other into the gardens (with or without cappuccino) to show off the new things that are there or call on each other for help: "What do you think of this?"

"Horrible," the gardener's wife says, and the gardener has to admit that she is right. Or the other way around.

Or the gardener uses his garden as some arbor birds from New Guinea do. The male birds create a whole garden of feathers and stones and bright flowers for the females and then stalk up and down their arbor to attract them.

Consider the garden as a place for courtship displays. A swing would fit in here because of its symbolism, and a grass bench is also an old and dignified member of the garden of lust. As the poet Hölty says, "Tumble he did from ball to ball, and forgot the grass bench where his love was awaiting him to the sound of the nightingale."

It is easiest to construct a grass bench when, somewhere in the garden, there is a hill to form it into. Otherwise, one needs a box made of brick or thick planks of wood filled with soil. One can then sow grass or put turf cut out from the lawn on the surface. Of course, the grass on the bench needs to be mown, which is best done with hedge shears. If the bench is created on a hillside, there can be a backrest. One can either build it as a slope and sow grass on it as well, or one can build a backrest from stones or strong planks of wood.

Even nicer than grass is a cushion of a low-growing species of chamomile or creeping thyme. When one sits down on it, one is surrounded by the scent of these plants.

Whether grass or herbs, when one gets up again, one will have a green backside.

Images of Death . . .

We do not give our cats names any more. At some point, they all end up being run over, and it is easier to bury a nameless cat than a Felix or a Trina.

Here the romantic image of arcadian life differs from reality. (Only in passing, I will mention the bees that a beekeeper placed at the back of the garden where there is a field of rapeseed. Rapeseed, a modern new breed, makes bees aggressive. They attack us and immediately sting, but later we get three jars of rapeseed honey.)

Much more emotionally touching are the pictures of death, and they are present every day. For example, when a fox has come at dawn and killed the goose that was always the bravest and the most vigilant or when a marten has decimated the chickens, there are ripped-up bodies, bitten-off heads, and wings covered in blood under the hedge.

One tries to account for the loss as some kind of payment owed to nature. After all, keeping poultry in the country means feeding a few wild robbers now and then.

But it also means feeling that powerless fury, regarded as unseemly for the part it played in fueling the ambition to take charge of nature and then denaturalizing it in the process. Yet the fury is there, seething. None of this is idyllic.

Under the cut-leaved elder is a large flower pot that has been filled through the years with white plant labels. These are the labels of death or, to put it in a friendlier way, the business cards of plants that used to live in the garden and have said good-bye. There are plenty of explanations to go with them.

The five hosta signs remind us that our little collection of hostas became a victim of the slugs—leaves and everything else—as soon as they were planted. I look enviously at the magnificent photographs of English gardens showing huge hosts of hostas in the deepest shade while I add them to the list of plants I simply cannot cultivate at Lindenhof.

Other business cards from the label urn accuse the gardener of forgetting to get the exploding cucumber into its winter quarters on time or to collect the seeds of the asparagus pea and plant them in the following year.

And then, of course there are those plants that the gardener's fingers simply were not green enough to keep. Disappointed, perhaps offended, and simply fed up with their life, they said "Adieu" or "Salu" or "Not like this" or whatever plants say when they leave.

The signs in my pot are like an abstract garden of lost things or a raffle from which I can draw names and go in search of the departed or its identical sister to invite back into the garden. It turns out to be a blessing that plants are not quite as individualized as cats are.

Death is everywhere in the garden, and most of the eating and being eaten remains invisible. Even the sun can bring death, as it indeed has done in the last few weeks. One is not always on time to save plants when they are dying of thirst. Some woody plants begin to show signs of dying when it is already too late, which should teach us a lesson for next year.

This dry heat also forces the slugs, which would otherwise bring death, to hide deep down in the soil, but this is little consolation; with the first sign of rain, they will all creep out of their holes.

Not only slugs but also snails with their beautiful houses will be back then, too, and the thrushes will be ready and waiting for them. They do not attack slugs, unfortunately, but they really clean up among snails. One can see "thrush anvils" everywhere, stones that thrushes use to smash snail houses to

Thrushes have been at work here. They smashed the beautiful snail houses on their "thrush anvils."

eat their inhabitants. Their ruins are a rather sorry sight because only then do they show how beautiful the insides of their spirals are.

Cats, however, are always in danger of death and yet are heralds of death themselves. Apart from mice which they have a right to, they also sometimes catch moles or get a wagtail drinking out of a puddle. The worst thing is when they manage to find a little frog by the side of the pond and continue to play with it until it stops hopping.

Images of death abound in the garden. And the simple wisdom that death is part of life does not stop the shivers—it merely softens the blow.

. . . And of Continuing to Live

Some well-educated ladies and gentlemen spent a day and a half in the bull stable, debating the morphology of plantains, the soul of the plant in Empedocles' writing, and the ability of plants to suffer. Above their heads, swallows fed their young and on the table was a collection of seven different plantains from the garden, their similar and dissimilar shapes being committed to memory. In exchange, the guests wanted to leave a tree as a kind of memento of themselves in the garden. They allowed us to choose which one, and we are to plant it in the fall.

Perhaps it will be a sassafras, an Appalachian fever tree, a miracle in scents and colors. Its timber and bark and roots smell of cloves and camphor with a whiff of fennel. An oil distilled from it can be used to add that tempting scent to soaps and tobaccos. And the magnificent orange and red of its leaves are said to be among the most beautiful fall colors to exist anywhere. Finally, its leaves have differing oval and lobed shapes, so it is just the right thing to commemorate unique people.

The conference tree will not be the first memorial at Lindenhof. My fatherly friend Friedrich first got me interested in looking at plants and animals and stones 50 years ago, so I have planted a velvet hydrangea (*Hydrangea aspera* subsp. *sargentiana*) for him. Its inflorescences are the size of saucers, its central florets are purple, its sterile ray florets are white, and the whole thing hovers above the large, downy leaves. This is my favorite of all the hydrangeas, and it needs most care—abundant water when it is dry and attention when late frosts threaten.

So this is Friedrich's shrub; we need not only plant trees in commemoration. In a friend's garden, there is a perennial that is simply called "Mrs. Melchers" because its correct name got lost along the way. Mrs. Melchers is the woman who brought the first shoots of the plant to the garden and is now remembered fondly by the family. Maybe only Miss Willmott is remembered more widely.

Miss Willmott was an English gardener. Throughout her life, she had such a liking for a particular, silvery gray relative of sea holly (*Eryngium*) that she always carried some seeds with her and dropped a few of them in every garden that she visited. She did this in secret, but not so much in secret that people never found out. Ever since, this plant has been called "Miss Willmott's ghost." If I did wish to live forever, I would like to live like that—not as a spiny sea holly but rather as a sassafras with its scents and colors.

Another way that life continues in the garden is usually anonymous, and therefore we rarely think about it. All those monks, traders, crusaders, botanists, and plant hunters who brought us the variety of plants we now enjoy in our gardens remain nameless. We recently commemorated them with a summer dinner. We had broad beans spiced with savory, potatoes with a few thinly sliced shallots browned in sunflower oil, and strawberries for dessert. That was the world on a plate.

Broad beans are from the Middle East. Savory is from the Mediterranean, and potatoes, as everyone knows, are from South America. Sunflowers, which gave us the oil, were imported from subtropical Central America; shallots were brought home by the Crusaders. And even though there is a native species of strawberry in Central Europe, it only became really enjoyable when breeders crossed it with an American one. From this cross, our commercial breeds with their large, aromatic, and juicy fruits were developed; we enjoyed them for a few weeks, but unfortunately their time is now over. We can only have more strawberries in our dreams which—according to an old superstition—herald a lot of money.

Caterpillars in May

We have not yet caught up and recovered from the ravages of a dry, late frost. This year has something tedious about it, and it is not really picking up speed. Everything needs a little longer, and some things have been lost altogether, such as the flowers of the wisteria and the peonies. Even our sneezewort, otherwise so robust, seemed to be in shock, vegetating with wilting tips.

Upon closer inspection, the sneezewort revealed the work of some animal. Inside its curled-up leaves, I found the small, olive-green caterpillars of plume moths. On many evenings late last summer, those small butterflies had danced around the yarrow bush, mated on it, and then deposited the eggs from which the little caterpillars now emerged.

Plume moths are the only butterflies with the gift of folding up their front wings at right angles to their bodies and of hiding their feathery hind wings in the pocket they thus create. Because of this unique and abnormal capability and because of their cute name, I have been fond of plume moths for years. It was unthinkable to destroy the brood of about 300 of them.

Yet neither was it easy to stand by and watch the destruction caused by these greedy caterpillars. I was consoled only by the thought that the plume moths would one day emerge. By taking this abstract view, we are acknowledging the contribution our companions make to the garden. For we are not alone in the garden, and the arrogance with which we decide what we will and will not tolerate is best tempered by letting other beings be and by realizing that the damage that these so-called pests cause is often not so large after all.

Our sneezewort, at any rate, showed itself to be quite unmoved. It surrendered its first shoots to the caterpillars and, right next to them, produced some tender new ones. The plant and the plume moths fought it out, and the gardener needed to do nothing but be patient enough to wait and observant enough not to miss the moment when he might have to intervene after all. Just like in real life.

Quarrels Around the Pond

Around the pond, there is real work to do. Water pepper (*Persicaria hydropiper*), which was once planted on the barren northern bank because it grows so fast, has colonized the entire eastern bank and is striding out to conquer the south. It must be decimated rigorously, and that means that wheelbarrow loads of the intertwined, thick, underwater branches must be pulled ashore and piled up in a separate compost heap and guarded ferociously; water pepper itself has no idea that it is called water pepper. It grows just as well on dry land and can easily become a nuisance.

On the western shore of the pond, grasses have grown far into the water. With their roots, they are creating huge floats to show us that a pond as we would like it is an artificial thing altogether. If we do not continuously intervene, many bog plants and some from the dry land, too, try to colonize it and turn it into dry land. A pond gardener needs to stay vigilant and interrupt this natural occurrence if he wants to salvage his human idea of a pond.

If not a fight, this is at least a little quarrel, and it is carried out not only between humans and plants, but also between humans and animals. Great pond snail, for example—something that our clever pond gardening books never warn us of—is supposed to eat only algae. In reality, however, it enjoys devouring all our tender bog plants, and when they are gone, it will go for the less tender ones, too. Great pond snail is impossible to get rid of, and one can only protect oneself by keeping all new plants in quarantine for four weeks and meticulously picking off any snails that may show their faces.

And ducks! On the last day of the water pepper campaign, a small pile of shoots and leaves remained on the shore. In the morning, a couple of visiting ducks in search of a nesting place discovered it, settled in it, and pulled it into shape, and the duck is now brooding while the drake stands on guard and secures the nest from the dry land.

So the pathway around the pond has been closed, our seat by the water remains unused for the time being, and if the ducks—and perhaps their descendants, too—decide to stay, a new pond will need to be built. For where ducks graze, the flora quickly gets reduced to the plants they scorn, and there are not many of them. Perhaps water pepper will be the only thing remaining alive. For even ducks cannot eat it as fast as it grows.

Sensitive Orloffs

The Orloffs were ill-mannered dukes. In fact, their titles were bestowed on them only because they were so uncivilized. Grigorij and Alexej Orloff, among others, assisted Grand Duchess Katharina in toppling her husband, Tsar Peter III. Alexej strangled poor Peter with his own hands. The now Tsarina Katharina was temporarily so fond of Grigorij that the Brobrinsky family descended from their liaison, and he gave her the Orloff diamond that was named after himself. However, he then behaved so rudely that Katharina finally decided that she preferred Lord Potemkin instead.

Our Orloffs are not rude; they are trusting and sensitive. It is inconceivable how anyone could have had the idea to christen this beautiful breed of chickens, imported into Germany from Moscow in 1910, with the name of Orloff.

Our Orloffs are usually in a hurry, running around rather too much on their long legs and therefore going to bed much earlier than our other chickens do. They carry their necks proudly upward. Their feathers are the color of mahogany with white dots, and their long eggs have something elegant about them. Even the rooster is thoroughly good-natured, in contrast to our other rooster, whose breed we cannot determine. The latter uses every opportunity to attack us, preferably in an ambush. Ever since I met a little boy who had had a hole pecked in this cheek by an aggressive rooster, I cannot find them funny any more. I now use a stick from the hazelnut tree to work my way up the pecking order, so far without success; our rooster does not seem to know that if I get fed up with him, he will have to make way for the Orloff rooster, just as Orloff had to make way for Potemkin.

Chickens are part of rural life. First of all, their eggs are unsurpassable. We not only eat them ourselves, we also give them as gifts. Secondly, we appreciate the noises they make to accompany our work in the garden—hens cackle and roosters crow and are answered from afar. Nicest, however, are the noises they make in the evening when they are already on their perches and notice that one is there to close the stable. Half asleep, they coo, probably talking of worms and grains, and the whole thing sounds very touching indeed.

Earthworm Piles of the Third Kind

The finely twisted little piles of earthworms are commonly known and valued as a sign of the existence of these night workers. Bunches of leaves looking like bags half dragged into the soil testify to their work.

However, there is a third sign of earthworm life that is often overlooked. I first found it on a bed waiting for some hellebores to be planted on it. Many little pieces of chalk, which I had used to enrich the ground, were still lying on the surface. Overnight, as if by magic, these bits had been arranged into round, neat little piles. What gave them away as earthworm edifices were the leaves, shoots, and larger twigs in between the bits of stone, all pointing to one point—the opening to an earthworm hole.

Ever since I first noticed these heaps of stones, I continue to spot them, both in my garden and in others. They obviously have existed always and everywhere, and yet they are hardly ever noticed. When earthworms become active, put out a few bits of chalk or brick dust in a regular pattern and check every morning to see if an earthworm has created its castle during the night.

These round piles probably are indeed a kind of castle, protecting the worm from enemies and disasters; underneath it, the worm is safe from birds, the entry to its hole is protected from the rain, and air can enter freely.

Marveling, we squat in front of this small citadel. It is the work of a blind creature capable of systematically searching the surroundings of its hole for stones of a suitable size; of transporting them with its body; of sensing distances, the condition of the ground, and the amount of work done so precisely and quantitatively that, in the end, it has built an orderly, balanced edifice that towers over the entrance to its cave.

Patient observers, perhaps photographers, are invited to investigate these nightly doings of earthworms and to show us in which order they happen, how the stones are chosen and transported, how long all this takes, as well as how much of the finished product is ascribed to chance and how much to directed planning. If one does not want to spend hours outside at night equipped with a blue light, one could try using a box of soil in a basement. This would be feasible even in winter, for earthworms continue to work as long as the ground is not frozen.

Wintry Things

Let Us Booze by the Embers

It is always the same. One simply does not want to accept the fact that winter is at the door. There is an admiral trundling along above the last Michaelmas daisies and our medlar is flowering for the second time, giving us hope of a respite. But it could all be over tomorrow, the medlar flowers brown and lifeless, the admiral retired. Perhaps it will try to hibernate in the barn instead of the Mediterranean, to which it should have flown ages ago.

There are a few things—and a few scents—we can store for the winter. Dried sweet vernal grass, for example, gives us the sweet scent of hay and memories of the warm, calm days of late summer. In Poland, this grass is added to the famous vodka Zubrowka, which is not so much a signal of loose morals as it is a signal of the versatility of some useful plants.

The leaves of *Aloysia triphylla* are also very versatile. We have to harvest them now, and they are used in perfumes as well as in a remedy for flatulence. In France they are also used for a refreshing tea called verveine. This small shrub, which can in milder climates grow to more than 10 meters in height, has spent the summer in our garden; it has not managed to flower and now has to be taken inside the house. There it either hibernates dry and seemingly dead or, if we water it, starts to shoot again after taking a short break, with no change in the sweet, lemony aroma of its leaves.

Lemon verbena was a popular indoor plant 100 years ago, whereas today it is nearly impossible to get hold of—fashions do change. If only the fashion for Christmas flowers would change. If only millions of sweetly scented aloysias were given away as presents instead of millions of miserable, chemically inhibited, poinsettias!

Oleander, too, has to be taken inside, along with the scented pelargoniums and rosemary. People often postpone lugging pots around, and then everything has to happen in the space of a few hours. But our camellias have become so heavy that one cannot lift them alone. One could really do with a few helpers now.

So one ought to announce a late fall party and then be as strict as Lord Haxthausen—a Westphalian freethinker, fairy tale collector, agricultural politician, and founder of the Maltese order—was 150 years ago. As was often the case, when he sent out invitations to his castle in Thienhausen, all guests had to roll up their sleeves and use hoes and spades in the garden before they received anything to eat, and the lord of the manor—so Lulu of Strauss and Torney tells us—"kept a strict watch that nobody shirked their duties."

We have not gotten this far with our guests. Instead, they bring us sweet chestnuts, which we do not have in our garden. Wonderful ones at that! Their devilishly spiny hulls are larger than tennis balls, and when they split open lengthwise or crosswise, two or three correspondingly large fruits appear.

In our former bull stable, we light a fire in the open fireplace and put a pan full of chestnuts onto the embers. Sometimes they are not altogether done, and sometimes they get burned, but they always signal a party. "Let us booze by the embers / with kittens and hampers," the poet Johann Fischart rhymed 400 years ago. In this, "kittens" are quinces, and "hampers" are sweet chestnuts. When it comes to drink, we have the Romans to thank for the wine we drink with the chestnuts, as well as for the chestnuts themselves. They brought us both. However, it is not true that sweet chestnuts grow only in regions that are warm enough for vineyards. There are large specimens far beyond that region.

Store-bought chestnuts are often somewhat crinkly, and when roasted they simply go hard, not soft. The only way to avoid this is by placing the fruits into a bucket of water overnight so that they can soak up some moisture—or by planting one's own tree.

With a tree, one will have to wait for quite a few years before the first fruits appear. To shorten the waiting time, fork out for a larger tree and, above all, insist on getting one of the larger fruiting varieties. Never try raising a chestnut tree from seed because you never know what may come out of it, and you will be 10 years older when you finally find out.

Chestnuts, too, have various uses. In southern Europe, they were a staple; in other countries, they became a delicacy. The English made them into soup and, of course, a pudding. Chestnuts were used to stuff poultry before it goes into the oven, chestnut flour was used to starch linen, and in France, people invented marrons glacés—candied chestnuts—and a chestnut purée for dessert. Its timber was sought after for many purposes, and its leaves, harvested in summer at the latest, were said to be an effective remedy against whooping cough.

We are going to plant a sweet chestnut, and we are going to try getting hold of a variety called 'Numbo' because it bears the largest fruits.

The Shades of Decay

Our local club is visiting our American sister city and is looking forward to the Indian summer—a grand eruption of glowing fall color illuminating large areas—while we sit in front of the fire in the old bull stable to warm ourselves. In fact, our friends' journey to Indian summer is more closely connected to our fireplace than one might first think.

A local directive on the use of open fireplaces obliges us to have open fires only on special occasions—weddings? St. Martin's day? driver's license renewal?—so that the atmosphere is not unduly polluted with carbon dioxide.

No one bothers to ask whether, in terms of the global atmosphere, it is reasonable and defensible to have 30 members of the local club dash to the United States to see the Indian summer, using enough fuel per head for each one of them to have driven 6000 miles.

And this is not the only case where, for good reasons, small and simple things and traditions are regulated while nonsense happily continues on a grand scale. They have lowered the fees for dumping poisonous wastes in rivers so as not to inconvenience the trade. By contrast, we are now paying an annual fee for the permission, so graciously granted, to let the rainwater from our roof seep into our garden. Rain, as far as the authorities are concerned, is not a natural occurrence that they are grateful for, if they were indeed capable of such emotions. No, as soon as it drips from the roof, it becomes a "substance" that we, as the owners of said roof are "discharging"—and we need permission for that.

Unthinkable what would happen if they withdrew that permission. We would have to pray to God to stop it ever raining on us again. So we pay the fee and settle down in front of our blazing fireplace, lit specially to celebrate the occasion. We then ask the fire spirits to make sure that the authorities never find out about the large amounts of carbon dioxide commonly discharged by compost heaps. For if they ever did, they would either prohibit compost heaps or charge fees for them as well.

But the local club is flying out to see the Indian summer. I can well believe that it is indeed breathtaking. Even so, we do not fly there; we make do with our own fall colors, and not only those of the trees. Even before our ginkgo leaves turn their sulfuric shade of yellow, our aronias display a whole range of oranges and reds; the mountain pear looks as if it is on fire; our raspberry leaves turn into three-colored wood carvings with clearly delineated red-green-yellow markings; and the leaves of our sunflowers, the flowers themselves long gone, don the blackest of blacks to announce their imminent demise. All those patterns are visible signs of the destruction of leaf pigments, of an orderly retreat of living matter into the roots of a plant, where it is stored for the following year.

In vain we try to archive the stages of these procedures by pressing and drying the leaves—everything shiny goes dull, and sometimes only a dirty shade of brown remains. So we have to go out into the garden every day to witness the changes—not just with our eyes, but also with our sense of touch—showing us how, with their magnificent glow, things start to slacken. Sparkling and passing away at once—signs of winter.

Before the Frosts Arrive

The yellow leaves of our poplars have spread across the entire garden like a thin yellow blanket. They are hanging in the shrubs, the last roses shining above them, along with an altogether untimely last flowering of delphiniums.

These leaves cannot stay everywhere. They stick together and can suffocate plants that spend the winter as a rosette or as a cushion. The hill of white-edged sedums and the thyme need to be freed, as does the Madonna lily, one of the two lilies whose basal leaves stay green throughout the winter while all her sisters are dormant deep down in the soil.

There is enough other work to last the next few weeks and months, though garden calendars usually do not mention much more than pruning trees and oiling shears. In reality, the short days are barely enough to manage all that we have planned—especially replanting. Woody plants and perennials are both quite insensitive to relocating right now, and if, when there is no frost, we work our way down last summer's list of necessary relocations, we will have gained some valuable time for the spring. The plants will not notice; they will simply reawaken in another place and will feel even less disturbed since their future place suits them better.

Our saffron crocus, which has given us only a modest harvest this year, will get a sunnier, warmer place to flower earlier and more freely. Enula (*Inula*), which has turned into an imposing shrub, needs a place where its large leaves can freely spread out and where its roots are easily accessible so that we can always dig out a few to dry and then chew on whenever coughs and sore throats befall us.

Yellow chamomile (*Anthemis tinctoria*), tirelessly flowering even now, needs a different place so that its warm yellow is not constantly competing with the more sulfuric yellow of the evening primrose. And fennel! It will have a whole area to itself, forming a backdrop to the purple flower candles of purple loosestrife (*Lythrum salicaria*) by the edge of the pond.

In our gardens, one normally can only find annual vegetable fennel, which has been bred to yield compressed leaves; as soon as these are thick enough, the plant gives up the ghost. Spicy fennel, by contrast, is perennial. The English alone have valued it enough as an imposing garden perennial to have bred a variety with a coppery sheen.

In spring, fennel produces its feathery greenery, and those who have a larger stand of it may well cut off a few shoots to use as a tender vegetable. (I can imagine a flounder, slowly oven-baked, surrounded by a mound of fennel green.) Later, fennel places one level of stringy greenery above the next, so that a thick jungle of slender stems and intertwined leaves develops, finally crowned by many yellow umbels. This shape gets mightier by the year and yet loses none of its grace.

Fennel leaves are a fine spice for salads and fish, similar to dill; its semiripe flowers can be used when pickling gherkins, and its ripe fruits make a tea that can cure a sore throat as well as indigestion. Its fruits mature late, so one needs to be extra careful to harvest them before they rot in the misty fall weather. The last display of fennel is its leaves, wilting and slackening in November, one more among many examples of the strange beauty of wilting.

We have already used up our walnut harvest—our mice were eager, and there was only a modest amount left for us. Mice probably also ensure that every so often a walnut seedling crops up in different parts of the garden, six inches high but already with a foot-long taproot that is quite powerful. Unfortunately, with these seedlings one can never be sure if they will bear good fruits or only poor ones. If one wishes to plant a walnut, go to a nursery and buy a reliable graft in order to make the wait worthwhile, for it can take 10 or 12 years or even longer for the first fruits to ripen.

Of course it is nice to harvest walnuts in one's own garden, yet care needs to be taken. A walnut has a large and spreading growth habit, and few other plants can live where its leaves drop.

One of our walnuts has a very rich inner life—in its deeply hollowed trunk, fine humus has accumulated and is constantly being refined by innumerable

In tree caves like this, one can find the finest humus, worked up by many animals and readily accepted by little plants as substrate.

animals living in it—wood lice, bugs, larvae, and worms. Remembering ancient gardeners, we passed a few handfuls of this mixture through a sieve and used it to grow cuttings—this is how things used to be done when gardeners still mixed their own compost and did not use plastic sacks of the stuff from compost companies.

At Christmas, we are going to try out the old custom of beating our walnut trees with a stick to make them bear a rich harvest in the following year. It is understood that we are going to beat them very gently, so as not to damage their wood. The ceremony was probably not intended to take out dead wood but was just a more rigorous form of the laying on of hands. We will see if it does the walnuts any good.

Roots and Horseshoes

One of this year's new discoveries was pineapple-scented sage (*Salvia elegans* 'Scarlet Pineapple'), which does not smell anything like sage but so much of pineapple that one is tempted to bite into it. Throughout the summer it grows into an imposing, light green shrub, and not until the end of October (as though it has forgotten the time and is now in a hurry) does it push up numerous small flower spikes with surprisingly magenta-red flowers.

Pineapple-scented sage is native to Mexico, and in our area it falls victim to the first night frosts. There is, however, a simple way of getting it through the winter, and it is well worth seeing. Cut off a few shoots—what am I saying? cut off whole bunches!—and you will be surprised by how readily they produce, in the space of only a few days, a rich network of roots in a vase. At the same time, they continue to grow and, at the slightest touch, give off their pineapple scent. Later they can be potted up and kept on the windowsill until spring. The more one prunes them and uses their leaves as a fruity spice, the more densely the bush will grow back.

A whole glass full of thin, white roots, intertwined strings, searching blindly, not yet fully shaped—this is the essence of the vegetative principle, abstractly, tangibly expressed in abundance. Pineapple-scented sage takes root with joy, the gardener would say. But one also has to think of the fact that hurry and abundance can be a sign of desperation.

Is it really right to indulge in such anthropomorphisms? Yes, as long as we do not give in to mysticism and are content to perceive the similarity of life's gestures only as an equivalence that has nothing to do with the fact that a plant is a plant and not a human being.

Among all the different plant genera, the ability to grow roots from shoots or even leaves is distributed most unevenly. Some species need only to sense the proximity of water to respond immediately by growing roots, while others cannot be coaxed into it even with hormonal stimulants.

In Goethe's *Metamorphosis of Plants*, with its beautiful image of a plant unfolding, roots are not mentioned, not even out of politeness. Roots have always been a trivial matter; the language of their shapes is hardly ever uttered except perhaps by psychologists using paintings to determine people's success or failure at putting down roots (and so use the anthropomorphic element in their readings).

It is also strange that roots—which are, after all, very secretive simply by virtue of being hidden in the soil—have so rarely become the subject of superstition. Exceptions are mandrake roots, believed to have far-reaching powers, and Pliny suggested that babies wear iris roots around their necks to facilitate teething.

With the abolition of superstition—not only the belief in mandrake and iris—a lot of nonsense has disappeared, along with many imaginative and beautiful images as well. These days, people are not superstitious enough. On New Year's Eve, one should really do some of the things that people who were not attached to their televisions used to do. For example, they picked some leaves from the boxwood tree, wrote the names of family members on them, and placed them in a bowl of water for the night. In the morning, those whose leaves were fresh and green would do well in the coming year, while a wilted leaf heralded sickness and death. Since a boxwood leaf can take weeks to wilt even without water, everybody could be reassured when starting the New Year. If people do not even try to get cheered up by such things—well, that is their problem.

I would rather not mention the old rural New Year's custom of "fitzling," which consisted of beating all the women on a farm with "Barbara's twigs." The twigs were cut on the fourth of December and had started to flower by the thirty-first. The practice was said to increase fertility.

Here at Lindenhof we "fitzle" very gently if at all. Instead, as was the custom in Silesia, we hang up a horseshoe on New Year's night. We always have an old one dangling from a beam in the attic with its ends pointing upward ("so that luck can drop into it"). We have never been able to decide once and for all whether the horseshoe ought to point up or down, so we will hang a second horseshoe pointing the other way, since we have a whole box full of old ones.

There is actually a sad reason behind this. Two years ago, a sprightly pensioner turned up and asked if we would rent out a stable, saying that he was unable to throw anything away and had run out of storage space. He was a seeker of things, a brother in the spirit of recycling. He got his stable and started to cart in a breathtaking array of things from all sorts of hiding places—screws, lawnmowers, more screws, ladders, boards, butter pails, and yet more screws. The stable filled up with things. The pathways in between got smaller and smaller, but if we needed something, it could always be found. We could count on it, especially when it came to screws.

He had wanted to establish some semblance of order in the collection but was hit by a stroke before he could begin to do that. The things were scattered to the winds. Among those that remained with us was this box full of horseshoes. So we will hang up one of them. And the others? We shall put them by the wayside, one after another, for our guests. For horseshoes must not be bought, they must be found.

Wintergreens

Sometimes in the winter a gardener feels like a rightful pensioner, stretching out his legs and reading a good book. When his glance wanders outside, he is greeted by a scented honeysuckle (*Lonicera* ×*purpusii*) covered with white, almond-scented flowers—everything else is only gray or brown, even if in the most delicate shades.

When the gardener finally goes outside to take a closer look, he can find some green things, and not only yew (*Taxus baccata*), boxwood, and ivy. Even among the herbaceous plants are some that weather the cold with fresh green leaves on them. Only the more severe frosts damage them slightly, and they immediately revive as soon as it gets just a little bit warmer outside. Outside one's window, one should have a consolation bed full of such plants against a backdrop of evergreen ferns—stinking hellebore with its dense, bushy leaves and its flowers in January and February; bushy pimpernel (*Pimpinella*), with its finely serrated leaves which taste of nothing but ennoble any salad just with their design; the hundreds of different species of houseleek that reduce their chlorophyll in the winter and mix their sparse green with deep shades of red; the untiring yellow cockspur that sometimes flowers out of the blue in mild winters; hyssop and thyme and, in between, the grayish green tufts of snowdrops.

These are only a few of those that are always green. There are others in the large group of biennial plants that, in the course of the fall, have produced a large rosette of leaves. They will flower this year. Evening primroses, which have self-seeded everywhere, are an example. If we think we have too many of their rosettes lying around, flatly pressed to the ground, we can use the very young ones in salads. And chervil! If in late summer one lavishly spreads chervil seeds on all vacant areas, there will be so many green plants that whole bunches of it can be picked for a sweet and spicy chervil soup. Hildegard von Bingen said that chervil gets one's juices going, drives out stomachaches, and is good for one's digestion. (She probably got this from Pliny the Elder.)

A few grasses, too, remain green throughout the winter, including that rather strange bulbous meadow grass that immigrated from the steppes of southeastern Europe. In tune with the climatic conditions in its native country, it wilts away at the end of May, spending the dry summers underground and only turning green again in September. In April, numerous little plantlets appear instead of flowers. They shrivel up and are blown away by the wind, and just like their parent plants, they do not come to life again until early autumn.

The Enjoyment of Papermaking

The gardener and his wife are always keen to turn the plants of the garden into anything they can possibly be turned into—jams and salads, herbal teas and dyes, gratins, dried flower arrangements, and medicines. And paper.

We started making paper when dandelions were in flower. Our first paper was densely studded with yellow petals that had woven themselves into a base layer of egg carton. This, in turn, had been ripped into small threads and left in a bucket of water for one hour to make a thick broth of uniform consistency.

Only advanced papermakers attempt the art of dissolving fibrous plants—by rot, chalk, or sodium—in such a way that their fibers swim around freely in a pulp, as cotton fibers do in the paper broth for old rag paper.

In the summer there is hardly any time for these things, so we collect our raw materials in bags and boxes—all kinds of flowers; the leaves of sword lily and Siberian iris; grasses; mosses; stinging nettle shoots; asparagus skins; and a glass full of dried elderberries, which will make their own, very particular marks, on our paper: thick black and purple accents.

In the winter we make the paper.

When the basic ingredients have been cut up, worn down, and had all their internal connections removed from them, two or three are chosen and placed in a tub filled with water. Some kinds of tender petals can be added—dried rose petals, for example, or blue larkspurs or the ray florets of sunflowers. They all immediately soak up the water and wake up to a new lease on papery life, albeit in a paler shade.

We sink our sieve into the pulp, lift it back out slowly, and let the water drain away. In seconds, the pulp turns into a kind of tissue. It is a fascinating process, and at that moment, the papermaker witnesses the coincidence that newly reorders the shapes and lines.

The wet paper felt is deposited or "gouched" onto a woollen cloth. Another piece of cloth is placed on top, the next leaf is "gouched," and so on. The pile that thus develops is then pressed to remove yet more water. Then one can pull the sheets of paper off the cloth and hang them up to dry.

Making wallpaper out of these sheets is easy to imagine, like those wallpapers that appear in many written and unwritten memoirs, a kind of map that one's imagination can journey on before going to sleep. Garden journeys this time, recognizable and unrecognizable fragments of the garden composed into an archive leaf. Every month could thus get its own paper—an asparagus leaf for June; a January paper with moss and the many yellow flowers of winter jasmine; in the August paper, we would add lots of leaves of stone clover so that paper will continue to smell of fresh hay for years.

Dried Beauties

Some women gardeners think the greatest virtue of hydrangeas is the fact that one can dry their flowers and then spray them with golden sheen. One can also dip them into white or blue lacquer.

Alternatively, one can let them be. Dry things left behind by the summer do not need to be ennobled by lacquer and gold but can also make an impact in their gentle shades of gray and brown, in the faded remains of colors that once were.

In flower shops, we can buy—and pay through the nose for it—never-ending spring. But if instead of buying Colombian carnations in December we search the garden for exotic wintry things, a whole new dimension of plant beauty will open itself up to us. Summer paints with an impressive array of beautiful color. Winter shows us the no less impressive and varied charm of lines, of contours, of shades of gray, and the nuances of the brown shades of rot.

Our eyes and soul need this quiet time. The joy we feel when we see the first colors appear in the spring is more profound when we have missed their sparkle for a while, enjoying instead the graphics that plants now offer us.

I am not talking of common dried flower arrangements. Anyone may deal with that as he wishes. Individual, single things are much more exciting—a dead branch, an unusual seedpod, a leathery dead leaf.

When dry, the static plant shapes reveal the structures of life. We can then perceive that some plants get their shape only from the water pressure in their leaves and sink down into a mere nothingness when the water escapes, while others show us that they have built a sturdy scaffold. Herbaceous mints perish, but woody absinthe withstands even the harshest winds; only a tangle of crumpled-up leaves remains of the velvety lady's mantle, but the large umbels with the seeds of fennel and parsnip continue to hover 6 feet high above the beds before they give up.

Irises show solidity and decrepitude at the same time. Their watery flowers have months ago wilted into a tender, papery skin, and their flat, firm leaves have now shrunk into scrunched-up pieces of string. In the meantime, seed capsules have developed in which the seeds are as closely packed as coins from the bank. These seeds are hard as stone and the capsules rigid as wood.

Seeds, capsules, pods, grasses, wilting umbels, bundles of herbs, dead wood, fungi, strange fruits, skeleton leaves and shoots—some of these we collect in late summer, such as the valuable spore capsules of sensitive fern (*Onoclea sensibilis*). Other things we notice only now, such as the tireless rose whose reluctant November flowering is gilded with ice. Once taken indoors, it shrinks down to a crusty ball.

Nearly every garden has its traditional harvests that take place every year, such as orange Chinese lanterns or silver pennies. The shining, white-gray walls that separate honesty seed pods could perhaps be enlivened in a vase by being paired with the strange seed pods of dyer's woad (*Isatis tinctoria*), with its flat black fruits hung up in rows.

And there are unusual things, such as the bark of paper birch (*Betula papyrifera*) that comes off in large strips. The Chippewa Indians used it to make little ornamental pictures by folding the paper-thin bark several times and then biting a pattern of holes into it with their teeth.

Every now and again, we notice some strange galls on leafless twigs, such as the "twisted braid" on willows, a woody and hoary construction that has the larvae of gall mosquitoes growing inside of it. The winter garden is full of those sharp, brittle shapes of dry things, every single one a filigree work of art.

"Twisted braids" that harbor the larva of a gall mosquito can be found on willow branches.

There are also rounded statues, such as the pumpkins that we took off and put inside in September to keep them from rotting in the moistness of cold fall nights. Once inside, they take endless months to dry and they keep their color for all that time.

It is only from their reduction in weight that we notice how life—that is, water—has slowly drained out of them. In the end, they are very light, with the seeds rattling about inside. From the shells, which are now hard as bone, we can make vessels. The seeds we can partly eat and partly keep for next spring, to raise new pumpkins in many different varieties, from our standard yellow edible pumpkin to the most amazing and playful multicolored varieties. These, even if carefully crossed and selected by breeders, are not unnatural but simply represent the whole range of possibilities for disguise within the species of pumpkin. They are goblins, and their dry rattling sounds just as joyous as the cap of Till Eulenspiegel, the famous German storybook fool.

When rot does at last attack our pumpkins, we do not throw them away. Instead we let the construction, multicolored and ornamented by several different types of rot as it is, shrink and dry up. It looks like the fantastic medal of a freemasonry sect—if indeed there is such a thing.

When it comes to silver pennies, honesty not only offers the usual, round ones of the biennial *Lunaria annua*, which needs to be re-sown every year, but also the pointed oval ones of *Lunaria rediviva*, an herbaceous perennial that sometimes grows wild in moist forests. It is a desirable variety in dried flower arrangements.

Winter's End

While eating breakfast at our east-facing window, we notice that the splendor of our pre-spring flowers is finally over. It was a captivating display—'Winter Sun' mahonia with its sulfur-yellow flower candles; *Hammamelis ×intermedia* 'Jelena', a hybrid of witch hazel with its coppery flowers; the flowers of our snowball (*Viburnum bodnantense*) that look as if they are made out of porcelain; the cream-colored bellflowers of our *Stachyurus* that hang from the shrub in grapes; and the intensely fragrant, white flowers of our scented honeysuckle (*Lonicera ×purpusii*).

They have all been flowering from February until far into March, and they have helped us bear the weather forecast ("northerly winds bringing cold temperatures from the sea") with some degree of composure.

Why are these shrubs hardly ever offered in nurseries? Salespeople, when asked, will tell us that such unusual things are simply not in demand. As if that was a reason not to offer them! Well, one does have to admit that customers are often very persistent in wanting to buy only what they know from their neighbor's garden. Of all these pre-spring comforters, they may plant winter jasmine and witch hazel, a yellow variety, of course—where would we be otherwise?

Otherwise we would be right here: curiosity about the unsung treasures of woody plants that make a mockery of winter would bring a lot more of them into our gardens, lighting up the darkness and reinforcing hope in a concerted effort of nurserymen (for that is what they are really called) and daring customers. And if then the apostles of naturalness should pass our garden and shout across the fence that all these plants are foreigners and therefore undesirable for ecological reasons, imports that are good for nothing with nothing to offer our native animals, then we would invite them into our garden and let them see just how much the first bumblebees and early butterflies enjoy these plants. Secondly, we tell them that in a certain sense, we count ourselves as part of the ecosystem, too, so that our own enjoyment is of considerable benefit in light of human ecology. And thirdly, we tell them that for reasons of diversity, it would be a crying shame if in the many gardens throughout the country, people grew nothing but the two dozen native shrubs that are suitable for garden use.

What could be more fitting than pointing to Tartarian honeysuckle (*Lonicera tatarica*), a particularly robust and fast-growing Russian shrub that does not flower in early spring but does start to grow particularly early—just what one needs if one lives in the Tatar republic. Its name reveals that it belongs to the same genus as climbing honeysuckle. This one, however, grows as a shrub. Its branches, which all start at soil level, can reach up to 4 meters in height. Its bark is thick and soft, and our cats love to use it for sharpening their claws. Its reddish flowers, which appear in May, are remarkable and decorative mainly thanks to their sheer number, as are its coral-red fruits in late summer.

Tartarian honeysuckle, present in European gardens for 200 years and even found in the wild here and there, is counted as an exotic decorative shrub. Yet it has all the virtues of an excellent hedge plant. It is fully frost hardy and totally resistant to wind and weather; its unusually early leaves are enjoyed by animals and humans alike, its flowers are visited by many insects, and birds like to eat its berries. One can (and even should) prune it hard; if it is growing in a hedge, one can easily chop it right down to the ground. By the way, it is happy in the poorest of soils and lets so much light through its lower reaches that not only spring-flowering plants but also low summer-flowering plants can grow in the semishade it creates.

There are many other shrub-forming varieties of *Lonicera* of differing heights. Nearly all of them have the same good qualities that Tartarian honeysuckle has, nearly all of them are native to different areas of Asia, and nearly all were imported into Europe several hundred years ago. The catalog of the famous English tree nursery Hillier's contains 31 different species, and in good German tree nurseries, one can find half a dozen at least. If one wants to plant a mixed hedge, one should not forget *Lonicera*.

Time of the Gardener

The flowers of white water lily (*Nymphaea alba*) open at seven in the morning and close again at five in the afternoon; dandelion flowers open at five o'clock in the morning, and white campion (*Silene latifolia*) starts to flower at nine o'clock at night, awaiting nocturnal butterflies. One can read these times on the flower clock that the Swedish naturalist Carolus Linnaeus thought up some 200 years ago. This flower clock is graceful and delightful but extremely imprecise. It stops in dull weather and is nonexistent in winter. Not surprisingly, botanists condemn Linnaeus's flower clock as a good-for-nothing game of an otherwise professional scientist.

In the garden, one does not need a flower clock. It simply does not matter whether the daily rhythm of plants can be related to any human or mechanical way of measuring time. What is more, the gestures of flowers are only a very small part of what happens in a garden in terms of changes, movements, alterations, and transitions.

The gardener uses other things to measure time, and his feeling for it derives from symbols. Since a garden is in many ways a mirror image of the world, a gardener's understanding of time—at least in part and with a large amount of caution—reveals a lot about how to deal with time outside the garden.

Patience is commonly held to be a gardener's most important virtue, but since a gardener without patience is unimaginable, patience is less a virtue than it is a prerequisite for being a gardener in the first place. The gardener's patience gives garden plants the time and space they need to unfold. Every flower and

The arches of time in a garden overlap; a late rosebud is surprised by the frost.

tree demand ample space and time for development, and these demands need to be taken into account when a flower is still a seed and a tree is no more than a cutting. The gardener mentally anticipates the final shape and uses that as a measure. One can often see how unsuccessful gardens, conceived impatiently, combine things that do not go together. Impatience seeks abundance but only succeeds in achieving overcrowding.

The gardener allows plants to unfold and supports their growth. He cannot accelerate the process at will; unlike things, plants are not available to hurry. It is a sign of patience to leave well enough alone. A plant's unfolding cannot be controlled, nor can its possible failure or its wilting or its dying. The questions that people in a hurry might ask do not arise—whether "the numbers add up," as is commonly said today, though people wisely do not say who is doing the adding and calculating and miscalculating.

Hurry is the opposite of patience. Impatiently, hurry tries to speed up anything that requires time. Impatience wants to gain time and urges beings and things to hurry, demanding results. Patience allows things to be unavailable; hurry counts on availability and feasibility. Just as hurry has become a primary prerequisite for success in life, the illusion that anything goes has been elevated to a position of prominence. The slow death of this illusion coincides with a rediscovery of gardens, which is certainly more than just a pretty coincidence.

All this may sound fatherly and deliberate and totally ill-timed in the face of all the urging to hurry these days. But the fact that hurry is a contemporary phenomenon and that it wants to push us along in a fast swirl of feasibility and availability is reason enough for so much confusion and destruction, which cannot be escaped by means of going even faster, but only by falling back.

In this, the garden as a parable can be therapeutic and is indeed used in therapies. Gardening is counted as a medicine that helps to reestablish orders and rhythms that have been damaged or lost. This has something to do with the fact that garden beings will not yield to any force or any will, they are not easily tricked, and in their own quiet and yet meticulous way, they live their lives in accordance with their very own rhythms. Interference means destruction that can be readily assessed and acknowledged.

At the same time, the gardener wins time by giving it back to his plants, by subjecting himself to the measures they exact. In doing so, he can escape the hurry that exercises its power all around him. Patience seems to lengthen time in the sense that it is measured by the slow unfolding of plants rather than on the wristwatches of people in a hurry. These people try to gain time, and the more time they manage, the less they end up having. For the patient person, time expands into great abundance but paradoxically is not in the end a driving force. For the patient person, time stands still, and once that happens, the need for hurry ceases. Aristotle described the tranquility derived from the continuity of time by defining *now* in two different ways. In one sense, it continuously disappears, drowning in the past the moment it is noticed while, at the same time, a new now appears from the future. In another sense, the present moment is continuous, flowing through time from the future into the past. On the flower clock, the opening of our evening primrose signals the evening. By late in the afternoon, the gardener can see which one of the blossoms is going to open today.

The gardener needs patience to observe the flower opening, its sulfuric yellow petals twisted into the shape of a pointed bag held together at the base by the yellow calyx. The flower opens when special petal cells slowly fill with

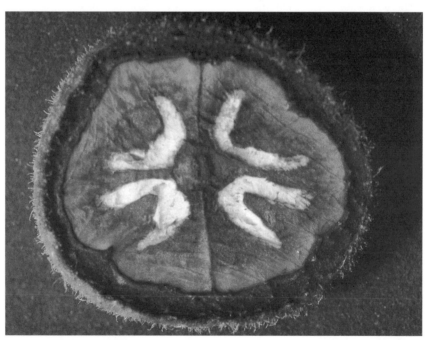

Curiosity rather than impatience made the gardener cut through a young walnut. What a mysterious sight!

water and, just like stretching joints, force the flower to unfold. The process takes about one hour. When one sits in front of the flower and takes a very close look, one can follow the process in fractions of millimeters. One can see how the tender petals split first at the top and then fold out more and more, until the whole flower of the evening primrose opens its shining face to the patient observer. Tomorrow in the morning sunlight it will start to wilt.

According to Aristotle, time flows from the future through the present to the past. It passes unnoticed, as every *now* at the moment of its existence is obliterated in the past and created anew from the future. If one were to speed up this process by forcing open the silky leaves, they would not survive. The flower would be ruined.

This is not only true of flowers. It is true of many things, including nearly everything that happens in a garden. Wherever things are hurried, something of the world, of matter, of beings, of people is destroyed. At the very least, silence is disrupted, since hurry is nearly always loud, drowning out all other sounds.

This sunflower leaf shows that wilting and dying are also part of the natural arches of time.

To describe the hurry of today's world means to portray everyday life, since hurry has come to be widely accepted as a part of success, freedom, and happiness, a colossal picture of acceleration that has taken hold of everything that exists and pushes it farther and farther. Speed has long exceeded the limits of a human being's ability to understand or react to it. Wares and humans, by using enormous amounts of energy, speed up. The faster they move from one place to another, the more it seems worth it—time is money—and the more enthusiasm people have for the technology that makes all this speed possible. Signals are transported and exchanged at a furious pace, information is created and researched with the help of computers, calculations and even thoughts are subjected to hurry, and people work feverishly to make these things faster and faster. All kinds of gadgets—from cars to electric shavers, from electric kitchen knives to telephones, from televisions to fax machines, from personal computers to Polaroid cameras, from microwave ovens to space shuttles—serve one goal. It is not exactly utopian but has been attained. That is, absolutely everything should be available at any time, in any place, without delay—information, lunch, a letter, a human being, strawberries. Everything should be there at the push of a button, ever ready, ubiquitous. Hurry wants to abolish time and space, to reduce the world to just that one point in time and space where an individual can, without any delay, absorb everything that exists, joining the here and now to the always and everywhere.

Even the work of genetic engineers is nothing but an attempt to speed up the traditional, much-too-slow speed of evolutionary processes, to rush evolution itself, mixing characteristics and shapes from all past and future genetic potential to create any being desired at any time. Only the beginnings of this have been put into practice, but that does not fundamentally change what these people aim for—omnipotence that annihilates distances in time and in space.

Hurry is destructive. Every time we mourn the destruction of something, we can find that hurry contributed to its demise, and wherever hurry manifests itself, we find destruction is its inevitable consequence. People are run over; daily and life routines are ripped apart, sometimes leading to psychological confusion; any privacy, even that of data, is tenuous; landscapes and habitats are destroyed; whole cultures are wiped out; and the earth itself is abused, damaged, worn out. All of this is fed and fired by an energy won from irreplaceable resources that only seem inexhaustible. Coal, oil, uranium: with its greedy hands, hurry grabs the substances that it needs, and when they are used up, it leaves behind waste that endangers the continuity of life in many different ways.

The garden, in the image that it creates, can quietly hint at the fact that the conservation of life must be an unhurried, slow process. Life falls apart and rots away if placed in the straitjacket of hurry.

The only thing that can spur a gardener to hurry is the threat of danger or emergency, such as taking precautions to protect sensitive plants from a sudden frost. Hurry is always born out of necessity. But what necessity is modern hurry fleeing from? In the final analysis, it must be the fear of death or the inevitable or the end of one's own life that is fueling a flight from time. I remember never wanting train journeys to end because I feared arriving at the destination; the faster the train went, the more anxious I felt.

For the gardener, too, death is everywhere, but he does not try to escape it for the price that life surrenders to hurry. Instead, he walks toward it under arches of time. The garden is covered by these arches of time. There are small ones—such as the one under which evening primrose flowers open—to larger ones—such as the floral clock that spans morning and evening. There are arches of days and weeks and years in which germination takes place or the 15 years a chestnut tree takes to mature from seedling to first harvest. These are very different scales, and sometimes one may even find something resembling hurry in the human sense of the word—fungi like ink caps, for example, live through that part of their life that we can see in a hurry that is not at all plant-like. Their fruiting bodies appear literally overnight, and it takes only a few hours for their spores to mature and for the fruiting bodies to dissolve into a black, inky substance. But this picture is deceptive. The hurried ripening is preceded by a long period of time during which the actual body of the fungus, its mycelium, was preparing itself for the grand and unique event of fruiting, which alone ensures its continued existence. Here, hurry is only a counterpoint to a quiet and secluded existence.

Hairy bittercress is in a real hurry throughout its entire short existence and has a vegetative period—that is, a life span—of only two weeks. During this time it germinates, grows, flowers with many small flowers, then produced pods in which its tiny seeds mature rapidly. Flung far away by the opening pods, the seeds spread in all directions. Behind this is a sense of urgency. Hairy bittercress can live only on ground that is otherwise unoccupied and therefore has to hurry up if it wants to hold its own, even for a very short time, against the competition. In its hurried fertility, there is also a subtle kind of destruction in the form of halting progress, for hairy bittercress can conquer and block entire areas.

A very different arch of time that spans months and years is the compost heap. Nothing flourishes on it, but everything slowly turns back into its mineral origins. Modern garden technology speeds up this process by first sending any garden remains through a shredder, that horribly noisy device with brutally rotating blades. The material this machine kicks out does rot quickly, while entire branches and trunks would perhaps have taken years to turn into nourishing humus.

Arches of time. There are annual plants that undergo germination, growth, and fertility in a single year. Biennials produce only a rosette in their first year and then go through the winter with it, forming a flower stand in the second year. Herbaceous perennials continue to live on for years. The age of trees and shrubs, which build one layer of wood after the other, is measured in decades and centuries—no chance for hurry here.

The arches of time overlap, just like humans and things in the world have (or used to have) their own time in consecutive or overlapping sequences—ages of life, seasons, short comedies, long tragedies, festivities, illnesses, sequences, and processes in their own forms and spaces. Many of these have been smudged and destroyed by hurry, truncated and shrunk. It takes 10 hours to get to New York and 10 minutes to have lunch in a fast-food restaurant; there are strawberries in winter and snow on ski slopes in summer; runners are getting ever faster and children learn to talk to computers before they have mastered their own language; an ad for telephone service tells us that Uncle Max is playing a game of chess in Toronto even though he is not there; our remote control lets us choose between seven different channels. Hurry makes us want to do everything at the same time, and barring that, we at least want to make sure that everything can potentially be done at the same time.

The gardener dispenses with such an enlargement of his capabilities (insofar as they have managed to find a way into the garden at all) because he knows that life is possible only if it restricts itself and adapts to the laws that govern unfolding and maturing. The gardener wanders beneath the arches of time; he knows many of them and continually is discovering others, either by chance or by actively seeking them out; he takes part in the life around him by perceiving gaps that enable development, that make beginnings possible; and he does not rush into anything, for things that are rushed are always damaged.

For the gardener, time is not linear. When one arch of time ends, it immediately starts again. Plants that die have already produced seeds guaranteeing the next generation. The arches and sequences arrange themselves into larger ones. They are a victory over transience, if that is even possible as far as a human timeframe is concerned.

Someone in a hurry flees time and death, but the patient gardener walks through time toward death, looking along the arches of time for the right way to show transience and overcome it simultaneously. This, too, is taught along the way. Arches can break off abruptly, there can be failures without new beginnings, there can be leave-taking with no return, there can be endings without perfection. In some things, the gardener fails. Some life simply eludes him or dies fighting with other life. There is no sense of infinite happiness and well-being. There is sadness, farewell, and irrevocable loss. Yet these, too, are

Spores and mycelia of fungi such as the shield-shaped cup fungus shown here take care of the next generation in a continuous life cycle.

integrated into the arches of time. And the gardener also knows that the truth—even that of a farewell—is more bearable than the deceptive attempt to hurriedly and forcibly fill time to the bursting point with life that ends in ruins.

All in all, hurry is aimless. It does not like arrivals because they can turn to stagnation. It immediately conceives of a new aim in order to remain on the go. This is illustrated by restless tourism that no sooner reaches its destination than it is thinking of the departure, destroying even the most remote corners of the earth. For people in a hurry, the future is more important than the past. They do not patiently watch the river of time flow through the moment that is now, but always try to escape as quickly as possible from now to not yet. They stumble in the attempt, getting sand in their eyes so that they cannot see the here and now anymore.

Thus do people in a hurry lose time in two ways. They do not perceive the current moment, nor do they see what the moment turns into, the point at which what was and what will be are one. They are blind. Those who watch patiently perceive the moment as well as its continuation because they lose themselves in contemplation of what was and what is coming. In this way, they are able to see becoming as being and being as becoming. They live the changes of time, but they also perceive the timelessness of being that underlies the changes.

What happens in the garden can be taken point for point as an image of our life outside it, of our ability to patiently let things be, and the error of reaching out too quickly. The destruction of our world is a work of haste, and patience is waiting for haste to fail. The gardener knows that haste is bound to fail. This is a partisan vision, not a utopian ideal.

Index of Plant Names